THE PRIMARY CURRICULUM IN ACTION:
A Process Approach to Educational Practice

THE PRIMARY CURRICULUM IN ACTION:
A Process Approach to Educational Practice

Edited by

Geva M. Blenkin and
A.V. Kelly

P·C·P
Paul Chapman
Publishing Ltd

Copyright © 1983. Chapter 1 Vic Kelly: Chapter 2 Geva Blenkin: Chapter 3 Marian Whitehead: Chapter 4 Stuart Ilsley: Chapter 5 Roy Richards: Chapter 6 Harriet Proudfoot: Chapter 7 Maggie Bierley: Chapters 8 and 9 Elaine Ball: Chapter 10 and Postscript Geva Blenkin and Vic Kelly: Chapter 11 Alan Goddard: Chapter 12 Gwyn Edwards.

First published 1983
Reprinted 1984, 1986
by Harper & Row Publishers Ltd
London

Reprinted 1988
by Paul Chapman Publishers Ltd
London

British Library Cataloguing in Publication Data

The Primary curriculum in action.
  1. Education, Elementary—Great Britain—Curricula
  I. Kelly, A. V.   II. Blenkin, G.
  372.19'0941   LB1564.G7

  ISBN 1 85396 030 6

Printed and bound by Butler & Tanner Ltd, Frome, Somerset.

v

CONTENTS

Acknowledgements   xi

Notes on the Contributors   xii

General Introduction   **1**

PART ONE   GENERAL CONSIDERATIONS
Introduction to Part One   **7**

Chapter 1 Research and the Primary Curriculum   *Vic Kelly*   **9**
The Primary curriculum   9
Research and the Primary curriculum   15
Summary and conclusions   22

PART TWO   ASPECTS OF THE CURRICULUM
Introduction to Part Two   **27**

Chapter 2 'The Basic Skills'   *Geva Blenkin*   **29**
Some hazards of teaching 'the basic skills'   32
Making learning individual   33
Making learning impersonal   35
Making the learner passive   36
Planning to teach 'the basic skills'   38
Resources to challenge competence   39
Tools for the young apprentice   41
Selection and influence of materials   43
Opportunities for discussing rules   46

Assessing progress	48
Implementing a unified approach: case studies	50
Discussing the rules	50
Extending strategies	51
Using the resources in the classroom	52
Co-operation	52
Integration of skills	53
Spontaneous application of skills	54
Summary and conclusions	55

Chapter 3 Language Development and the Primary Curriculum
Marian Whitehead **57**

Major trends and influences in language study	57
Framing language policies	60
Continuing language development	61
Into literacy	65
Becoming independent writers and readers	69
Generating research and theories in schools	75
Back to 'the basics'?	78
Summary and conclusions	80

Chapter 4 The Development of a Mathematics Curriculum
Stuart Ilsley **81**

Getting started	82
Turning to books and mathematics schemes for help	82
Published guidelines	83
Discussions with other teachers	87
Assessment as a basis for responding to children's understanding	87
Development through relevant experiences	89
Summary and conclusions	94

Chapter 5 Learning through Science   *Roy Richards* **96**

An historical perspective	96
What is science?	98
Using the senses	101
Aids for the senses	102
Questioning	103

Devising fair tests   104
Recording and finding patterns   105
Communication   105
Knowledge   106
What does science offer?   106
The Learning Through Science Project   108
  A school policy   108
  Resources   110
  Pupil material   111
  Slow learners   113
  Slide/tape sequences   113
Summary and conclusions   114

Chapter 6 Development through the Creative Arts *Harriet Proudfoot* **115**
Creative work as the starting-point for all learning   116
  Art work   119
  Writing   120
  Drama   128
  Other arts   130
Four case studies   130
  Giovanni   130
  Joanna   134
  Kwok Leung   138
  Tom   145
Summary and conclusions   153

PART THREE   STRATEGIES FOR IMPLEMENTATION AND CHANGE

Introduction to Part Three   **159**

Chapter 7 The Development of a Record-Keeping System
Maggie Bierley   **162**
The evolution of a record-keeping system   163
  Early stages   163
  Extending the scope   165
  Reappraisal   171
General issues and principles   175
Summary and conclusions   181

Chapter 8 An Approach to School-Based Curriculum Development
Elaine Ball   **183**
    Preparing for school-based curriculum development   184
        Recognizing the need for curriculum development   184
        Defining the task   189
    Implementing curriculum development   190
        Communication   191
        Responsibility   192
        Time   192
        Organization   194
    Support for school-based curriculum development   195
    Summary and conclusions   199

Chapter 9 Supporting Curriculum Development: Case Study of a
school-focused support scheme   *Elaine Ball*   **200**
    Background to the establishment of three support teams
      in one ILEA Division   201
    Towards a philosophy for Curriculum Support teams   203
      The role of the support teams in relation to the
        staff of schools   204
      The role of the support teams in relation to
        Headteachers   204
      The role of the support teams in relation to the
        Inspectorate   206
    Strategies for supporting schools   208
      Task definition   208
      Models for the team's work in a school   209
    Towards a contract for schools and support teams   213
    Summary and conclusions   215

Chapter 10 The Education of Teachers   *Geva Blenkin and Vic Kelly* **218**
    A 'process' approach to teacher education   219
    The major elements and emphases of this kind of course   222
    Recent and current developments and their implications   231
      Some common inadequacies of teacher education   231
        programmes   235
      Recent trends and developments

Induction and in-service education   238
Summary and conclusions   242

PART FOUR   BEYOND THE PRIMARY SCHOOL

. Introduction to Part Four   **245**

Chapter 11 Processes in Special Education   *Alan Goddard*   **248**
The dominant influence of behavioural objectives on the
    development of Special Education   252
A process approach to curriculum development in
    Special Education   258
A process curriculum in practice   263
Some recent developments in Special Education and
    other related issues   272
The myth of structured teaching   273
The myth of 'basic skills'   275
Summary and conclusions   .277

Chapter 12 Processes in the Secondary School: MACOS and Beyond
Gwyn Edwards   **279**
The school setting   280
    The Humanities Department   280
Man: A Course of Study   281
Beyond MACOS: theoretical considerations   286
The process curriculum in action   289
Some constraints   305
Summary and conclusions   306

POSTSCRIPT   *Geva Blenkin and Vic Kelly*   **310**

Bibliography   **317**

Author Index   **328**

Subject Index   **331**

ACKNOWLEDGEMENTS

The gratitude of the editors must go first to all those people who, from many quarters, offered comments on our first publication, *The Primary Curriculum*, of a kind which emboldened us to take things a step further with this follow-up volume. We hope that they are not disappointed in what their comments have prompted. We must also thank the contributors to this book who have responded heroically and, as we are sure what follows will demonstrate, most successfully to the difficult brief we set them. For there is no doubt that the most difficult task for any educationist is to write convincingly about educational practice. Thirdly, we must make mention of the reviewers, mainly anonymous, whose comments on the first draft, as they will themselves see, have led to many improvements in this final version. In this respect, we would like to make special mention of Tracey Argent who provided us with a lucid and extremely helpful student's-eye view of what we have endeavoured to do. And finally, we must again thank Jill Thorn and Sue Scott for their work in turning manuscripts in many different hands into decent typescript.

Geva Blenkin
Vic Kelly

NOTES ON THE CONTRIBUTORS

Elaine Ball is Deputy Headteacher of Craven Park Primary School, Hackney, and has many years' experience of teaching in Primary schools within the Inner London Education Authority. She recently spent two years working as a member of a curriculum support team in the same borough and thus gained considerable insight into the problems of curriculum change.

Maggie Bierley was until recently Head of the Infants Department at John Scurr Primary School, Tower Hamlets, and now has special responsibility for literacy at the same school. She has many years' experience of teaching young children in London's East End. Her major interest for some years has been in methods of recording the progress of children working in informal situations.

Geva Blenkin is a Senior Lecturer in Education at Goldsmiths' College and is particularly involved in Curriculum Studies and in the professional preparation of teachers for work in Infant schools. She was formerly Headteacher of an Infant school in the East End of London.

Gwyn Edwards is a Head of Upper School at Meopham Secondary School, Kent, and is also a member of the Humanities Department there. Much of the work of that department has focused on the project, Man: A Course of Study, and he has been closely involved in the development of a curriculum from the underlying principles of that project.

Alan Goddard is Headteacher of Mayfair School, Darlington. This is a Special school and his interest and experience in Special Education extend over many years. His major professional preoccupation has been and continues to be the establishment of a truly educational basis for the development of the curriculum in this sector of schooling.

Stuart Ilsley is Deputy Headteacher of John Scurr Primary School and has special responsibility for the mathematics curriculum there. He recently spent a period of secondment as a mathematics consultant for the Inner London Education Authority and this provided him with an opportunity to study the development of mathematics in a number of schools.

Vic Kelly is Dean of the School of Education at Goldsmiths' College. He also has special responsibility for the advanced courses for teachers offered there and for the work in Curriculum Studies.

Harriet Proudfoot is Deputy Headteacher of St. James and St. Peters Church of England Primary School in London's Soho. The location of this school gives it a highly cosmopolitan and ethnically diverse population, and this in turn offers not only a challenge but a very broad range of possibilities, especially for a teacher whose major interest is in the development of pupils through the encouragement of their creative abilities.

Roy Richards is a Principal Lecturer in Education at Goldsmiths' College, currently seconded to the Schools Council as Director of its 'Learning through Science' project. This is a project which has not only emphasized the need for young children to be offered experience in the scientific field but has also advocated strongly that this experience should be such as to promote conceptual understanding rather than merely the acquisition of knowledge.

Marian Whitehead is a Senior Lecturer in Education at Goldsmiths' College. Her main involvements there are in the professional preparation of teachers for work in Infant schools and in Language in Education. It is in the development of children's language that her major research interest lies and her work provides her with ample opportunities to pursue this through regular contacts with a wide range of teachers and schools.

GENERAL INTRODUCTION

In *The Primary Curriculum* we attempted to pick out the major features of a theory of education which emphasizes the processes of education rather than its content or its products, to describe the consequences of this theory for curriculum planning, to argue its importance for individuals and for society as a whole and to identify certain current trends which seem to us to be counter-productive to its continuing development. We also made the claim that this is a form of education which is not and should not be confined to the Primary sector of schooling.

The response to that book has been interesting and perhaps significant. For, on the one hand, we have received expressions of welcoming approval from people at all levels and in all sectors of the teaching profession, suggesting that there are more individual teachers around than some may have thought who recognize the merits of this kind of educational theory. On the other hand, these expressions of approval have often been tempered by expressions of doubt concerning the problems of implementing it in practice.

The relation between theory and practice in education, as much as, and possibly more than, in other fields, is a complex matter. To produce a book that has practical significance for teachers is thus a difficult task. Certainly, it is now clear that statements and detailed analyses of elaborate statistical researches have had little if any effect on the practice of teaching. The most one can hope to do is to offer teachers some thoughts about, or observations on, the kinds of possibility that exist for them in their work with children and hope that they can develop such ideas in the individual context of their own practice. This is what *The Primary Curriculum* attempted to do.

We have been led to believe, however, that there is a little more that can be done through publication, and that is to offer teachers not only some, perhaps sometimes abstruse, theoretical considerations, but also some examples of good practice, accounts of how other teachers have attempted to translate certain ideas into reality within their classrooms, to show both that this can be done and to offer some suggestions as to how it can be achieved.

We know of at least one group of teachers who, with the support of their local authority, have arranged to meet regularly to discuss the ideas.we offered in *The Primary Curriculum* and to help each other to relate them to their own practice. If all teachers who are sympathetic to this approach to education had similar opportunities there would be no need for us to do more. Since they have not, we now offer a companion volume to that work which attempts to provide such teachers with some insight into the thinking and the practice of some of their colleagues in the hope that this will in turn lead them to productive insights into their own work and assist in its continuing development.

In one sense, it is a pity that in the titles of both these books we have had to focus attention on the Primary school. For it is our conviction that the approach to education which they attempt to explicate is applicable, indeed we believe it to be essential, at all levels and in all truly educational contexts. To reinforce this view, we have included in this present volume descriptions of work undertaken outside the Primary sector of education which is based on these same principles.

The converse is also true, of course, since recent studies have revealed that there are many teachers in Primary schools whose approach to their work does not reflect the principles outlined here. However, it is in this sector, and perhaps especially in the very early years of schooling, that this form of education is currently most readily to be found, and it is our belief that, if we can help teachers to articulate both its theory and its practice, this will prove to be the best route towards its continuing development and its expansion into all sectors of education. It is to this end that this book, like its parent volume, is directed.

We have seen our task as fourfold and have thus divided the contributions into four sections. Firstly, we felt we ought to lay out the groundwork, to remind readers briefly of the basic principles of the view of education we are attempting to explicate. We felt too that we ought to offer some justification of our approach to the task we had set ourselves, if only by drawing attention to the inadequacies of some other approaches to research in education. Part One, then, is entitled 'General Considerations' and contains just one chapter, an article by Vic Kelly, originally published in the *Journal of Curriculum Studies*, in which he attempts briefly to lay out the major features of this form of curriculum, and to establish the importance of the approach to curriculum research and development adopted in this book by emphasizing the ill-effects which other approaches have often had on the growth of this form of educational planning.

The second major section we have called 'Aspects of the Curriculum'. Here we include several accounts of work undertaken in the major areas of the Primary curriculum, all of which reveal the need to look at these areas not only in their own right but also, and more importantly, as aspects of a unified set of experiences rather than as separate subject areas. In the first of these, Chapter 2, Geva Blenkin explores the notion of 'the basic skills' and attempts to reveal some of the confusions and the fallacies that are to be found in many current pronouncements in this area, as well as to identify the harmful results these can have for educational practice. A series of chapters follows in which contributors consider the major areas of learning experience within the Primary curriculum and attempt to emphasize the importance of a 'process' approach in all of them. Marian Whitehead examines the crucial area of language development; Stuart Ilsley considers the development of mathematical understanding; Roy Richards develops the idea of learning through science from the perspective of the Schools Council's project of that name, of which he is Director; and Harriet Proudfoot explores the important area of development through the creative arts.

Part Three turns the reader's attention to 'Strategies for Change and Implementation'. It begins with a discussion by Maggie Bierley of the important question of how to develop an appropriate form of record-keeping, one which will support and promote rather than hinder and inhibit what the teacher is attempting to do in the classroom. She shows, by describing the development of her own system, that it is possible to do this adequately, properly and successfully without adopting the prespecified objectives or the check-lists which many local authorities are now purveying and thus without doing violence to the principles we are concerned to outline. Next, in Chapter 8, Elaine Ball examines some of the issues raised and the problems encountered when schools embark on policies of change, or when they recognize the need for continuous change and appreciate that, to be effective, this must be in some sense school-centred. We then turn to the question of what outside help might be needed to support this kind of development. This is the theme of a second chapter by Elaine Ball describing her work with a curriculum support unit and one by Geva Blenkin and Vic Kelly on the problems and the possibilities, in the present context of Higher Education, of producing teachers adequately prepared to undertake work of this kind with children.

Part Four takes us 'Beyond the Primary School'. For, as we are repeatedly to be heard saying, in discussing Primary education, we believe we are discussing education itself and we believe that we are elucidating a form of practice that is not merely applicable but even essential at all levels. To demonstrate and to emphasize this point, we have included accounts of practice outside the Primary school which seemed to us to reflect the same essential principles. Thus, in Chapter 11, Alan Goddard explains and describes from his own practice how the needs of pupils in Special Education must be catered for according to exactly these same principles which we are advocating for every other pupil, and, in Chapter 12, Gwyn Edwards demonstrates the inadequacies of the arguments that this approach cannot be adopted in the Secondary school, and that it is incompatible with the public examinations system, by outlining his own work both in using the Man: A Course of Study (MACOS) project and in developing further work from that project predicated on the same principles.

In a final 'Postscript', we, perhaps rashly, attempt to pull together many of the strands which run through all the contributions by returning to an examination of the basic principles of the view of education all have been trying to give reality to. In doing so, we suggest that there are many factors in present-day society which may be seen as prompting a major overhaul of our thinking about education, and that the form of education we are purveying may offer some clues as to where such rethinking might begin and the directions it might take. For again we reiterate that, while we have looked mainly to the Primary sector of schooling, we have done this only because it is here that the need for some rethinking has been acknowledged officially and here that the major attempts have been made to translate this rethinking into practice. Both the Hadow (Board of Education 1931) and Plowden (CACE 1967) Reports suggested that Primary education should be seen as *sui generis* and thus evaluated in its own terms. It is our contention that it is education itself which is *sui generis* and that it should not be confused with any of the many other inferior articles currently on offer at all levels of the educational system.

PART ONE

GENERAL CONSIDERATIONS

INTRODUCTION TO PART ONE

This opening section is deliberately brief, for it sets out merely to lay out the ground as a preliminary to the accounts which follow and we feel that this should be done as speedily as possible.

There are two aspects of this groundwork that we wish to stress, two 'general considerations' which we feel must be clearly spelled out at the very outset. The first of these consists of an outline of the general theoretical principles upon which the practice which subsequent chapters will describe is based. These are the principles which we fully explored in *The Primary Curriculum*. We offer a brief reminder of them here as a guide to understanding some of the principles which are implicit in the accounts which follow.

The second 'general consideration' we offer concerns the approach we have adopted. It is our view that teachers and student-teachers are likely to learn far more that will be of productive value for their practice from some attempt to explicate for them what might be regarded as good practice than from detailed surveys of general trends and occurrences. Global statements are of limited value in education, as the fate of many major curriculum projects and other attempts at research has revealed only too clearly. Teachers need help in translating or relating these general principles to the realities of their own classrooms and thus they need an opportunity to see how other teachers in similar circumstances have themselves made such translations. This is the essence and the value of the personal case-study.

We have adopted this approach because we are aware that most other kinds of research in education have been largely ineffective in influencing practice. They have done little more than provide fodder for endless debate among educational theorists. Sometimes, indeed, their effect on practice, especially on practice of the kind we are attempting to describe and analyse here, has been a negative, inhibiting one, since it is clear, often from their very approach and the assumptions which underlie it, that they have failed to understand the basic principles of the activity they purport to explore and examine.

It is our intention to recognize the essential subjectivity of all judgements about education and about the curriculum, to demolish the myth of objective, scientific research in education and to point teachers towards the development of the kind of sensitive and self-critically subjective perspective Lawrence Stenhouse spoke of.

Part One, then, consists of just one chapter, an article previously published in the *Journal of Curriculum Studies*, which attempts to offer these initial considerations — the essential principles of the approach to curriculum we are advocating and the major inadequacies which appear in some attempts at research in education when they are viewed from the perspective of these principles.

CHAPTER 1

RESEARCH AND THE PRIMARY CURRICULUM*

VIC KELLY

'The primary school has its own canons of excellence and criteria of success; it must have the courage to stand by them.' (The Hadow Report 1931, p. xxii).

The purposes of this paper are, firstly, to argue the truth of the above assertion, secondly, to propose that the proper development of Primary education has great significance for all levels of education and, thirdly, to show that the development is currently at risk, not only from pressures external to the teaching profession but also, and more seriously, from the attitudes evinced and the approaches adopted by those within it who have in recent times attempted to promote curriculum innovation and change or to engage in critical analysis or research at this level.

The Primary curriculum

Exactly half a century has elapsed since the publication in 1931 of the Hadow Report on the Primary School which, it could be argued, along with its predecessor of 1926, created, or at least identified, Primary education as a distinct entity. It is thus a good time to re-examine that entity, to appraise its subsequent development and to assess its appropriateness to the contemporary context which is different in so many ways from that of 1931.

The Primary sector of education in the UK has afforded outstanding opportunities for curriculum development. For it has from the beginning been largely free of those external constraints, focusing on and symbolized by the public examinations system, that have inhibited change in the Secondary sector. The demands of the selection procedures at 11+ did have their 'backlash effect' on the work of many Junior schools, but the lower Junior classes, and certainly the Infants schools and departments, remained mostly

* First published in *Journal of Curriculum Studies* (1981), Vol. 13, No. 3, 215-225

untouched by this, and the sense of release that was apparent immediately upon the removal of the 11+ 'examination' by some local authorities is itself evidence of the point that is being made. It is clear too that advantages have accrued from the absence of those constraints created for other educational institutions by internal administrative structures, especially the existence of autonomous subject departments. The looser, and more flexible, internal structure of the Primary school has thus combined with the absence of strong external pressures to create a soil ideal for the rapid growth of the curriculum.

To say that such a context was created is not, of course, to claim that every school can be seen to have taken advantage of it. It is to suggest, however, that curriculum development in some Primary, and especially Infants, schools has been more extensive than that to be observed in any other sector of education. Such development has been shaped and influenced by three major traditions which Blyth (1965) calls the *elementary*, the *preparatory* and the *developmental*. The first two of these derive from the older traditions of English education: the last has emerged during the half-century that has elapsed since the publication of both Hadow Reports (1926 and 1931), that is since the creation of the Primary school. It can be seen as the fruit of those seeds sown much earlier by theorists such as Rousseau, Froebel, Montessori and Dewey which have taken root in the rich and uncluttered soil offered by this newly created Primary sector of education.

It is this tradition, therefore, that holds the greatest interest for and offers the most useful lessons to the student of curriculum. It is this too which has attracted the attention and admiration of educationists throughout the world although it has also inevitably brought out the critics. And it is this approach to education that has been given the official approval and sanction not only of the Hadow Report (1931), but also of the more recently published Plowden Report (1967).

It must, of course, be acknowledged that the recent survey of Primary education undertaken by HM Inspectorate has revealed that far fewer schools have been a part of what the Plowden Report described as the 'quickening trend' towards child-centred education than many people have appeared to believe. Nevertheless, there are some schools, particularly among those concerned with the very young child, which have been developing in this way.

It is also possible to discern a similar trend in certain areas of the curriculum of the Secondary school, as, for example, in some of the attempts to implement the Goldsmiths' College scheme of Interdisciplinary Enquiry (IDE) (James 1968), the Humanities Curriculum Project (HCP) (Stenhouse

1975) and Man: A Course of Study (MACOS) (Stenhouse 1975; Goodson 1976), all of which have recommended that educational planning should begin from a consideration of the processes to be promoted, rather than the bodies of subject-content to be transmitted or the extrinsic objectives to be attained There have been noteworthy attempts to plan education in this way in the private sector too, particularly at schools such as Summerhill, Bedales, Salem and Gordonstoun, whose practices have attracted a good deal of attention and, indeed, admiration.

Furthermore, among those Secondary schools which have in recent years introduced mixed-ability forms of grouping, there have been those who have recognized that a change of pedagogy in this direction is required by the new educational principles they have thus embraced (Kelly 1976), and it has in general been argued that the shift away from the view of education as trans- mission should on other grounds be assisted and accelerated (Goodson 1976). These would appear, then, to constitute further reasons for attempting to elucidate the central features of this alternative pedagogy.

In fact, even if only one school is endeavouring to develop a different form of curriculum, that school is entitled, firstly, not to be forced into adopting a different model before a proper attempt has been made to understand the principles underlying its own; and, secondly, to be recognized as offering a new approach to curriculum which deserves to be considered on its own merits before being rejected.

There are thus several good reasons for regarding the curriculum that has emerged from this tradition as being worthy of study in its own right, without reference to the degree or breadth of attempts at its implementation.

This approach to the curriculum has several major features which it will be helpful to identify at this point. Its central characteristic and all-prevailing principle is its insistence that education must be planned and assessed in terms of its own intrinsic values and merits rather than as instrumental to the achievement of goals or the creation of products that are extrinsic to it (Blenkin and Kelly 1981). This note is first struck by Rousseau who attacks the traditional view of education as concerned with 'man in the making' and as 'always looking for the man in the child, without considering what he is before he becomes a man'. Thus from the first this tradition has urged us to view education as concerned with activities or processes and to evaluate it in terms of its intrinsic merits rather than to see it as a means to extrinsic ends, whether these be social, economic or vocational. Many attempts to explain or to review Primary education have missed this vital point.

Secondly, as a corollary of this, there has been an insistence that education be thought of, in the time-honoured words of Hadow (1931), 'in terms of activity and experience rather than of knowledge to be acquired and facts to be stored' (p.75). It has been the intention that the curriculum be planned by reference to the developing experience of the individual pupil and to his educational needs or requirements rather than to the demands of those bodies of knowledge that are felt to be useful to society or even those which are claimed by some philosophers to have a right to inclusion in the curriculum on their own merits. This view has been strengthened by the work of the developmental psychologists which has suggested that the main concern of education should be to assist in the intellectual development and to improve the cognitive functioning of each individual child, rather than to promote the learning of certain kinds of subject content, and, further, that this can best be done by providing opportunities for active forms of learning (Blenkin and Kelly 1981).

Allied to this has been the idea that knowledge should be seen as largely undifferentiated (ibid.), that subject boundaries, far from being sacrosanct, are arbitrary and ephemeral, that they should impinge on the individual's learning only when they have relevance and meaning for the organization of his developing experience and that they should, like knowledge itself, be constantly open to revision and restructuring, a point that has recently gained strength from the claims of the 'new sociology' that knowledge is socially constructed (Young 1971).

A further and increasingly important aspect of this view of the curriculum as unified and largely undifferentiated has been its rejection of the idea that a division can be made in education between the learning of 'basic skills' and other apparently more sophisticated forms of learning (Blenkin and Kelly 1981). This is a division which, in the first place, it is difficult, if not impossible, to make, since there has been no adequate definition as yet of what constitutes a 'basic skill'. It is also a division which it is dangerous to make since to attempt to teach those things that appear to fall into this category in isolation from other kinds of learning have often proved counter-productive. Many children are put off the activity of reading, and thus never come to appreciate the value of literature, by teaching which over-emphasizes the development of mechanical competence, just as many have been denied for ever access to the wealth of Latin literature by teaching which set about the development of grammatical and syntactical knowledge in isolation from literary appreciation. This, then, is a further important feature of the Primary curriculum.

These features can be seen to add up to what is currently being dubbed as a 'process' model of curriculum (Stenhouse 1975), the main characteristics of which are a concern to define the curriculum in terms not of its subject content nor of its goals but rather of the principles that must underlie and inform the work of both teachers and pupils, and an emphasis on the developmental processes that education is concerned to promote.

This is the main thrust of Richard Peters' analysis of the concept of education (1965, 1966), whose main strength lies in its identification of those processes that are integral to the notion of education and which is weakened by its attempt to graft onto this analysis the incompatible idea that it can also be defined in terms of certain bodies of subject content. It is also borne out by our normal use of the term, since there are few people, except for the ardent followers of 'Mastermind', who would call a man 'educated' merely because he was knowledgeable, even in the most esoteric areas of human knowledge. As Alfred North Whitehead (1932) said, 'The merely well-informed man is the most useless bore on God's earth'. Nor are there many who would call a man educated because his behaviour had been moulded into certain preconceived shapes or modified in certain predetermined ways. What we look for in the educated man is the ability to value things for their own sake, to raise his thinking above the concrete by the use of appropriate forms of conceptualization, in fact to operate successfully in all 'modes' of thinking, to examine issues critically, to see them in perspective and, above all, to think for himself. In short, education is a matter of processes and this the exponents of Primary education have been trying to tell us for some time.

There are two particular approaches to educational planning which are totally incompatible with this basic philosophy. The first is that which has tended to dominate curriculum planning in the Secondary, and, indeed, the Further and Higher sectors of the educational system, namely a concern with subject content as the central determinant of the curriculum, what we might call the 'content' model of curriculum planning. There are two main reasons why this approach is incompatible with the view of education I have just outlined. In the first place, it wrongly assumes that only certain kinds of subject or 'discipline', only certain bodies of knowledge can be suitable vehicles for the kinds of development that constitute what it means to be educated, so that it concentrates on what appear to be the demands of those bodies of knowledge rather than attending to the process of learning. And secondly, it is this approach and the consequent forms of institutional organization that it has led to that have sometimes resulted in the complete rejection of, and have always made difficult the implementation of, the idea that knowledge might be 'integrated' or at least reorganized into new structures to enable us to respond to new kinds of question or enquiry.

The second kind of approach to curriculum planning that is incompatible with the view of education I am suggesting underpins the Primary curriculum is that which requires us to begin with a statement of the objectives or goals of our teaching. For this 'objectives' model of curriculum planning is essentially instrumental and thus at odds with the developmental approach to education whose major characteristic, as we have seen, is its concern with the process of education itself rather than its end-products. There are many other reasons why this model is incompatible, such as its base of behaviourist psychology and its consequent concepts of man, of education, of learning and of knowledge, but the core of its incompatibility is its instrumental stance, its product ideology.

It can thus be seen that of the four elements of the curriculum identified by Ralph Tyler (1949), usually summarized as objectives, content, procedures and evaluation, the view of education we are discussing here stresses procedures, and this, far from being the weakness that Paul Hirst (1969) supposed, does in fact constitute its strength as a model for curriculum planning of a kind that is in the full sense educational. It is this that makes it a unique form of curriculum and one that must be assessed on its own terms rather than measured by the application of templates which are inappropriate to it.

These, then, are some of the major features of the development that has been going on in some Primary schools for a good many years, development of a kind which led one commentator, in contemplating a much wider canvas, to say as early as 1961 that 'in primary education, a notable expansion of the curriculum is perhaps the century's major achievement' (Williams 1961, p.165). It is also worth noting that much of this development had occurred and a tradition of development had been established long before the notion of deliberate curriculum planning had reached the consciousness of those engaged in other sectors of the education system, long before what Lawrence Stenhouse (1980) has called 'the curriculum development movement' of the mid-1960s. It must also be noted that this development has been inhibited rather than advanced by much of the research that has been generated by that 'curriculum development movement', both by the kinds of solution and of innovation which have been proposed for the Secondary sector and by the perspectives that have been adopted by some of the subsequent research that has been directed specifically at the Primary curriculum.

The Primary curriculum, however, is not only to be viewed, examined and assessed on its own terms, it must also be seen as providing a model that all other sectors of the education system would do well to consider with care and attention. In part, this is because it seems to represent the most developed version to be seen in practice of what is now being hailed as a 'process model' of curriculum planning, but also because it increasingly appears to be the only basis for genuine educational planning.

This approach to education, even at Primary level, has of course always had its critics and contrary views have been expressed. Indeed, those other traditional influences on the Primary school which Blyth (1965) calls the 'elementary' and the 'preparatory' have brought to bear a different set of values and have encouraged the development of a different ethos. It is only recently, however, that deliberate attempts have been made from outside the schools to influence the development of the Primary curriculum in directions different from those described here, and positively to inhibit further growth of this kind. Moreover, in addition to these deliberate attempts to impose upon it a different stamp, it is also clear that similar pressures have sometimes resulted from attempts at analysis or research in this area which have failed to appreciate the basic principles of this form of education and have thus inhibited this kind of development by applying unsuitable criteria to it. It is to a brief consideration of some of these that I now wish to turn.

Research and the Primary curriculum

It is quite clear that those external pressures on the schools which have been rapidly gathering momentum in recent years have as much significance for the Primary sector as for any other sector of the education system. Demands for increased teacher accountability, for the monitoring of 'standards' and for greater public control of the curriculum are having their effect on the work of the Primary schools as much as on that at other phases of education. Indeed, it might be argued that it was the sequence of events at one particular Junior school, the William Tyndale school, which triggered off this very process. What is not always so clearly understood, however, and cannot, therefore, be stressed too often is that this process consists of attempting to force the curriculum of many Primary schools into a mould that is unsuited to it or, what may be worse, to evaluate it by reference to criteria which are inappropriate to it. For the general thrust and direction of these external demands and pressures has been towards an emphasis on the teaching of subject content as justifiable in itself rather than in relation to its contribution to the growth and development of the pupil, on the consequent introduction of subject divisions and teaching of 'basic skills' in isolation from their wider educational context, and the prespecification of curriculum objectives as a prerequisite for simplistic forms of external evaluation. In short, the needs of society are being held to take precedence over the needs of the pupils, so that a totally different philosophy is being foisted upon the Primary school without, one suspects, any real appreciation of what this entails. In particular, it is doubtful if there is any real awareness of the extent to which these pressures are inhibiting the continued development of a special kind of approach to education.

It is much more serious, however, when the same process is assisted from within by the theoreticians and by those who have been responsible for major research projects in this area. For one result of this has been that much of the research undertaken has had and is having the effect of inhibiting rather than promoting that curriculum development we noted earlier. It is to this that I want to devote the rest of this paper.

The first thing one must note when considering research into Primary education is its paucity. Less than 25 per cent of Schools Council funds have been spent on this area of schooling, although, if one leaves aside demographic variations, there must be at least as many pupils between the ages of 3 and 11 in Primary schools as there are between the ages of 11 and 18 in Secondary schools. One's second reaction, however, is to be grateful for this, since most of the work that has been undertaken in this area has reinforced this process of forcing it into unsuitable moulds by using inappropriate techniques of measurement and/or by failing to appreciate the peculiar and particular principles upon which it is based.

There are three major kinds of mistake that have been made here and I want to look briefly at all of them in turn; firstly, that of viewing the Primary curriculum in terms of its subject-content, secondly, that of separating out for teaching purposes the so-called 'basic skills' and, thirdly, that of too readily and uncritically accepting the idèa that all curriculum planning must begin from the prespecification of objectives.

It is understandable — although not excusable — that a University teacher of biology might be heard opposing the development of a programme for the initial education of the intending Primary teacher on the grounds that it contains no identifiable 'teaching subject'. It is neither excusable nor understandable when teachers of education are to be heard making the same point. One of the strengths of the Primary curriculum is, as I tried to show earlier, that it has been able to emphasize the processes of growth and development rather than the teaching of bodies of knowledge. That old adage about teaching children rather than subjects has more substance to it and is worthy of more thoughtful consideration than most educationists have been prepared to concede. Yet a major feature of many of the attempts that have been or are being made to promote the development of the curriculum of the Primary school has been a concern with the advancement of learning in particular subject areas.

The recent survey of Primary schools carried out by HM Inspectorate (DES 1978a) reveals an ambivalence on this issue. For while it notes the strengths of the 'one class to one teacher system' and acknowledges the dangers of diminishing these strengths by introducing organizational arrangements which might fragment the children's experiences, it also recommends the employment of subject specialists in Primary schools and thus adds its weight to the view that the central concern of education at that level is with the acquisition of certain identifiable bodies of knowledge rather than the development of children's capacities. The reluctance of HM Inspectorate to make such a positive commitment and the general ambivalence which the Report reveals in this area are not reflected, however, in the reaction of most local authority inspectors or advisers to suggestions that they should be exercising more control over what goes on at this level of education. For, in most authorities, the recent demands of the advisory service for more detailed accounts of what teachers are planning to do and what they are actually doing have taken the form of requests for statements of policy and the keeping of records in discrete subject categories. Nor is this to be wondered at when one realizes that most authorities appoint and employ such advisers on the basis of their expertise in particular subjects rather than their knowledge and understanding of the processes of Primary education.

However, this general trend has also been reinforced by most of the formal research that has been sponsored at this level. For most of the large-scale projects in this area have taken as their point of reference the kind of curriculum theory that has been generated by the subject-centred approach of the Secondary school. The largely subject-based structure of the Schools Council, in spite of the fact that there has been from the outset one committee concerned with Primary education, has had the effect of keeping curriculum development within subject areas and most of the experts whose advice and guidance have been sought have been subject specialists, usually from University departments. This has led many people, in turn, to view curriculum development in the Primary school in terms of content only (Blenkin 1980).

The two subjects that have received most of this kind of attention have been mathematics and science; and a case could be made out for claiming that much of what has been attempted there has been counter-productive to the work of the Primary school, because it has not been based on a sufficiently clear understanding of what many teachers at that level have been attempting to do and has thus been offering them directives or blueprints that were incompatible with other general features of their work. In this connection, it is interesting to note the very different line that is being taken by the most recent Schools Council project in Primary science, whose very title 'Learning through Science' (Schools Council 1980) indicates that there is now a recognition that what the Primary teacher needs is guidance on how a subject can be used to promote those processes he or she is concerned with rather than on what devices can be offered to assist with the learning of the subject itself. In this area at least, then, the penny has dropped and the approach to curriculum development is now being made from the pupil's end of the process rather than from that of the content of the subject.

The failure to appreciate this is also a feature of some of the theoretical analyses that have been attempted of the Primary curriculum. For these have often taken the form of attempting to foist upon or at least adapt to the Primary school those knowledge-based theories of education, which no matter how much they have been dressed up in epistemological arguments, have been prompted by the subject-centred ethos of the Secondary school. Thus most of the work of Dearden (1968, 1976) has consisted of attempts to adapt to the Primary curriculum the notion that the 'forms of knowledge' should be the central concern of the curriculum planner, a notion that runs counter to the essence of the philosophy of education that has developed at that level. For the epistemological basis of that philosophy is fundamentally empiricist and that is why it will reject any form of rationalism that one tries to graft on to it (Blenkin and Kelly 1981).

In these ways the work of the researchers and the theorists has reinforced the attempts of many outside the education service to impose a subject-centred model on a curriculum whose development has taken a completely different form.

The same kind of incompatibility is apparent when we consider the main features of the earlier development of the Primary curriculum with current demands for an increased emphasis on the teaching of the 'basic skills'. For again we can see that such demands run counter to the main thrust of that development.

Again we can perhaps understand how the layman comes to take this kind of simplistic view of what schools are for and of how they can best achieve what he sees as their central purposes. Again, however, one feels there is less justification when people inside the teaching profession adopt a similarly unsophisticated attitude. Nevertheless, this is another area in which we can see this happening. It is not only parents, industrialists and politicians who are ready to evaluate the work of the Primary school by reference to the scores its pupils can attain on tests of reading and/or mathematical competence; local authority advisers can also be seen to be yielding too readily to the pressure to make the same kinds of narrow evaluation of the work of the schools. And the effect of this again is to distort the curriculum by pressing it into a mould that is not fitted to it.

This process has been further reinforced by the work of some of the researchers. The most obvious example here is the work of Neville Bennett (1976), among whose basic assumptions were that the effectiveness of a Primary school can be measured by reference to the attainment of its pupils in a narrow range of cognitive skills and that pupil progress is to be defined in terms of achievement in reading, mathematics and English. Such an approach invites not merely an emphasis on cognitive achievement but, worse, an emphasis on that narrow range of cognitive achievement that can be measured by the primitive and limited techniques that psychology has been able to develop. It will be readily apparent that such an approach ignores most of what might appear to be of lasting value in the educational experiences a child can be offered at this stage.

What is not so apparent is the degree to which it may also be counter-productive to these wider aspects of education. We noted earlier that it is possible to train children to a high level of competence and achievement in tests of reading and arithmetic by methods which have the effect of simultaneously deterring them from ever using them to educational advantage. In short, it is possible to lead pupils to a high degree of competence in, say, reading and by that very process not only to fail to develop in them any love of literature but perhaps even to inhibit that development. Conversely, it is worth noting the findings of the recent survey of Primary schools by HM Inspectorate (DES 1978a) that the highest levels of competence were attained by those pupils whose learning of such skills had not been isolated from the totality of the educational experiences the schools were attempting to offer them. It is also interesting to compare this with similar claims made for the learning of basic motor-skills in the broader context of education in Craft, Design and Technology (Schools Council 1969).

Again, therefore, we must note that not only external pressures but the basic assumptions of some people, including research workers, within the profession can be seen to be opposed to a major feature of the recent development of the Primary curriculum.

Lastly, I turn to a brief consideration of what may well be the most seriously disturbing feature of current pressures on the Primary curriculum, namely the attempt to force upon it an approach to planning through the prespecification of curriculum objectives.

The most depressing feature of the recent flurry of activity in the area of curriculum planning at all levels of the education system is the adoption, particularly by local authority advisers, of the idea of curriculum planning through the use of prespecified objectives as though it is a great, new discovery. For it reveals just how long it takes for the ideas of the theorists in education to filter through to the consciousness of those in the field. And it suggests that we must wait another fifteen years or so before they catch up with the mass of work that has more recently been published on the inadequacies of this approach. In the meantime, we must recognize that teachers are now being asked to state their aims and objectives in written form for the benefit of such advisers and others and, sometimes, also to keep detailed written records in the same format, and that this is being done without reference to the fact that it is in conflict with that approach to education we described earlier.

Again it is even more disturbing to find this process being reinforced by the assumptions and approaches of those engaged in research into, or other kinds of theoretical analysis of the curriculum of, the Primary school. Among the best examples of this are two projects which, having avoided the Scylla of taking a subject-based approach and thus having held out hope of an examination of the Primary curriculum in terms appropriate to it, were immediately sucked into the whirlpool of the 'objectives' model of planning. The first of these is one of the few attempts the Schools Council has made specifically to explore the Primary curriculum in its own right, the 'Aims in Primary Education' project, which not only adopts, largely uncritically, the 'objectives' approach but also embraces an overtly behavioural version of it — 'If the teacher's aims are to help to guide his practice, then they should be expressed in behavioural terms. That is to say that they should state what the child will actually be able to do when the aim is achieved' (Ashton, Kneen and Davies 1975, p.15). It is not merely the adoption of this kind of approach that is to be questioned; it is more the failure to recognize that it is diametrically opposed to the main direction taken by the curriculum of many Primary schools. Similarly, the more recent Schools Council project 'Record-Keeping in the Primary Schools' (Clift, Weiner and Wilson 1981) adopts an approach that is even more directly derivative of Bloom's taxonomy than the 'Aims in Primary Education' project. Not only does it accept the need for aims and objectives as a basis for effective assessment and record-keeping, it also advises teachers to list the aspects of pupils' behaviour — cognitive, affective and psychomotor — which need to be recorded. Again, one feels that this approach is adopted without due consideration of the extent to which it may be quite unsuited to the curriculum of many Primary schools, and in particular of the Nursery schools which were the subject of the report of a parallel project (Bate and Smith 1978).

Again too Dearden's attempt to reconcile the view of Primary education I have attempted to describe here with demands that it should state its goals and purposes, misses the point (Dearden 1976). For, even when we have distinguished our 'relational' aims from our 'directional' aims, we are still viewing the process of education as an instrumental one and thus are adopting a perspective which is not only incompatible with that particular view of Primary education but also with that very rationalist epistemology on which this distinction purports to be based (Blenkin and Kelly 1981).

To view and to evaluate the curriculum of the Primary school, or of any other educational institution for that matter, by reference to goals or purposes external to it, no matter how those goals or purposes are defined, is to put at risk the essence of that curriculum which is its focus on the processes of education. If education is concerned with intrinsic value, then it cannot be defined by reference to any kind of extrinsic goal. That is the message of fifty years of curriculum development at Primary level. It is a message that cannot and should not be ignored.

It is not being suggested that a 'progressive' or 'process' approach to education should be accepted uncritically, merely that its existence must be acknowledged and that, where it does exist, it must not be ignored and trampled down if our concern is to promote a proper form of curriculum development. It would be reassuring if we could assume that those responsible for current attempts to erode it do in fact have a full understanding of what they are doing and are acting from an appreciation of its basic principles. However, if the attempts to replace it with other approaches to curriculum planning were the result of careful consideration and a conscious decision to reject it, then those attempts in themselves would be more thoroughly planned. Merely to ignore years of evolution, particularly at a time when the effects of that evolution might be said to have begun to influence other sectors of education, is something which cannot be justified on any grounds.

There are, of course, indications that some of the people working in this field are attempting to look at the Primary curriculum as something which is *sui generis*. The survey of HM Inspectorate (DES 1978a), to which reference has been made on several occasions, is an example of an attempt to evaluate Primary education in its own terms. Several curriculum projects too have been based on a clearer appreciation of the essential and peculiar elements of the Primary curriculum. Projects such as the 'Progress in Learning Science' project (Harlen, Darwin and Murphy 1977), the 'Learning through Science' project (Schools Council 1980) to which I referred earlier, and, perhaps especially, the 'Communication Skills in Early Childhood' project (Schools Council 1976) have all, in different ways, attempted to promote the development of the Primary curriculum in a manner more in keeping with its earlier history and have thus pointed the way to its continued evolution. In doing so, they are also making important contributions to the development of curriculum theory itself, since they are revealing new perspectives and exploring the implications of a planning model that is fundamentally different from that which has been adopted largely uncritically by others. Research, development and proposals which run counter to this kind of evolution must at least take account of its presence and make some positive response to it.

Summary and conclusions

The Primary curriculum, at least in the form in which it has evolved in certain schools and through the work of certain theorists, offers a different and interesting model of curriculum planning and one which, because of its central concern with the intrinsic value of education, may be the only model which provides the blueprint for a form of schooling which fully merits description as educational. This paper has endeavoured firstly to pick out the major elements of that model, secondly, to argue that it is worthy of deeper analysis, further research and the careful consideration of people engaged at all levels of the education system, and, thirdly, to suggest that it is currently at risk and needs to be protected from those attempts to press it into a different and unsuitable mould which are being made not only overtly from outside that system but also, covertly and, one fears, through ignorance, by the implicit assumptions and unsuitable approaches of some of those who have already attempted such analysis and research.

Primary schools must be declared a protected species before we destroy something that may be uniquely valuable in an educational system that daily appears to have less and less to be proud of.

PART TWO

ASPECTS OF THE CURRICULUM

INTRODUCTION TO PART TWO

One of the things we attempted to do in Part One was to reveal some of the inadequacies of traditional approaches to research in education. It is our view that few, if any, teachers have been directly influenced in their practice by the findings of educational research. If any effect can be discerned, it is indirect, a result of thoughts which the research findings may have sparked off, since the research itself, if it genuinely sets out to be scientific, must restrict itself to offering descriptions of what happens rather than prescriptions for future development. Chapter 1 endeavoured to show that in the case of the Primary curriculum, as that was defined there, the effects of research of this kind has been inhibiting rather than helpful.

In fact, the major positive influences on the development of this approach to education have come from rather different sources, such as the ideas of many thinkers from Rousseau to John Dewey, who have been inspired far more by certain notions they adhered to about child-nature, or indeed human nature, than by any scientific or pseudo-scientific data. It is equally plain that a major influence on the development of this kind of curriculum has come from practitioners — not only those, such as Pestalozzi, Froebel, Montessori and Dewey, who have engaged in extensive theorizing about their work, but also some, such as J.H. Buckley at Bedales School, A.S. Neill at Summerhill, Susan Isaacs at Malting House and Kurt Hahn at Salem School and later at Gordonstoun, who have been largely content to let their work speak for them. This approach to educational research has been lost in recent years. The attempt made in the United Kingdom in the 1960s by educationists such as Richard Peters to inject rigour into educational theorizing was important and necessary but it has led to the loss of much of that essential sense of commitment that the contributions of the practitioners provided. Our approach here is intended to bring the committed practitioner back into the debate.

In Part Two, then, we introduce several practitioners and invite them to give an account of their work in several areas of the curriculum.

There are of course certain difficulties with this kind of approach. Teachers are likely to find it no easier than anyone else to stand back and look at their work with detached objectivity. However, this is something they must learn to do if they are to play a full and proper part in accountability procedures, in the evaluation and thus the continued development of their work. Besides, if we invite their contributions in order to regain that lost sense of commitment, we must beware of stifling it by pressing too hard for detachment. It is the essence of dialogue that people should put and support their own point of view. Their listeners, or readers, must accept this.

A second difficulty stems from the fact that we have had to ask them to address themselves to specific aspects of the curriculum. We were conscious in doing this that we might be putting at risk that sense of the unity of knowledge and of educational experience which we see as crucial to educational development. We were reassured, therefore, to discover that the editors' problem turned out instead to be one of overlap, since all the contributors to this section have found that they could only describe their work in the aspect of the curriculum we asked them to consider by showing also its interrelationships with other areas of the curriculum.

And so, albeit with a full awareness of the risk of introducing another set of rigid categories and of attempting to divide the indivisible, we have identified several aspects of this kind of teaching and asked contributors to concentrate on these in describing their own work.

CHAPTER 2

'THE BASIC SKILLS'

GEVA BLENKIN

"I couldn't afford to learn it," said the Mock Turtle with a sigh. "I only took the regular course."
"What was that?" inquired Alice.
"Reeling and writhing, of course, to begin with," the Mock Turtle replied, "and then the different branches of Arithmetic — Ambition, Distraction, Uglification and Derision."
(Lewis Carroll)

When parents send their children to school they do so with the expectation that, at the very least, the children will be taught 'the basic skills'. Teachers too, share the conviction that one main purpose of schooling is to advance literacy and numeracy. There is overwhelming evidence (DES 1978a; Galton, Simon and Croll 1980; DES 1982a) to show that Primary teachers hold this conviction so firmly that they will spend most of their time attempting to teach children the 3 Rs, despite the alarmist claims to the contrary which were made so vociferously in the 1970s. Even the youngest children in our schools would re-echo the Mock Turtle's surprise and scorn if they encountered someone who did not seem to understand that this was in the nature of things when one goes to school.

It is remarkable that this consensus of opinion concerning the importance of 'basic skills' which has existed at least since the establishment of compulsory schooling in 1870, has not brought us nearer in our practice to an understanding of the significant impact that skills learning makes on the day-to-day work in schools. It is even more remarkable that, in spite of (or, perhaps, because of) the overwhelming emphasis placed on learning 'the basics', we have not succeeded in changing most children's experience of skills learning from that parodied by Lewis Carroll over a century ago.

Part of the problem is that our view of 'the basics' is too naive. The growth of competence is rarely considered as central to the processes of education and vital to the learner's experience, not just in the early years but throughout childhood and beyond. Too often the teaching of 'the basic skills' has been seen as an issue separate from and often therefore outside of the main curriculum debate, to be dealt with as early as possible in the child's school career and then forgotten about. If the child at seven is thought to have failed to have achieved basic competence he is considered for remedial help in order that he may then proceed with his education. And for many children this 'regular course' dominates their experience in school in the same way as it did for the Mock Turtle.

Another difficulty lies in the fact that not only has skills learning been designated as a purely psychological matter, but also it has been seen as systematic in nature. The predominant influence on skills teaching, therefore, has come from behavioural psychology. The emphasis has been on analysing the levels of difficulty in skilled behaviour and arranging these into steps. Materials have been selected, schemes of work devised and time allocated by the teacher so that the learner can work through the sequences, practising as much as is necessary, until he emerges as a skilled person at the end of it all.

If we doubt the influence of this model on teachers, we need only to note the fact that, throughout the twentieth century, reading schemes and structured mathematics programmes have become big business and are now accepted as essential to the equipment of most schools. It is valid to argue, therefore, that a 'step-by-step' procedure has seemed more plausible in explaining the acquisition of skills than it has seemed in any other part of the teacher's work.

In addition to these aspects of the problem, teaching 'the basic skills' is still the source of most anxiety for teachers and parents alike. It remains the sphere in educational debates that provokes from teachers the most heated responses and reveals the most entrenched positions. It is not difficult to understand the apprehension of teachers when on the one hand parents are watching their children anxiously for signs of progress and on the other hand the local education authorities are pressing for clear, written evidence of success in 'the basics'. Adults who have achieved a certain level of competence in literacy and numeracy forget that it can present difficulties and often view as shameful any problems that teachers may face in helping children to a similar level of competence.

Finally, and most curiously of all, studies of teachers at work in the classroom have shown that skills teaching is dealt with quite separately by many teachers who profess to being committed to a unified approach to the curriculum (Barnes 1976; King 1978; Galton, Simon and Croll 1980; Adelman 1981). This separation is often made unwittingly by the teachers concerned. It is in this sphere that we are most likely to find a gap between the teacher's aspirations and the reality of her work.

It is in an attempt to help those teachers and student teachers who are finding difficulty in making practical reality of their beliefs that the following exploration is undertaken. The picture is incomplete, as is our understanding of what constitutes a 'basic skill'. However, sufficient work has been undertaken recently, especially in the teaching of reading, to offer practical guidance to teachers who are helping children here, as well as in other areas such as numeracy, enquiry skills and study skills.

My basic premise is that it is possible — indeed desirable — to teach skills in such a way that they hold meaning for the learner and provide him with the means to grow in competence and confidence. I have found that many teachers agree with this assertion but they have often received insufficient help towards seeing its practical implications. It is the identification of some of the principles which underlie this assertion and the practical implications they lead to that form the theme of this chapter.

It is becoming increasingly apparent, both from observational studies of classrooms and from the evidence of the numbers of young people who leave school feeling bewildered by the experience and alienated from the skills that have been offered there, that many of the teacher's efforts have been misdirected. Our first task, therefore, must be to identify some of the pitfalls that occur in current practice. For, if the teacher has a clearer picture of these hazards, she will not only be in a better position to know what she must avoid but she will also be able to deduce principles that will help her to evaluate and improve her daily practice.

Next we must examine the planning and preparation that must be undertaken if the teacher is to equip herself with the right kind of support. We may accept that many of the current approaches to skills teaching are inappropriate. In order to change these, however, we need to give considerable thought to the practical preparation and planning that are necessary. Without a fundamental change in the context of our work, we will remain ill-equipped to develop a more appropriate approach. Practical guidance on the planning of a suitable context is offered, therefore, in the second part of the chapter.

In the final part, we will examine briefly some attempts at implementing an approach to skills teaching which seeks to unify skills learning with other aspects of the child's experience. It is hoped that these brief descriptions of real encounters will 'flesh out' the more general points which are made.

Some hazards of teaching 'the basic skills'

I will begin this section by sharing what was for me one of the most enduring images that I have witnessed on television. It occurred some years ago in a comedy programme which was a compilation of the mishaps and errors which are normally edited out of films and other programmes. A pretty and intelligent girl of Primary school age was cast as the compère of a sports programme. She appeared confident, relaxed, even somewhat precocious until, through employing a conventional English phonic strategy, she mispronounced her introduction of the Grand Prix, to howls of amusement from the studio audience and the adult supervisor of the programme.

The image endured not because it was funny — I didn't find it so — but because of the confusion and alarm on the face of the child when she recognized that she had made a monumental blunder. She clearly understood that she was introducing a big motor race but did not understand why her mispronunciation should be so hilariously funny to the adults on the set. I remember watching uncomfortably as her mood changed from one of confidence to one of panic and anxiety.

Here was a child who had a degree of competence — in literacy at least — in advance of her age and was happy and poised when demonstrating it, until one simple slip led to her feeling humiliated in a way that she is unlikely to forget.

This fear of revealing incompetence can extend far beyond childhood. For example, a team of researchers who set out to investigate the mathematical needs of adults in daily life found their work largely frustrated by the widespread reluctance on the part of adults to participate. In reviewing the responses of the small numbers of adults who were persuaded to take part, the Cockcroft Committee comments that 'the extent to which the need to undertake even an apparently simple and straightforward piece of mathematics could induce feelings of anxiety, helplessness, fear and even guilt in some of those interviewed was, perhaps, the most striking feature of the study' (DES 1982b, p.7). And there was no significant difference between the response of men and women or between the academically qualified and unqualified.

These episodes draw attention to the fact that learning 'the basic skills' can be a hazardous business for children. To reveal incompetence is painfully embarrassing. This simple truth, however, is rarely considered because we are in the habit of viewing the situation from the teacher's rather than the learner's viewpoint. In perpetuating this habit, we often increase rather than alleviate the hazards that children face.

In the course of this first section, therefore, I will pick out elements of skills learning from the learner's point of view. In doing so I hope to mark the pitfalls that exist when we embark on teaching children 'the basics'.

Making learning individual

The first element to highlight is that skills learning is essentially a social experience. This is why it can lead to the negative consequences described above and also why it can provoke powerful and unpleasant emotions in the learner.

The social nature of skills learning, of course, is not totally negative. There are very positive dimensions that have direct implications for teaching. The learner, for example, needs the support of someone who is more skilled and able to demonstrate and share the pleasure that can be gained from being competent. Adults who enjoy sharing books, who see the purpose of being numerate, who research and write when necessary, who are expert enquirers and above all who spend time sharing the delight in these skills in their daily contact with children are always the most inspiring teachers.

The second dimension is that the support offered, as well as giving a model, should be collaborative in nature. The less experienced the child is at the skill, the more dependent he is on the support of others alongside him. Further than this, the teacher who is offering support must be able to see the problem from the child's point of view — must be able to 'decentre', as Margaret Donaldson so powerfully puts it (Donaldson 1978) — and collaborate with him on the task in hand until he can make sense of it.

Now this kind of co-operative approach may seem very idealistic until we pause to watch even the most inadequate parents willingly and spontaneously helping their children to walk and to talk. For here the striking feature is the delight in sharing which provides a truly social experience for all participants. We cannot but be convinced that this is how 'the basics' should be learned.

Teachers, however, are under more pressure than parents, as they are often dealing with 35 or more children, so that the sheer problem of numbers can put them off even attempting to provide experiences of this kind. Later in the chapter we will examine some of the practical measures that can be taken to make it possible for the teacher, despite the obvious pressures, to work in this way. At this point, however, we must identify the first pitfall to be avoided when teaching 'the basic skills', which is making learning individual.

The importance of the social nature of skills learning, briefly described above, is too often overlooked by teachers who tend to place most stress on individual performance. As was noted above, teachers are very busy people and often become harassed by the sheer size of their classes. This problem is exacerbated, however, by the teachers themselves when they make persistent attempts to provide individual programmes for every child. These attempts are most likely to be made in relation to the 3 Rs.

The main problem seems to be that it is often assumed that, in order to ensure that each child is cared and catered for, teachers must not only be aware of the individuals' progress themselves but must also give the child his own work sequence to follow. Several children may be following the same schedule but each is working alone. It is not difficult to see how the teacher's time and attention can become filled by this mammoth task.

The demand that such an undertaking places on the teacher must explain one of the most disturbing findings of the ORACLE study of Junior school classrooms, which was the solitary nature of most children's experience in school. Many children were, in a very real sense, alone in a crowd. The research team describes the scene as follows:

> Individualized teaching (or interaction) is not 'progressively' oriented . . . it is overwhelmingly factual and managerial . . . the teacher's interactions with individual pupils are in fact primarily of a task supervision or 'routine' type; that is, they are centrally concerned to keep the pupil working or involved on his task (Galton, Simon and Croll, 1980, p. 157).

The report goes on to show a situation where children spend most of their time in the classroom sitting in groups but working alone on individual assignments planned by the teacher, two-thirds of which are related to the skills of numeracy and literacy.

The most worrying aspect of this glimpse of life in our classrooms is that there seems to be no opportunity for the kind of collaborative experience that is so vital to skills learning. Children are left to make what they will of numeracy and literacy whilst the teachers depend heavily on the effectiveness of preplanned programmes.

Of course, some children succeed in this setting. It is not difficult to imagine, however, that many more will be put off by the experience. For many children reading, writing and calculating are reduced to a lonely exercise of working through programmes and schemes. One must assume that many children never gain an insight into the power and enjoyment that comes from becoming literate and numerate. The work which has been carefully devised to help the child can serve to alienate him from the very skills that it was designed to advance.

Making learning impersonal

If the first element in learning skills is its social character, the second is that it is a very personal matter. It is characteristic of children — and adults too — that they will strive to make sense of their experiences and they do this, in part, by bringing their own meanings to the task. They need to meet situations in school and at home, therefore, where they can experience what it is like to be a reader, a writer or a mathematician.

At first glance this may seem to be an unreasonable demand to make on a young child. Recent work has shown, however, that a compelling case can be made for the adoption of this approach in the teaching of reading at least. Margaret Spencer, for example, argues that, when this is done,

> Children no longer have to perform actions with words in ways that bear no re-lation to what a successful reader does. 'Behave like a real reader' is the invi-tation; guess, sort out the meaning from the text. The young reader is to go about reading as readers do, and the teacher has to stand behind the child's head to see what the task looks like from there (Spencer 1980, pp. 52-53).

If the teacher chooses to acknowledge this, she has a powerful base from which to work. Her attention is immediately drawn to the material that is being handled — in the case of reading, the books, stories etc. that are shared — and to the reason for spending time on the task. These become two con-siderations that are at least as important as the third — the performance of the individual. For they are the means by which the learner makes sense of the task and makes the skills part of himself. And this is as true of the adult who is extending his competence by meeting new and challenging materials and seeking to make sense of new experiences as it is of the child at the earliest stages. The material and the reason for involvement are intimately connected with the learning of the skill.

This takes us, then, to the second pitfall to be avoided when teaching 'the basic skills', which is making learning impersonal.

One way of alienating children from skills learning is to give them a sense of isolation. Another way is to make their tasks impersonal. As was noted above, children expect learning to make sense and if we neglect to build on this inclination, they are unlikely to grow in competence. Margaret Donaldson warns us that 'the process of becoming literate can have marked — but commonly unsuspected — effects on the growth of the mind. It can do this by encouraging highly important forms of intellectual self-awareness and self-control' (Donaldson 1978, p. 97). There is every reason to suppose that the same applies to becoming numerate or to learning any other reflective skill.

And yet so much of the work that is undertaken in schools under the name of 'the basic skills' is off-putting to children because it ignores this important point and becomes senseless and mystifying. The impersonal, technical approach to learning has resulted in reading and mathematics books whose sense has been sacrificed in order to promote a small part of a skill. It has spawned cards and exercises to be practised which, when disconnected from any meaningful context, become dull, incoherent or just plain insulting. And it is the children who are already finding the process difficult to make sense of who are most likely to be exposed to this kind of activity for the longest period of their school life. Small wonder that most people make minimal use of these skills in later life.

Worst of all, the impersonal approach has made it difficult for teachers to discuss with children in a meaningful setting and in an honest way the kind of venture that they have embarked upon. The 'magic rules' that are invented by teachers to explain the inconsistencies in language systems, for example, compound the situation for many children.

Making the learner passive

We have explored the social and personal aspects of skills learning and must now turn to the third dimension. This is the active nature of the learning. Part of the invitation to behave like a skilled person implies an intellectual activity on the part of the child. He is to explore, try things out, guess if necessary. Most important of all, he is to approach the task as if it makes sense and is worth doing. The teacher is there to share the experience with the children in her class. Her role is to help them gain the most from their attempts by offering assistance, showing them further possibilities, helping them to find the rules and consistencies that govern the activity and encouraging them to ask for help when necessary.

Too many children, however, are given quite a different impression. For they are encouraged to think that they will learn skills as a result of what the teacher does to them. Thus we come to the third pitfall that we need to be aware of when teaching 'the basic skills' and this is making the learner passive.

Children are very quick to learn how to behave as pupils and they do this by subtle and indirect means — mainly by watching the teacher's reactions to their classmates. Mary Willes, in her study of reception classes, has shown, for example, that in a sample of forty-two newcomers to school, only four children gave clear evidence of not knowing what was required of them. She goes on to argue that, on her evidence, 'the pupils' part is one in which real initiatives are rarely taken and real choices rarely available. In so far as the pupils' role is typically that of a recipient, it does not commend itself as more than a limited and rather inflexible medium for learning' (Willes 1981, p.58).

Children at every stage of the Primary school are fully aware that the teacher is at an advantage — not least in the sense that she controls and limits the kind of behaviour that is acceptable and the range of activities that are available in the classroom. The problem is that too many of the measures which teachers take in order to maintain control over the behaviour of the children encourage them to be passive in their learning as well as orderly in their behaviour. It is only very recently that we have begun to question the impact that certain kinds of classroom control have upon the child's disposition to learn. The development of different ways of maintaining an orderly classroom, ones that will positively encourage active learning, therefore, have been slow to emerge and most schools rely on traditional routines.

Again one can appreciate that, once the teacher has found an approach that seems to work and that quickly establishes order in her classroom, she will be reluctant to seek alternative ways of working. This is especially so at a time when she is pressured by claims in society at large that schools have become disorderly places. However, the way to establish control that is too often adopted by teachers is to give children a daily routine of tasks to undertake. These routines extend far beyond registration and the distribution of milk to include such rituals as, for example, a story to write, a reader to practise and a mathematics card to complete. The option 'to choose' is offered as the reward for the completion of these tasks before the day is ended.

In this way 'the basics' — often referred to by the children as 'the real work' — become divorced not only from reality but also from pursuits that actively engage the minds of the children. They become the means for controlling the child rather than the means by which the child comes to have more control over his own life.

It is clear from the discussion so far that there are serious pitfalls that the teacher encounters when she sets out to teach children 'the basic skills'. If she recognizes them, however, and examines their causes, certain fundamental principles emerge which give her a basis for evaluating her work.

She is able to consider, for example, whether the children are given opportunities for genuine collaboration with her and with others in their work and whether the activities which are offered are encouraging them to experience the social significance of their increasing competence. She will be alerted to the fact that, if the child is to grow in competence, he needs to be able to see skills as part of himself and his experience of them must, therefore, be personal and invested with meaning. She will also be aware that the tasks that she invites children to participate in must be such that they encourage active learning and give each child the opportunity to see himself as in control.

Most important of all, the teacher's attention is drawn to the fact that, far from being a cause for concern to be remedied as soon as possible so that children can proceed to 'the real stuff' of education, the teaching of skills is of central importance in every aspect and at every stage of education. The reflective skills of literacy and numeracy have a powerful influence on how the individual views himself and on the scope he has for extending his personal experience. And this is true whether he is five years old or fifty. Skills are not a preliminary to education; they are an integral part of it at all stages.

It is one thing for the teacher to recognize these important dimensions of teaching 'the basic skills'. It is another thing, however, to translate them into practice. We must now consider, therefore, some of the practical implications of our discussion.

Planning to teach 'the basic skills'

In such a limited space it is impossible to cover all the practical problems that the teacher will need to resolve in relation to skills teaching. In addition to this, the approach that I am concerned to elucidate views skills learning as intimately connected with other kinds of activities that are planned for in school. As I have argued elsewhere (Blenkin and Kelly 1980), categories we may use in making written plans will overlap in practice. They are also partly dependent on the teacher's sensitivity towards children and this is a quality which cannot be planned for in a deliberate way.

With these reservations in mind and in the interests of coherence, I have been guided into making selections by the aspects of skills teaching that have proved to be of the most significance to the teachers and student teachers with whom I have worked. I have grouped these selections into five areas for consideration.

Resources to challenge competence

I begin with the premise that, if children are faced with a genuine challenge and are helped judiciously by their teachers, they can marshal together all the required competencies and attempt to improve these in order to meet the challenge.

An indication of the truth of this occurred recently when the London Museum of Childhood — 'the toy museum' which is much beloved of many children — was threatened with closure. It was remarkable to see the written protests of even very young children which were sent to the minister concerned. Some were angry, some persuasive, some informed the minister of the information and interest that had been gained from visits to the museum and most were direct and to the point. The combined impact of these responses must have placed an irresistible pressure on him and the museum was saved, at least in part, as a result of children using 'the basic skill' of writing to great effect.

In our day-to-day life in school, of course, we rarely face crises of this kind. What we need to ensure, however, is that the experiences that we involve children in, and the resources that we offer them, encourage them to see the purpose of developing and employing skills.

There are many instances of the ways in which this might be done in later chapters of this book — through pursuing scientific enquiries or through trying to resolve mathematical problems, for example. For the purposes of this discussion, however, I have chosen to show how an Infant teacher was able to extend her children's book and study skills through supporting their interests. Part of the work involved her in helping the children to make five home-made books during the course of several weeks.

In the Autumn term the six- and seven-year-olds in this class were naturally interested in and excited by the prospect of the entertainments that they would be involved in both at school and at home during the Christmas festival. They were constantly telling their teacher about the pantomimes, plays and other entertainments that they would be visiting. In response, she collected these together and offered simple explanations of some of the traditions that they would be participating in.

BOOK ONE 'OUR BOOK ABOUT ENTERTAINMENT'
(A reference book made by the teacher)

The children became closely involved in this simple reference book and it led them to look for other, more sophisticated published references which they added to their book corner and browsed through constantly. In the course of their discussions it became clear that they were particularly fascinated by masks. One of the parents shared this fascination and loaned masks from his own collection for a display in the classroom. The children made their own masks and used these in improvised play. Their own masks were stored on the display when not in use and they were keen to write about how they made their masks and about who they were when they were wearing masks.

BOOK TWO 'OUR BOOK OF MASKS'
(The first collective book made by the children as a development from their interest in masks)

In the course of compiling this second book, the children had asked many questions. Some of these were to do with how books work. They were interested in how to arrange their material for most effect, they wanted to be able to find their own work quickly and they wanted to find out more by referring to the contributions of other children. The teacher also organized a visit to a local museum which had a larger collection of masks, some of which they were allowed to handle and wear. The children decided to make another book.

BOOK THREE 'A BOOK ABOUT OUR VISIT TO
HORNIMAN'S MUSEUM'
(Previous discussion on the book-making process brought a more polished result — use of index, contents page etc.)

The interest in masks continued throughout the term. At the museum, however, the children had also seen and handled different kinds of puppets. They remembered that their teacher had included the traditional puppets, Punch and Judy, in her reference book. They set about making their own puppets and used these in improvised plays. Some children who showed a particular interest in this activity decided to stage their own performance in order to entertain the other members of the class. This group became busily engaged in writing a play.

BOOK FOUR 'A BOOK ABOUT OUR PLAY'
(An account of the children's production of a play. This group illustrated that they had grasped the idea of sequence by the telling of a factual story)

Throughout all this activity the children had shown as much interest in books and how they work as they had in entertainment. With the help of their teacher, they spent much time learning about indexing and sequencing, and they sought extra material in the school library, the museum and the local library. In doing so they decided that their own collection of books should be properly classified and they devised a simple system for doing this. One child became so fascinated that she decided to make and write her own book. She insisted that every detail should be correct and even included a blurb about the author on the cover.

BOOK FIVE 'MY BOOK OF ENTERTAINMENT'
(A solo effort showing a child's use of book and study skills as a showcase for her own ideas)

These five carefully produced books were, of course, a favourite source of interest during the term. They also remained as a class resource in later terms and provided a means by which the children could recapture past experience and also compare and take pride in their later progress.

To develop work in this way, the teacher needs an informal and well-equipped environment which is full of resources that invite curiosity and challenge the young learners. In arranging her classroom she must also pay due regard, however, to materials and equipment that will support the children as they try out the skills that are required to meet these challenges.

Tools for the young apprentice

The skilled craftsman places great store by the quality and appropriateness of his tools. Similarly, the teacher should consider and constantly review the equipment that she makes available in her classroom. She should also think over the ways in which she is encouraging children to select, use and care for the items that can loosely be termed as the tools that are necessary to the development of 'the basic skills'.

All classrooms are equipped with basic items: pencils and other drawing and writing implements; paper, books and sentence makers; dictionaries and alphabets; counters and number lines; measures of various sorts — the list is endless. In recent years more sophisticated tools such as cameras, calculators and computers have also been added, in some schools, to these basic items. Some teachers have introduced their own home-made equipment — classroom word banks, charts, word lists, cards of writing patterns and so on — which are designed and made specifically for their own group of children, and these are often the most effective tools of all.

Too often, however, insufficient time and attention is given to helping children to make an appropriate selection from available materials for the task in hand. For example, how often is the child expected to add a beautifully composed story to his writing book during the course of a morning when most adult writers know that, unless it is an intimate letter that is being written, several rough drafts are often attempted before any risk is taken and the final draft is made public?

If the teacher encourages experimentation with tools that are well cared for and thoughtfully designed to help, many opportunities can arise for discussion and the children are more likely to learn and to practise techniques that lead to the most polished results that are possible at their stage of development.

Finally, it should be noted that some of the equipment used can be designed to help the children to be independent of their teacher. A word bank, for example, can provide a comprehensive and readily accessible home for words that the children often need and they can, with help, be encouraged to use this before consulting their teacher about the spelling of a word that they are unsure of.

In order to highlight some of the practical implications of the above points I have included a student teacher's notes about writing. She has decided to try to increase the interest that the children are showing in writing by making a special collection of the tools that can be used and the effects that can be gained when we write. These are her thoughts about introducing a writing area into her classroom.

General considerations

1 To provide an area where writing can be done.
2 To find ways of interesting the children.
3 To broaden their understanding of the reasons for writing and the different types of writing that can be undertaken.

I intend to locate the writing area near the book corner since it will be quieter and the two activities complement each other. Green will define the area — it is a restful colour and also blends with my existing equipment (word bank etc.).
I have plants and furnishings which will lend a more 'homey' and relaxed atmosphere to the area.

Materials prepared

1 A home-made book about writing which gives examples of:
    —different types of writing (newspapers, typing, letter writing)
    —history of writing
    —illuminated lettering.
2 Cards and posters about lettering (including alphabet poster).
3 Collection of pens (ancient and modern) to extend their experience of writing

implements.
4 Paperweights, pen and pencil holders, paper store.
5 Handwriting practice cards — examples of decorated borders.
6 Collection of simple books about writing etc. (e.g. 'Anno's Alphabet').
7 Trays for unfinished and finished work.

From these notes we can see that one way of stimulating an interest in 'basic skills' is by considering tools and materials as a source of stimulation in themselves. As was noted earlier in the chapter, however, other practical considerations need to be made in respect of the materials to be used.

Selection and influence of materials

There is no doubt that the effects of the materials can be more far-reaching than merely providing the teacher with an indication of the child's performance. We need to give some thought, therefore, to how we can ensure that the selections we make have a positive rather than a negative influence.

The first judgement to make is whether or not the materials are impoverished. If the teacher tries to discuss a reading book with a child as if it was a real book worthy of serious consideration or if she shares his attempts to make sense of a page of his maths book, it often becomes clear to her that the materials that she has given the child are very limited indeed and sometimes even harmful or confusing. It is important, therefore, for the teacher to assess and reject the poor illustrations, muddled instructions and meaningless scripts of some readers and maths schemes, most of which have been designed with the sole intention of taking the children on a sequential route through the early stages of the skills.

If these manufactured schemes are rejected, however, they must be replaced by a wide range of real books to read and more productive ways of presenting mathematical problems which will provide children with experiences that are both meaningful and match their level of competence.

In the past this presented teachers with an impossible problem. In recent years, however, this problem has been alleviated by the increasing availability of more appropriate materials. Some guidance on how to select from what is now available is offered in later chapters. At this point it is worth noting that it is not only published material that needs critical attention. Teachers must direct the same assessments at the home-made work cards and schedules that they have made themselves for children.

Other judgements that need to be made concern the values that are implicit in the materials. Often these promote stereotypes, particularly in relation to social class, race or sex, and it has been shown recently that distortions of this kind occur as frequently in the supposedly factual reference books as they do in stories and readers (Klein 1982). It would be wrong to suggest that the materials that we use can be free from values. However, teachers have a responsibility to ensure both that children can identify with the materials that are presented to them and that they are neither harmed by these materials nor have their prejudices confirmed and indirectly legitimized by the teacher.

Finally teachers must take care that they do not bend the materials and experiences that are presented to children in order to promote skills teaching. This is probably the most difficult judgement that the teacher will need to make for sometimes the interest leads naturally to the promotion of skills. To illustrate this point, I have included a simple flow plan which shows the work that was undertaken by a group of reception class children as a result of hearing the familiar story, 'The Three Bears' (Figure 2.1).

This example is not unusual. Indeed, it is likely that the story has been used in a similar way by most teachers of very young children. In this instance the counting, matching, measuring and sorting that occurred did so naturally as a result of the original experience.

However, there are two dangers that might ensue if we include materials and experiences only if they can obviously be extended to serve our purposes in advancing skills learning in an interesting way. One is that a story (or any other experience, for that matter) might be selected only because it has potential for direct development of skills and the children might be alert only to the utilitarian potential. How many times do we hear children say, 'Oh, we don't have to write about it, do we?'

The other danger is that important stories might be rejected because the potential is not so obvious. This is a point that Marian Whitehead explores in more depth in the next chapter. At this point it is worth heeding Bertrand Russell's warning that 'to kill fancy in childhood is to make a slave to what exists, a creature tethered to earth and therefore unable to create heaven' (Russell 1926, p. 71). We are likely to kill fancy if we only include materials and experiences that have an obvious potential for development today or tomorrow.

Much of the discussion so far has been concerned with provision and experience. We must now turn to considerations that are more to do with how the teacher makes use of the time that is available.

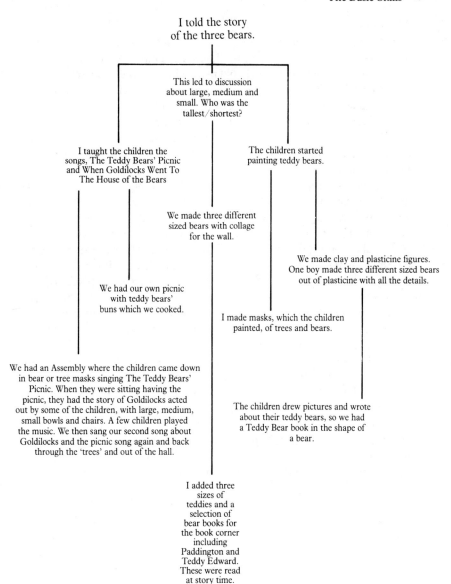

Figure 2.1 Simple flow plan indicating work undertaken by children as a result of hearing a familiar story (Age: rising fives and five-year-olds)

Opportunities for discussing rules

To plan, establish and adapt a setting that will continually provide stimulation and support for the development of children's competence is an important responsibility for the teacher. It should not lead her to underestimate the fact that she herself is the most important resource that is available to children in school. The way in which she organizes the use of her time when school is in session, therefore, becomes the most important factor in her planning. And part of her use of this time must be directed at helping children to identify and come to an understanding of the rules and generalizations that govern the reflective skills that they are employing.

As we have seen already, many opportunities for her to do this will arise naturally in the course of a day's work in the classroom. Whether or not opportunities can arise and what happens when they are taken, however, depends on her approach, which must take account of several factors.

Firstly, her contact time with the children must not be governed entirely by the routine tasks that were discussed earlier in this chapter. If her attention is filled with ensuring that children complete a daily ritual, she is unlikely to have time to react to or even notice the interesting problems that occur. Task management and anxiety to ensure task completion will clutter her own thinking and she will be unable to assess how to respond to the children in a way that will help them positively.

Secondly, her approach must be flexible, and this flexibility must extend to the amount of time that she allows the children to spend on activities. The balance of the child's experience must not be measured by the arbitrary divisions of the day but must be seen in a wider setting which takes account, at the very least, of his preoccupations at any particular time. Both the teacher and the children need time to explore and question, experiment and mull over, listen and share. This may mean that a child hasn't read his book to the teacher more than once during a week or it may mean he spent all his day reading.

Parents, of course, may be confused and anxious about such flexibility. They, too, feel reassured by a routine that makes it appear that 'the basics' are being attended to. Through open discussion, however, where they are helped to understand the important learning that is occurring and are encouraged to see that they too play a positive part in a responsibility that they share with the teacher, parents can become the teacher's greatest allies rather than her strongest critics. Flexibility also allows for experiences to spill over from school to home and back to school again.

Thirdly, the teacher must be sensitive to the children and what they are engaged in so that she can choose an appropriate time for drawing their attention to the rules. If his main interest is in finding out what happens at the end of his story, he is unlikely to welcome a discussion of word similarities.

If these features are incorporated into her general approach so that adequate time is given to the on-going activities that the children are involved in, many opportunities will occur for discussion. Moreover, these opportunities will not only present themselves when the teacher is working with an individual child — when she is hearing him read, for example, or helping him with a mathematical activity. Vital as these contacts with individual children are, other equally important instances can be cited which occur when a group is working on a task or when the whole class is together. Indeed, a communal setting can provide the best opportunities of all.

One reception-class teacher, sensitive to the importance that her children attached to seeing and recognizing their own names in print, encouraged them to draw self-portraits and wrote a name card for each child. These portraits were proudly displayed on a large frieze, captioned 'Our Class'. The random collection of pictures and names was carefully arranged by the teacher in the following way:

As she mounted the display she drew attention to the fact that Diane's and Debbie's names began in the same way.

In this instance, the children not only took delight in identifying their own names but also began to compare and contrast the similarities and differences that occurred in the names of the other children. They scrutinized with great care 'the beginnings', 'the middles' and 'the ends' of the words. Furthermore, they extended this game to other print that they met in the books that were in their book area and the labels that were around their room. Throughout the activity, they sought an explanation for the similarities and differences. Sometimes they offered solutions themselves whilst at other times they listened to their teacher's explanation. In short, from key words (their own names) the teacher encouraged these children to pursue a game of detection based on the assumption that, by and large, the skill of reading makes sense.

From this example we can also see that the essence of working in this way is that, having found an opportunity, the teacher and the children must spend time exploring it. As was noted earlier, however, this may lead the teacher to feel that, although it has been important to spend an extended period on one aspect of work, other aspects are being neglected and the child's growth in competence is thus being impeded or distorted. This takes us, then, to the final consideration — the keeping of records.

Assessing progress

It is of great importance that the teacher should have the child's progress and the coherence of his experiences under constant review. This becomes especially significant if the approach that she adopts is one which seeks to unite the learning of 'the basic skills' with other aspects of learning rather than to teach them in isolation. It is likely that the interests that the children have shown and the opportunities that have been taken for using the skills will have led to a balanced progress, even if the child has not completed a task related to the 3 Rs each day. The teacher needs to be sure of this, however, so that careful and efficient record-keeping must become part of her daily responsibility.

Many of the records that are needed have been discussed already. We have examined, for example, the flow plans of interests that developed, the notes on the arrangement of the classroom and the children's work used as a record of experience. In these instances, the records were kept as an integral part of the work under way and served, later, as a description of what had happened. They served to record the general life of the classroom and care was taken to indicate the part that skills learning had played in this.

In addition to these kinds of record, however, it is important that a means should be found to record the experiences and track the progress of individual children within the class. Individual records will ensure that progress is being maintained across a range of skills. These records may also be designed to help the child and his parents to share in this process. The sharing of records can begin in the earliest stages, as is shown in the following example.

During her time in the reception class, one young teacher designed small folders to replace the conventional name cards that are usually available. Each time a child read his book to the teacher, an entry was made. Parents, too, were invited to record books read at home on the same card. The following extracts are taken from two of these cards.

Honza's reading card
'School'
Honza doesn't think this book is about our school. We have different things.
'Bears in the Night'
Honza liked this story — he likes books about bears. He thought their mummy was cross because of her eyes.
'Inside, Outside, Upside-down'
Honza thought this was a funny book — especially when the bear was upside down.
'Anno's Alphabet'
Honza found and said the letter 'b'. He drew a picture of a bear and a bed.
'Jill's Toys'
Honza liked looking at the numbers in the book as well as the writing.
'Jack and the Beanstalk'
We both read this book. Honza liked the last page best. He liked to read 'Fee fi fo fum'.
'Mog's Mumps'
Honza liked to read the big words best of all. He especially liked 'catastrophe'.

Kim's reading card
'Hospital Day'
Kim liked the pictures of everyone talking on the bus.
'Daniel's Mysterious Monster'
Kim thought that this was a very funny book. Kim said, 'My dad's name is Daniel'.
'Link up 3'
We talked about the letter 'k'. Kim noticed that the doctor was wearing a

stethoscope and she knows what it is for.

'The Little Red Hen'

This story was rather long. We read a bit of it and looked at the pictures in the rest of the book.

'Grandfather Clock'

Kim liked this story. She liked the bit when it's 12 o'clock. 'That's the best bit,' she said.

'The Enormous Turnip'

This is Kim's favourite story. She read this story to some of her friends today. She likes the bit when everyone's pulling up the turnip. It made everyone laugh.

In addition to recording the books that had been shared, these cards served to remind the teacher of the interests that each child had shown in addition to the strategies that each was beginning to employ. They also gave parents an opportunity to participate actively in their child's early attempts at reading. Most of the comments came from the teacher, but some parents quickly joined in whilst all of them appreciated the brief glimpses of their children at work in school. Most important of all, each child loved to recapture the experiences that were unique to him and also to share in his teacher's recording of his progress.

During this exploration of some of the problems and opportunities that arise when a teacher embarks on teaching 'the basic skills', one significant point has recurred. Advancing the children's competence in these skills in a coherent and meaningful way presents the teacher with a complex challenge. In the final section, therefore, we will turn briefly to the accounts, collected from professional records, of teachers who have sought to meet this challenge.

Implementing a unified approach: case studies

Discussing the rules

Context: hearing a child read. (Part of a study made by a student teacher)

When hearing Ann (6.0) read I would let her continue even if errors were being made if she was still making sense of the text and grasping the meaning. I did this because it was likely to build up her confidence — a very important factor if she was to see herself as a reader. An interruption may have caused her confidence to be undermined or even destroyed. Often she would realise her own errors (although not always immediately) and self-correct.

Ann (6.0) was initially rather self-conscious when reading to me. However, gradually we built up a satisfactory relationship and she would look forward to our chats about the pictures. When looking at one page in her book Ann originally said 'slide' for the word 'see-saw' and then later self-corrected. I decided this was an ideal opportunity to capitalize on her own strengths. Naturally I praised her and asked how she knew the word was see-saw to which Ann replied, 'Because there are two words'. This led to a discussion on dashes and their purpose; we also looked back to the word 'slide' and remarked how that also began with an 's'. Ann felt very pleased with herself because she felt actively involved in the discovering process.

Extending strategies

Context: writing a book about a personal interest. (A page from a child's book with teacher's notes)

Things you take to the seaside

swimming ring	goggles
food	swimming hat
armbands	camera
sunglasses	sunhat
spade	lilo
bucket	frisbee
swimming costume	hoola-hoop
beach ball	boat
towel	deck chair
flip-flops	book

Joanna (8.7) was involved in making a book about the seashore. She decided that it would be useful to write down all the things one takes to the beach. We discussed the various ways this information could be presented and decided that a list would be both the clearest and simplest way. Joanna also decided to draw a picture of each item. She explained this was so that people like her little sister who could not read would still know what to take. This exercise involved Joanna in several constructive processes. Firstly she had to decide the method of recording the information, then she had to consider the nature of the list — that is, whether it was just for her own use or to be under-stood and used by other people. It also put Joanna in a position where she could appreciate the functional value of the writing.

Using the resources in the classroom
Context: writing news. (Notes from a teacher's record book)

On one occasion Michael (6.9) was working on a piece of writing about a play that he had seen at the theatre. He was searching for the word 'cast' in order to tell me about the characters in the play. He knew that on one particular poster in the theatre corner, about a 'Robinson Crusoe' pantomime, the word 'cast' was actually written down, because we had discussed this word earlier on in the morning and I had used this particular poster as an example.

Michael went over to the poster and began searching for the word. He called me over to give him some assistance, but did not ask me to tell him the word; he wanted to find it on his own. He had already established that the word began with a letter 'c' and was searching through the words for something to fit this clue. He pointed to the word 'Crusoe', and said to me, 'That's "cast" it starts with "c".' My reply to this was, 'What letter do you think "cast" ends with?' Michael thought about this for a while and then replied, 'That's not "cast" then, it should end with "train" sound'.

He then proceeded to search the words on the poster to find a word beginning with 'c' and ending with 't'. In the process of doing this and repeating the word to himself he also established that the word had an 's' sound in it. At last, he found the relevant word with very little help from me. He fitted the clues that he had 'solved' to the word 'cast' and decided that this must be what he was looking for.

Although this task of finding one word seemed to have taken ages and a great deal of effort on Michael's part, I feel that persevering with it was a really worthwhile experience for him. Actually using this printed material, which was a bit of a novelty in the classroom, seemed to be a stimulant to get him to try on his own and to persevere with what he was searching for. From his point of view, I think that the perseverance came about because he was faced with a challenge in something he was interested in — he was writing about the theatre and was able to use *relevant* material to help him in this.

Co-operation
Context: writing about a play. (Notes from a teacher's record book)

The children would often help each other to find words they needed. For example, on one occasion Sally (6.10) and Zoe (6.11) were working together and Sally went to consult the theatre key-word chart for the word 'scenery'. Both this word and the word 'scene' were on the chart and Sally wrote down 'scene' instead of 'scenery'. On showing this to Zoe she was told in no un-certain terms that: 'That's not "scenery"; it doesn't end with a "y" like "silly".' On realizing the mistake, the two of them then returned to the chart and after further consultation found the correct word.

The co-operation between the two girls on this occasion struck me as being very important in the process of learning to read. Zoe, who has mastered the art of using the last letters of a word as a clue to the whole as well as the beginning letters, was passing on the skill to her friend Sally. In this situation Zoe was taking on the role of teacher.

Integration of skills

Context: a child reading her own book, 'My book of food and shops'. (From a teacher's notes on an individual child)

Liza (6.2) is a reasonably able child and her main strength is her ability to apply herself for long stretches of time. Once Liza had begun to make her book she organized a work programme for herself; her whole approach was very methodical and well thought out. Liza would ensure before commencing each piece of work that the paper was of the correct size and proportion; she showed a special concern for presentation and layout. I also noticed how Liza set herself certain standards and, if her work did not measure up, she would reject it and start again. I was aware that Liza was self-motivated and it was not a question of my having to do all the thinking. This was probably because she was working from first-hand experiences which interested her. Liza certainly had no problem in collecting together enough work and had plenty of ideas.' the content of her writing. The gutting of the herring served as a real stimulus for Liza and sparked off an interest in the larger topic of 'fish'.

Liza was extremely pleased with her book and seeing it in its finished form with all the work mounted and attractively laid out made her feel that all her efforts had been worthwhile. Liza was initially somewhat surprised and disconcerted when I asked her if she would like to read her book to me. Liza assumed that I or any teacher was only interested in listening to readers and thought this was a very novel idea. I was surprised but pleased to note how many new words Liza had picked up, 'scales' (page 8), 'tie-dye' (page 12), and the extensive information she had obviously assimilated which revealed itself in our discussion of her pictures etc. I noticed how Liza found her illustrations very helpful when in difficulty, probably because they are very personal and done to accompany her text, making them very meaningful. On page 4 Liza was struggling over the word 'face' but deduced this from her picture of the cake with its smiling face. Similarly on page 5 Liza was again faltering but because the experience of making butter was so vivid she was able to recall how she felt and worked out the word 'horrible'.

Again I was aware that Liza was concentrating more than usual by some of the observations she made. On page 7 she pointed to the word 'liked' which she had writted as 'like d' and somewhat indignantly inquired what the letter 'd' was doing there? Moreover, on page 11 Liza remarked how she had written the word 'pat' instead of 'put', going on to mention how it was only one letter which was incorrect. Liza was not only being observant but also self-critical, but in a positive and constructive way which permitted her to learn through the situation, one which was much more meaningful to Liza than any contrived by the teacher beforehand.

When Liza read her book she did make some errors but was coping with both vocabulary and sentences whose complexity was of a far higher level than her official reader. Obviously the work was familiar because she had written it herself but one must remember that some of the work had been done almost a month ago.

Spontaneous application of skills

Context: six-year-olds playing in the shop. (Extract from teacher's weekly review)

I was very pleased to note how the shop was being used this week and the impact of the introduction of paper bags and a notepad for making up bills. The children during their play strictly adhere to the price list and the tendency is now for them to write down carefully the item being purchased and its price so they can add it up.

It was also pleasing to note how in the shop situation children of differing mathematical abilities could constructively play together. It was interesting to note their sense of fairness and how they organized their play — they instigated a system whereby there were two shop-keepers and two customers and swapped over periodically. I noticed that Marlon was able to do maths in this situation which he had difficulty with the day before and successfully added up four items totalling 27p and gave the correct change — admittedly he did have Joanna as the 'pushy' customer demanding to know the total price so she could check her change! The price lists also came into their own because although at one time I had thought them to be too simplistic I noted how Lee used the rows of pennies to count on and add up his prices and the satisfaction he derived from being able to solve the problem.

Summary and conclusions

The exploration of 'the basic skills' undertaken in this chapter has drawn attention to many considerations of a theoretical and a practical kind which teachers need to take account of, both as they plan their work and as they make their daily contacts with children. The serious pitfalls that can occur if the wrong approach is adopted have been examined and it has been argued that a failure to teach skills in such a way that they have meaning for the learner has undermined the confidence of many children in the worth of what school has to offer and, worse than this, has made them disinclined to grow in competence and independence.

This led to an examination of the principles that can guide the teacher towards more productive ways of working, principles which clearly showed that skills learning must be an intimate and vital part of all learning if the processes of education are to be forwarded. The practical implications of adopting such a stance were then discussed and we glimpsed at the classroom encounters of some teachers who have already taken up this challenge in their work with very young children.

Before ending, however, one point remains to be stressed again. This is that the reflective skills which are so prized in our society are not 'basic' in the simple sense of that word. They are fundamental to the educational process at every age and at every stage of the learner's development. It is when all teachers begin to perceive 'the basics' in this way that education will begin to be a reality for all children. In this context it is worth returning to Bertrand Russell's view of the relationship between skills learning and education.

> Education consists in the cultivation of instincts, not in their suppression. Human instincts are very vague, and can be satisfied in a great variety of ways. Most of them require, for their gratification, some kind of skill . . . the secret of instruction is to give a man such kinds of skill as shall lead to his employing his instincts usefully. The instinct of power, which in the child is crudely satisfied by identification with Bluebeard, can find in later life a refined satisfaction by scientific discovery, or artistic creation, or the creation and education of splendid children, or any one of a thousand useful activities (Russell 1926, p.71).

(I am indebted for examples given in this chapter to many of my students past and present and, in particular, to Madeleine Luxon, Wendy Otterburn and Julie Search.)

CHAPTER 3

LANGUAGE DEVELOPMENT AND THE PRIMARY CURRICULUM

MARIAN WHITEHEAD

> As we have developed our view of learning as interactive, of the curriculum as negotiable: we have recognised the dramatic effect of intentions upon performance — by teachers as well as by students: as it has become clear that teaching consists of moment-by-moment interactive behaviour that can only spring from inner conviction — I think we are, perhaps for the first time, ready to admit that what the teacher can't do in the classroom can't be achieved by any other means (James Britton 1981, p.10)

In ushering in the eighties as 'the age of the classroom teacher' James Britton in no way minimizes the importance of the professional help which teachers should receive. However, he puts the emphasis squarely on supporting teachers as they come to theorize from their own experience. One aspect of such supportive back-up must be accounts of the present state of play in theoretical research and of the influences such theoretical 'positions' exert on procedures and outcomes in the classroom.

Major trends and influences in language study

The major thrust of current research strengthens the view that language development can be seen as a paradigm of the 'progressive' or 'process' approach to education. Language is a form of knowledge created by human beings and infinitely adaptable to their changing purposes and needs. The development of language in young children is explained in terms of increasing experience of the world and of social relationships. The crucial feature of these experiences is the part played by social interaction with significant persons and the ensuing sharing of meanings. Early language learning is a dynamic process in which the infant is an active participant and frequently the initiator of exchanges. A language may be described as a public system of agreed signs but its meanings are recreated by the young child in processes negotiated with others, rather than learnt by passive initiation into the language community.

Perhaps the key idea underlying recent work in language and learning is interaction. It is a concept which emphasizes the part played by an active involvement with experiences and a reconstruction of their significant features in order to achieve understanding. It is helpful to chart the progress of research into early language development in terms of four major areas of experience with which the child interacts. These areas of interaction are the spoken language, significant persons, the environment and the written language. Although it is clear that these areas all come together in the infant's early experiences there has been a tendency for theoretical research to go through periods of emphasizing one at the expense of the others. A concern with the child's interaction with the spoken language dominated research in the fifties and early sixties and led to a concentrating of attention on how the child acquires syntax, the forms and structures of the language. The work of Chomsky (1957, 1965) stressed the need for a theory of language which could account for the highly original and creative nature of language learning and use. The young child produces eccentric and irregular forms which are clearly not imitations but evidence that the child is forming and testing linguistic hypotheses. Chomsky's assertions were supported by the long-term studies of child language made by Roger Brown and his associates (1973). These approaches were further illuminated by evidence that very young children play with the spoken language as they acquire it, practising its forms and stretching its possibilities to suit their own interests, fantasies and emotional needs (Chukovsky 1963; Weir 1962). All this work gave insights into the sequential acquisition of grammatical structures but was less helpful when it came to explaining how the all-important representation of meaning in language comes about.

The first tentative answers to this most complex of issues began to emerge from the work of research psychologists. One major influence was the work of the Russian psychologist Lev Vygotsky, who died in 1934 but was not published fully in the West until 1962. Vygotsky's writings (1962, 1978) suggest that meanings emerge in the process of the child's joint activities with an adult. The co-operative ventures which the child initially engages in with the adult are internalized to become the source of independent thinking and independent actions. These early postulations were strengthened by the findings of psychologists studying the abilities of new-born infants. From this work on the surprising social competence of young babies a continuing flow of observations of infant/caregiver interactions suggests that language and communication begin long before the first recognizable words are uttered by the child. Jerome Bruner has also directed his research (1975) towards the shared games and rituals of mothers and babies. He sees in these games of 'peep-bo' and exchange the prototypes of the meaning-bearing patterns underlying the structures of language. It now appears that the key concepts for language learning are shared intentions and the mutual exchange of meanings, and the typical form this takes is the 'conversation'. This approach underlies the current long-term research in Bristol by Gordon Wells and his team. The first book arising from the project is tellingly titled *Learning through Interaction, The Study of Language Development* (1981).

Interaction with persons and with the spoken language takes place in a particular environment. Recent research projects look at children and their caregivers in their homes and stress the need to observe language in a natural environment. This emphasis on the normal setting for language has also highlighted the amount of important learning which goes on in homes and has led to several research developments which focus on the relationship between schools and homes (Wells 1981; Clark 1976; Tizard et al. 1981; Southgate et al. 1981).

It is in schools that a new significance is placed on the child's hitherto informal interactions with the written forms of the language. Recent increases in our understanding of linguistic and cognitive processes do challenge some of the traditional views of learning to read and write. The emphasis has now shifted to the business of extracting meaning from text by processes which utilize intelligent guesswork and the knowledge of the world and of language which the reader brings to the text. Reading is an active involvement with the text at all stages of competence and not a passive receptive skill. And, similarly, writing is seen to be concerned with encoding messages which serve human purposes and expand the possibilities of language.

Some of these theories and their practical implications have already been brought into the school context by government reports. The Plowden Report (DES 1967) is a synonym for 'progressive' Primary practice and it did acknowledge the centrality of spoken language in learning and the interrelatedness of language and thought. It identified language as a powerful tool for organizing experience and facilitating planning and action. The stress on the importance of talking about experiences was seen as crucial in all areas of the Primary curriculum. Language is one of the most powerful systems we have for identifying experience and symbolizing it, that is, giving it significance. The Bullock Report (DES 1975) was a report on reading standards which turned into a statement on the central role of language in learning. This is held to be true for all stages of individual development and for all the traditional curriculum areas. Language issues are not just the concern of the Primary school or the Secondary school English department and talk, or oracy, is the matrix for the skills of reading and writing. There is an emphasis on teachers monitoring their own talk in the classroom and listening carefully to their pupils. The Report's theoretical background reflects a concern for the role of personal expressive language as the source of the individual's varied linguistic skills.

Framing language policies

This brief indication of the nature of some relevant theories and research suggests implications for language policies in the Primary curriculum which may be expressed as three main insights. Firstly, the child's role in language learning is an active one and the child frequently initiates the moves. Secondly, this learning is a creative process and exhibits innovatory and exploratory features. Thirdly, this process is most typically an interaction between partners in a conversation and is strongly affected by feelings and relationships.

It has been the norm — post-Bullock — for schools and groups of teachers to frame their language policies under headings which reflect the main language modes — talking, listening, reading and writing. These aspects of language in use are undeniably central to any rational language planning but categorizing them so neatly may lead to practices reminiscent of traditional subject-based approaches. Furthermore, such clear distinctions make a nonsense of the interrelatedness of these language activities in daily thinking, communicating and coping. The speaker hopes for at least one listener; the listener continuously plans appropriate responses and predicts the spaces for his contributions. Who would write if he could not read back his own message? And does the reader never desire to make his own permanent mark, the traditional testimony that 'I lived and was here and made this mark'?

Clearly the Primary curriculum can be unhelpfully slanted in the direction of discrete subject categories by lists of listening, talking, reading and writing activities, as much as by arbitrarily timetabled units of mathematics, nature study, history and geography. A real trivialization of language activities may occur when we begin to cast around for lists of things to do in daily 'listening' or 'writing' sessions. The clearest way out of this particular dilemma is to avoid taking on a traditional subject-based curriculum model with all its subtly pervasive assumptions and biases. The most successful Primary practice arose from independent and innovatory approaches to child development and learning, not from following established models of schooling. A more appropriate way of tackling language across the Primary curriculum would be to build on the strengths of the learner-centred process model (Blenkin and Kelly 1981).

I have already suggested that current linguistic knowledge and research gives us some useful insights into the nature of language learning and this can provide a rationale for a school language policy. Thus choices and arguments can take place against a background of shared knowledge which emphasizes the role of the learner and of the interactive nature of learning.

To summarize, in first-language learning the child is active and frequently initiates moves in the game. The process owes little to passive imitation but is highly creative and experimental. The typical situation for language learning is the conversation or interaction between interested and highly motivated partners.

Given these background assumptions I would put forward three main aims for a language policy in the Primary school. Firstly, the school must continue to enrich the language development of the individual pupils, bearing in mind that this process is well under way before formal schooling begins. Secondly, the move towards literacy should certainly be an aim, but one which is most usefully seen as crucial in extending and enhancing the individual's language development. Thirdly, the school should aim to generate research 'projects' and theories about its own language procedures and activities involving teachers, pupils and parents. These aims and the thinking behind them are relevant and illuminating in any educational setting, be it Nursery school or University department. They underlie my own teaching on initial and in-service teacher education courses and I hope that they come to inform the thinking and the practices of the students and teachers I have worked with when they are in their own schools. But what really happens when these broad aims are translated into classroom practicalities?

Continuing language development

There is no shortage of books about language in the classroom and there are several lists of language functions which can be used to pin-point the identifiable types of language used in the classroom. However, these lists may well raise all the problems of crude stereotyping inherent in neat tick-sheets and over-simplified categories. Understandable doubts have been raised about the validity of attributing preconceived functions to young children's remarks (Francis 1978) and the difficulties of assessing young children's language are considerable (Clark 1979). The complexities of the situational context and the subtle nuances of interpersonal relations should alert us to the fact that language and gesture are only at full stretch when natural situations and powerful human purposes propel the search for satisfactory linguistic expression.

Relevant planning and provision in the Primary school must tap the sources of language development in such real-life concerns. Wells (1981) has indicated a significant link between the rate of language development and real involvement in routine household activities with interested caregivers. Although interaction in the classroom may call for the exchange of information and the verbal display of knowledge (Wells 1979), the stimulus for such talk can still be household business.

Children delight in cooking and preparing food in school and are usually able to contribute as much practical knowledge of the subject as their teachers. Outings to local shops to buy the ingredients for cooking or food for school pets have been exploited by teachers over the years, but the simplest ideas work just as well. The unpacking of a supermarket carrier bag containing some basic groceries can release the most surprising confidences. The bold blue lettering on the bag of a well-known brand of flour reminded one four-year-old that all the front doors on her estate had just been painted that colour. 'Teachery' attempts to draw another child's attention to the forms of the print on the same flour bag inspired a delightfully idiosyncratic recognition of the digraph 'll' in the brand name as 'eleven' — the age, about to be celebrated with a birthday party, of a much admired older brother. To launch into the conversation of the classroom is to be continually surprised! Children are actively concerned with making sense of their experiences of the world and use objects, persons and language to achieve this end.

Knowledge of the nature and extent of the connections between language in use and school learning is still somewhat tentative (Francis 1978). In the face of such partial understanding it is unwise to be committed to approaches which assume simple cause and effect connections between speaking and learning. Language policies which emphasize a naive kind of intervention frequently come down to little more than a barrage of narrowly focused questions directed at children. Just as unsatisfactory is a sloppy policy of immersing children in language, in practice the overwhelming running commentary and rhetorical questions of an adult with didactic intentions. An approach which allows the child language-user to be actively involved in the experimental recreation of his language, in partnership with others, is the most promising way forward in the light of current incomplete knowledge. The varieties of language and the extension of the things that language can do only emerge in response to real intentions shared with interested persons in an environment which is stimulating, yet offers a fair degree of predictability; in other words, an educative setting which has not become utterly divorced from the real world of normal human purposes and practical concerns. Situations which favour the loosely structured ebb and flow of talk are most likely to produce language which moves towards new formulations and extends understanding.

It is significant that some of the best examples of this language for learning have been captured on tape almost by happy accident. Thus, Janet Ede and Jack Williamson (1980) are able to catch a moment of self-knowledge when a five-year-old, chatting with his teacher, realizes that he is frightened of a lot of things. Even more interestingly the most extended and varied tape is of two six-year-olds, mainly unsupervised, observing a classroom collection of snails. The children's talk ranges across modes of self-assertion, co-operation, commentary and scientific speculation in tones of sheer delight and enthusiasm.

This natural extension of the range of language functions happens in response to actual events and situations. The teacher is crucially present as trusted adult and as the organizer of an environment which challenges some assumptions and provides time and space for the exploration of new ideas and new relationships.

It would be both pointless and impossible to list all the materials and experiences which promote language development. Such a list would turn out to be the story of a lifetime and perhaps this is the surest touchstone! Classroom materials and experiences which are firmly rooted in the environment and reflect the concerns of children and adults organizing and making sense of their lives are the most fruitful. It is when our immediate attention is focused on real problems and outcomes that language is unselfconsciously employed as a communicator of existing ideas and a formulator of new insights and impulses.

So the best Primary practice does arise in a world of play with basic materials. It is a world of people who love and hate, cook and clean, build and break, paint and sew, care for pets and go on visits. It is a world of estimating, measuring, matching, counting, drawing, story-telling and talking. In all this real-world business it is difficult to maintain clear lines of demarcation between the traditional subject disciplines.

In our daily lives a tight adherence to such categories would severely limit our flexibility of response and, consequently, our ability to cope. Similarly, the many kinds of language in use blur and merge into each other and the simplest utterance is likely, in its context, to serve several purposes. Language clearly expresses our sense of self or identity and it is also the means by which we establish and maintain co-operation with others. It is the vehicle for sharing and enriching the meanings we evolve in our encounters with objects and persons. Most significantly, language is a symbolic system which enables us to represent to ourselves possibilities at some remove from actions in the real world. We can handle in talk and in thought actions, events and objects not present or occurring and thus we are able to recall the past and predict future possibilities.

Language can both represent the actual world as we have known it and create alternative worlds by a process of infinite recombinations of features from the known. This activity usually appears as an endless telling of anecdotes or stories about ourselves, our past, and our predictions for the future. Like most story-telling the activity gives order and shape and evaluates experience. This natural narrative is probably the sole means of organizing experience symbolically in childhood (Moffett 1968) and remains important throughout life as the dominant mode of memory and literary expression. Telling stories and listening to stories are the primal activities from which all later skills of literacy evolve. Literacy is an extension of the possibilities of language, not a totally new activity.

So we all develop, with ever-increasing experiences and information to process and add to our pool of linguistic resources. The circles widen out from shared experiences and talk with one consistent caregiver to the differing language demands of other relationships and situations, and to the stories and experiences of many unknown others.

The negotiation of so much that is new needs time, and some sort of breathing space. It is an assimilative activity which can be identified in the earliest pre-sleep monologues of infants (Weir 1962). Alone in a darkened room, the young child will try out new words and new sounds and mull over strong emotional responses. At a much later stage of development unsupervised small-group discussion in the Secondary school enables adolescents to handle language and feeling in similar ways. This situation is structured by the need to come to some understanding of the book, poem, film or topic at issue and by the group's need to negotiate contributions and explicate meanings. Tentative formulations and complex responses should be just as carefully nurtured in the Primary school.

Such talk is only likely to arise in response to tasks and experiences which seriously engage the interests and feelings of children. The most likely triggers are stories, poems, shared group experiences or family relationships, rather than invented or anonymously produced topic titles or ideas for discussion. Good talk also needs small informal groups, a physical environment that is comfortable, homely rather than institutional, and a network of supportive relationships throughout the school. The fleeting, mainly unrecorded, nature of this language work should not detract from its significance. It is second only in importance to talk between teacher and child on a one-to-one basis. These interactions must also be allowed for and safeguarded in a crowded day. The informal grouping of children, arranging the physical environment as a well-organized workshop with quiet bays or areas, and the planning of fairly uninterrupted blocks of time help. Such opportunities for talk are crucial because they develop and build on the skills which first launched the child into the language community. The conversations of the classroom can be a creative and experimental series of interactions which the children use to make school learning a sensible extension of their previous experiences.

Into literacy

Perhaps all of us who set out to teach reading and writing should ask ourselves, Why read? Why write? What is in it for the individual? Without minimizing the value of literacy as a practical survival skill in a print-dominated society we may propose other kinds of answers. Margaret Meek (1982) argues that no one should be victimized by print into believing all he reads or buying everything he sees advertised. But Meek's most compelling reason is bound up with the quality of life for the individual, 'Readers are at home in the life of the mind; they live with ideas as well as events and facts' (Meek 1982, p.17). The way in which these arguments touch our own lives as readers and writers, the differing priorities we give them, will affect both the style of our teaching and the very materials we use.

The move into literacy for the individual should be seen as a continuation and enrichment of the process of language development. Learning to read and write depends on our ability to think symbolically and order our experiences in story-like fashion. These abilities are bound up with our development of a first language and the establishment of mutually satisfying relationships. Clearly these processes originate well before the age of formal schooling but it is essential that we continue to build on them in our teaching rather than plunge into a fresh-start policy of formal schemes, 'rules' and exercises.

Towards the end of the sensori-motor period of thinking in infancy a crucial development occurs which precedes and facilitates symbolic thinking and the use of language as a sign system. This is the development of mental imagery (Piaget and Inhelder 1971) or iconic representation. Jerome Bruner (1964, 1966) describes iconic representation, or thinking in mental pictures, as a technological advance in the use of mind. Certainly it is the first stage in thinking about the 'not present' and speculating about alternatives. Furthermore, this potent source of highly personal images makes up that inner private world of the imagination which colours all our dealings with external reality.

The significance of this for literacy lies in the fact that the image comes before the word and continues to affect the significance we attach to the agreed meanings of our language. Reading and writing are as much about feeling as thinking and rely on our ability to re-enact in mental pictures the vivid particularity of the meanings intended (Iser 1978). In Chapter 6, Harriet Proudfoot considers in some detail the power of these images in the child's creative development.

The early stages of literacy need to stress the reading of pictures and the drawing of messages. These basic skills can continue to support and extend the development of reading and writing throughout the Primary school years. Young children's first encounters with books, in or out of school, need to retain some of the features of early language learning. For some happy children the two activities may have run parallel (Butler 1979). What is required is an interested and more experienced partner to share the process, a full acceptance of the child partner as an active participant, with his own intentions and expectations, and a shared feeling that the activity is meaningful and enjoyable. The quality of the books chosen is obviously central to the experience and this raises complex issues about the role of literature in human development.

There are some excellent discussions on these issues, complete with suggested book titles, available for the guidance of parents and teachers (Butler 1980; Tucker 1981; Meek 1982; Heeks 1981). Suffice it to say that the earliest experiences with books must be with real books. Books which present a story, a sequence of events in time, complete with some evaluation of the experience described and an implied invitation to the reader or listener to consider this view of the world.

This rather sweeping claim is not quite as abstract and vague as it appears. I have already indicated that the first story experiences mesh with the narratives of memory and the story-like ways in which young children handle and evaluate their experiences. These processes are further strengthened by the fairy stories and nursery rhymes which children hear and participate in at an early age. 'Humpty Dumpty' will as well fulfil my definition of story as *Rosie's Walk, The Iron Man* or *The Owl Service*. Stories, heard and read, may confirm our experience of the world and offer the young child the security and confidence of recognition: 'I've been there', 'I've got one of those'. Stories can extend and challenge our knowledge and experience and the young child may try out new roles and different attitudes. At their most powerful, stories offer symbols for the expression of disturbing fears and desires. *Where the Wild Things Are* ranges across anger, rejection and forgiveness and the traditional folk and fairy tales explore a similarly full repertoire of emotional responses.

The young reader or listener, concerned to make sense of the story, brings to bear on it his experiences of the world, his knowledge of language in use and all his previous book and story encounters. This powerful collection of expectations and predictions is tested against every picture, incident and recognizable piece of print. In essence this approach to getting the message off the page remains unaltered in the most fluent and confident of readers. But there must be a message! Few reading scheme books offer this kind of material in the early stages.

The appropriate provision for learning to read is a collection of books immediately to hand and one or two enthusiastic readers eager to share their pleasure in story-telling and reading. The book collection need not be large but it does need to offer a variety of forms: picture books, pop-ups, holes-in-the-page, as well as a progression in the dominance of words over images. (Although we do need to remember that some modern picture books are designed to make considerable demands on the 'reading' skills of sophisticated readers.)

New books should regularly come into the collection but a core of familiar and well-loved books is essential to provide examples of known texts for the beginner reader who is matching the words in his head to the marks on the page. This activity helps to focus attention on the distinctive features of print. The importance of discriminating significant features within a meaningful text is essential if children are to learn to read by reading. Collections of nursery rhymes provide plenty of familiar text and reflect the child's natural delight in experimenting and playing with the possibilities of language.

But all the books are of limited value without an enthusiastic story-teller who puts the human voice back into the words on the page or breathes life into the ritual phrase 'Once upon a time . . .'. It seems to me essential that children should know that *people* produce the writing in books and that the opening lines of the traditional tale serve the same function as the familiar, 'Here, Miss, guess what?'

Story-telling should not be restricted to the last part of the day or week, nor to whole-class sessions. Young children should regularly, throughout the day, be able to look at a book with an adult reader or listen to a story. If this is a priority on the teacher's timetable it can be achieved. It can also be supplemented by other helpers in the classroom and by tapes of the teacher telling familiar stories. These tapes can be used by the children and matched with the available text.

There is growing awareness now that as children move up the school system they should not lose out on story listening and sustained periods of reading. Many Secondary school teachers read to their pupils regularly and some schools now institute a daily freely chosen reading session in which the whole school, quite literally, reads for pleasure.

If we have any lingering doubts or anxieties about spending considerable amounts of school time on reading for pleasure they should be dispelled by the recent discussion document by HMI, *Bullock Revisited* (DES 1982c). A major part of the document (Section 4) is devoted to the importance of imaginative literature and it expresses a fear that literature is still neglected while schools focus narrowly on the teaching and extending of early reading skills. The document is a timely reminder, seven years on, that the most important message pupils need to get from learning to read is that people do it for pleasure.

'Magic in the Yard'

This is my favourite book because it is very funny. A cat called Tobias put some magic in the cakes. Aunt May and Miss Miff float about. Then the cat got them down.
Alexander, 6 years, June 1982

Some of the most exciting books I see in Primary schools have been made by teachers for their pupils or produced by the children themselves. When reading and writing are approached together as closely linked processes literacy makes sense. It makes sense for the child because he can bring his knowledge of the world as he knows it, and his skills as a language user and producer of graphic symbols, to the task of conveying a message or celebrating an event. All this is evident when the young child draws or paints a picture and tells an interested adult about it. When the child's name is written on the picture he is already in the role of author or maker. This is the start of an exciting phase in the development of every individual: what we think or say can be written down, captured and made permanent. Even if the words do sit there and accuse us they can also be gloated over, worked upon and altered, or left simply to testify, as does every cave drawing and graffito, to the fact of existence.

This sort of excitement can and should pervade the process of writing and reading in the Primary school. In fact much of children's early reading should consist of books which they have themselves created. Initially these will be put together by the teacher and consist of pictures with captions dictated by the child. The value of such books lies in their relevance to the child's own interests and concerns and their presentation of a small amount of known text. But they also exemplify the fact that books are made by people, and older Primary children will be interested in achieving greater resemblance to the published article. The typing of text and the investigation of the conventions of indexing, pagination and chapter heading will support this interest. These activities are important if literacy is to be seen as giving the individual independence and control over his life.

Becoming independent writers and readers

Childen can be helped to observe and collect many different types of writing in the environment. Discussions about writing and other kinds of conventional signs such as lights, trade-marks and pictures, help children discern some of the uses of communication systems in society. The topic of graphics and conventions in writing was beautifully presented by one Infant teacher in a book which contained such examples as a newspaper headline, a greetings card, a knitting pattern, a recipe, an informal note and an advertiser's leaflet. Older children can be introduced to other systems for conveying messages such as sign languages, picture writing and hieroglyphics. This work may need to be researched by the teacher from sophisticated sources and then reproduced as a good teacher-made reference book for the children. Armed with this material the children can evolve differing ways for conveying messages and information. Even the more lengthy written work of older Primary pupils can retain the immediacy of drawn symbols if it is suggested that sometimes they intersperse their personal writings with a small drawing or vignette which shows the exact detail or effect they are after.

All of the routines and events shared by a class or school can lead to the production of books and many teachers use photographs of these activities to supplement the drawings made by the children. One of the best picture books I have seen in a Reception class was a collection of photographs of the previous winter's spectacular snow and ice. A written and photographic record of visits to local parks, street-markets, building sites and the school kitchen produced a series of books which linked learning to read with environmental studies in another Infant class. Obviously the care and observation of plants, pets and mini-beasts and the rituals of shopping, cooking and eating provide material for books in the classroom.

One group of 'Top Infants' moved on from their experiences of handling clay to a general interest in what can be found in the soil. This culminated in a thorough investigation of a bucket of earth brought in from the adjacent Junior school garden. Several of the children wrote up their observations with a truly scientific passion for recording the facts. The following example also shows the child consciously taking up the role of writer.

'There was lots of tiny ants in the soil. I saw a little creature in the soil that looked like a worm but it had red spots on it. I picked it up and put it on my hand to look at but when I picked up my magnifying glass and looked at it it wasn't there so I looked on my arm and there he was, so I put it back. I then saw another creature but it did not have spots, it was black all over, it climbed out of the soil and he fell off the table. Talitha, Eve and me all crowded round to have a look. Then I said look, What said Eve it's climbing up the wall. then when I got my magnifying glass and that wasn't there so I had another look but there was nothing there so I got a piece of paper and started writing'.

There is no shortage of starting points for written records in the Primary school but other familiar formats, apart from the conventional book or folder, can be exploited. The use of the comic strip technique has proved highly successful in the schools I know and its use need not be restricted to the younger children. Indeed, a best-selling author/illustrator has recently used this convention for the exploration of catastrophic issues (*When the Wind Blows*, Raymond Briggs). The meaning-crammed details of pictures in sequence and the small amount of text with much stress on the immediacy of informal speech encourage a greater freedom of written style combined with considerable sophistication of content. It is also tapping the children's knowledge of the conventions of one of their favourite out of school reading activities. For beginner readers it reinforces the basic procedures of reading in our culture, the left to right, top to bottom, organization of printed symbols on the page. And, following this order, the import of the message is gained by a careful scanning of the images.

If children are using the books of a reading scheme as a part of their reading activities in school it is still possible to bring their own interests and skills as authors to bear on this type of material. Once they have been introduced to the main characters in the scheme young children can draw pictures and dictate captions for tiny books of adventures. The results can be surprising! The children's own reading books thus created reflect their family experiences, their own environment and a strong input from the real stories they have heard. This combination produces life and death issues and passions which are a long way from the sanitized worlds of the families in the schemes. I have seen South London re-workings of a popular scheme with a rural village setting in which the main issues become the sudden deaths of baby siblings and frequent road accidents. Similar concerns surfaced in a project which aimed to get Junior school children writing their own reading books (Otty 1975). Children do not live in safe, cosy worlds and their innocence is not the bland, passionless stereotype which some adults like to cultivate. If we invite children to write in ways which do not restrict them to the copying of neutral messages and predigested information we will sometimes receive disturbing material.

This brings us back to the major functions of language. Just as language is not only for communication with others but serves in self-development to organize and clarify our own inner life and identity, so it is with the written language. One of the first audiences for which we write is our own self and the purpose of the writing is often to explore feelings as much as ideas. Much of the poetry and prose written by school children expresses fear and anxiety as well as joy and affection. A lively collection of children's explorations of their emotions and experiences is offered in Harriet Proudfoot's chapter on 'Development through the Creative Arts'.

This kind of writing does raise the issue of what is an appropriate response from the teacher. It seems to me that such writing is offered to be shared with a trusted friend and should not be routinely graded and corrected. The expression of pleasure in its existence and some tentative comments on its theme and form may be appropriate and, perhaps, an introduction to poems, stories, pictures or music which handle similar experiences.

If children seem reluctant to write it may be that the initial struggle with the conventions of 'correct' letter formation, pencil manipulation and standardized spelling have been allowed to over-shadow the real purposes for which we write. Unless children are writing to exchange and preserve ideas, feelings and facts which they see as important it may be difficult for them to cope with the demands of the writing process. Of course the difficulties of writing are also the source of its great advantages. The endless fluctuation of responses and thought is steadied, new connections and possibilities become apparent, words and ideas can be recombined and formulations and messages can be preserved over time and distance.

But the beginner writer must not be fobbed off with totally pointless writing tasks in which he has no involvement. The first aim of the Primary school writing policy should be to nurture young writers who know that they must have in mind the audience for which they write. This can be helped by organizing a range of real recipients for the children's writing. The teacher is not the only person in the school and it is important for children to share their writing with other adults and with each other. The children can write to friends in the class and in the school and contacts can be established with other schools so that genuine letter writing is possible. Children can write brief notes of greeting, information or enquiry to their own parents, to the Headteacher, the Secretary, the Caretaker or any of the many adults who regularly come to the school. Letters of enquiry or of thanks to outside agencies will extend the children's experience of writing in more formal modes.

A second aim, closely tied up with having an audience in mind, is developing an understanding of what purpose the writing is to fulfil. Children need to know for themselves what the writing is for, as well as who it is for. The development of varied and appropriate written styles depends on this awareness. A wide experience of books and many other reading materials in school can foster this development and the children can be encouraged to write about favourite games, hobbies, outings, investigations and pets.

The third aim of Primary school writing should be to ensure that while the children's writing becomes increasingly sensitive to audience and purpose it yet retains the unique voice and stance of the individual writer. Children's first writing will be very close to their habitual speech forms but gains in variety and mastery of the conventions of written language should not be at the expense of the individual's use of written language to express a view and record a way of looking at the world. Nurturing 'voice' is no simple matter but it is bound up with respect for the individual learner and helped by a determination not to impose received opinions, formula answers and linguistic exercises on the writer at any level of education.

This is particularly relevant if young children are to be successful in writing about topics which belong to disciplines with traditionally established conventions of recording. Writing about scientific investigations by Primary school children is fully considered by Roy Richards in Chapter 5 but the following example illuminates some important considerations. The young child's writing is most fluent when it uses the form of narrative. Within the framework of a story the child's understanding of lengthy play and of experiments with water and floating is formulated and ordered. (The original story, by a six-year-old girl, covers eight pages and I have selected two passages.)

'Once upon a time there was a plastic spoon which some one had thron in the sea. the plastic spoon did not have truble with the water because it floatied . . . he was just about to go on to land when they throw a tin in the sea. the tin floatied because it has air in it. the plastic spoon thought he would stay in the water and make friends with the tin. So he stayed in the water and made friends with the tin. then the tin sead. you could have a little riyed in me so the plastic spoon got in the tin triyed to swime and they foued that they were moving so the tin went on swiming. the tin did not know he could swim and he felt very proud of him self. but the plastic spoon got heveya and heveya and soon the tin was sinking because he had water in him. and ther was no air because the tin was full of water and there was no room for some air so it was sinking. the plastic spoon jumpied out of the tin. so taht he would not sink too . . .'

The best example of 'voice' in a familiar kind of writing is the diary or private journal. The keeping of such a personal record is a practice which is growing in this country, particularly in the Secondary school (Paquette 1982). This private journal is usually shared with the teacher, by agreement, but is not marked. It is however replied to in written form by the teacher and gradually develops as an ongoing record of a relationship, rather than a school assignment. The book is a written dialogue in which the participants mull over issues and concerns which touch them most deeply. There is now some evidence (Britton 1981) that children in the Primary age range can keep journals in which they use written language to record and come to terms with feelings, social relationships and the demands of classroom life.

It is possible to organize writing tasks in the Primary school in such a way that children help and support each other. Geva Blenkin has already indicated in the previous chapter the need for the 'basic skills' to be developed as social and co-operative undertakings. There is some research evidence (Graves 1976) that shows children as young as seven participating in 'writing conferences' in the classroom. This can be one-to-one talk with the teacher or small-group discussion. It may be a pre-writing talking out of initial ideas or it can come after a first draft stage of writing. The children read their work to each other and discuss ideas for improvements before further drafts are attempted.

The value of this approach lies not just in mutually supportive learning but in the independence and control it gives the young writers over their material. It also emphasizes the fact that writing can be re-worked and altered in order to achieve a satisfactory result. This fact is emphasized by Geva Blenkin in her consideration of 'The Basic Skills', and well illustrated by Harriet Proudfoot's examples of individual children's development through the creative arts. How different from the 'slap it down and get it over and done with' approach to the task! When so many chilsen in school dare not voice an interest in anything in case they are told to write about it, we might seriously consider advocating a little less writing in schools. It is not appropriate, or normal, to write about everything and the cause of literacy might be better served if we aimed for quality and not quantity in writing.

If I have been less than precise about the process of learning to read it is because the current state of knowledge does not justify dogmatic assertions. We do not know enough about how individuals learn to read. It is clear that there are considerable differences in individual approaches and rates of progress and this alone justifies the Bullock Report's warning, 'there is no one method, medium, approach, device or philosophy that holds the key to the process of learning to read' (DES 1975, p.77).

Some of the most successful young readers do in fact achieve fluent reading before starting school. To cite such evidence (Torrey 1969; Clark 1976; Bissex 1980) is not an attempt to minimize the significance of the professional teacher of reading but a serious effort to increase our understanding of a complex process. All these successful young readers and writers had access to books and the very wide range of informative written material encountered in a literate society. They were also able to find plenty of pencils, 'markers' and scrap paper in their immediate environment. The children studied spent most of their day in the company of at least one caring adult and sometimes had the company of older siblings. The adult caregiver was not ostensibly concerned with teaching but gave the necessary linguistic information when asked, in the midst of normal daily activities and affectionate exchanges with the child. For these pre-school children there was also plenty of time and freedom and a total absence of anxiety about reading.

Under these conditions the children used a range of interesting strategies in their daily encounters with print. Firstly, they had the clear expectation that all words and sentences in print conveyed meaning, that there was a message to discover. Secondly, they used all their knowledge of the context — situation, pictures, objects — to predict the likely meaning. Thirdly, on meeting words they did not know, they would unhesitatingly ask an adult for the necessary information. Fourthly, they were reluctant to slow down their reading for meaning by lengthy struggles with individual words, preferring to read on while enough information was being extracted to keep the message intelligible. It is worth noting that these children often used writing to print out strongly felt messages concerned with desires, rights and privileges (Torrey 1969; Bissex 1980).

This evidence strengthens the arguments of Frank Smith (1978) that understanding reading requires understanding language and how children learn. Further, it is clear that 'information brought to reading by the brain is more important than information provided by the print' (Smith 1978, p. v). And, above all, children learn to read by reading. The challenge of this concept of reading has led to an interest in the process which goes well beyond the concerns of the Primary curriculum. University students of literature may now begin their researches into the nature of response to novels with careful analyses of the act of reading (Iser 1978). Such studies suggest that reading is an active recreation of the possible meanings of the text and involves the development of a special relationship between author and reader. We have come full circle, back to first language learning, with this emphasis on an active, creative and experimental process, negotiated with a more knowledgeable language partner.

Generating research and theories in schools

Throughout the working day teachers are involved in research procedures. We evolve theories and plan possible approaches and activities; we predict likely outcomes and organize the environment so as to maximize the chances of success for our work. Once the work is in progress we monitor it closely, watching and listening and generally thinking on our feet. The bustle of activity is followed by a crucial period of reflecting, recording and analysing our perceived successes and failures. In the light of these reflections we modify our theories and approaches, or even abandon the hypothesis and start again. The children too are busy setting up hypotheses and evaluating the outcomes of their experiments: 'I tried so-and-so but it didn't work'. The classroom is a learning laboratory and it is surprising that its potential as a power-house of research has been neglected until recent years.

However, the professional researcher is coming back into the classroom in order to draw on the unique contribution which only the teacher-researcher can make. This contribution is in fact the relationship the teacher has with her pupils and the remarkable insights into the personal nature of learning which this allows. This point is sensitively discussed by Minns (1981) when she writes of her daily interaction in her classroom as a constant inquiry into the learning that is taking place.

Some recent inquiries into aspects of language in education have taken great care to base themselves firmly in homes, schools and classrooms. Not only does this research carry the conviction which springs from hearing the genuine tones of people using language to cope with their lives, it also constitutes a rich collection of suggestions for classroom activities and procedures. The material coming out of the long-term Bristol study (Wells 1981) points up the subtly differing responses children make to various adults; the problems children may experience in making sense of some school learning tasks; and the significant effects of pre-school experiences of talk, stories and book language on children's progress in literacy in school. The work of the Crediton Project (Wilkinson et al. 1980) provides a lively collection of children's written work and is another research tool for analysing and classifying children's writings throughout the years of formal schooling. This research is a useful indicator of audience, purpose and voice in young children's development as writers.

Teachers and children are important in research but parents are also involved in the educative process and significant adults are crucial in children's language development. The Bristol study began with infants in their homes, their exchanges with caregivers being randomly sampled from the age of fifteen months. Other research projects led to a quickening of interest in the possible advantages to be gained from involving parents in the work of Nursery and Infant schools (Tizard, Mortimore and Burchell 1981). What emerges from this is the immense concern parents have for their children's progress in school and their desire to be involved with teaching their children, rather than just sharpening pencils. The considerable difficulties to be overcome in these home and school co-operative ventures do not detract from the powerful energies released when child, teacher and parent are working together.

The success of some of this work has led to a widespread interest in involving parents of Primary school children in the teaching of reading. Many teachers and schools are committed to this approach which links the two major centres of the child's life experiences, home and school. The approach has been particularly effective in communities which have not always appeared to be at ease in the world of formal schooling. One particularly well-documented account, *The Belfield Reading Project* (Jackson and Hannon 1981), highlights not only the considerable reading progress made by the individual children but also the sense of purpose and dignity the project has brought to a whole community.

These recent innovations in the teaching of reading emphasize the pleasure of sharing the learning in a supportive and informal setting. This is crucial for the beginner reader but once the initial stages are passed there is still a need to ensure sustained and varied reading experiences and lengthy informative contacts with an adult who is also an enthusiastic reader. The Schools Council research project, *Extending Beginning Reading* (Southgate, Arnold and Johnson 1981), tackled these issues by returning to the Primary classroom and investigating in depth what happens to the 'established' school reader of 7+. The intensive school observations were one feature of the research, the other equally practical aspect was the involvement of practising teachers who formed reading research groups and worked with the children in their own schools.

The main recommendations of the Report have received some publicity and give the teacher eager to question and evaluate her own classroom practices important matters to consider. But it is the end-of-chapter summaries and the 'Implications for Teachers' sections which make this Report such a useful handbook for working teachers. Many people are aware of the Report's criticism of the practice of listening to large numbers of children reading aloud for extremely brief periods each. But how many realize that this is accompanied by detailed suggestions for using the longer contacts with individual children advocated? Such a positive approach to the new partnership of teacher and research worker is both an implicit and an explicit characteristic of the Report. 'If researchers will take teachers into their confidence, state clearly their aims and the practical results which may be expected from the work, and, most important, supply them with as many of the results of

their work as soon as possible, an extremely valuable partnership can exist'
(Southgate et al. 1981, p.313).

Back to 'the basics'?

The approach to language development in school which I have outlined has
sometimes been dismissed as only suitable for the youngest children, but I
have indicated the rich possibilities which this approach holds out at all levels
of education. In particular, the seminal influence of informal small group discussion, the significance of reading for meaning at all stages of response to text
and the role of writing in increasing the potential of language for the individual. However, the most damaging and misleading criticism of this particular view of language development is that which accuses its advocates of
failing in their duty to teach 'the basics'. It is damaging in its suggestion that
there are basics of language which are being wilfully neglected in favour of
more frivolous pursuits. It is misleading in its assumptions about what
constitute 'basics' in language. Most frequently this view confuses the sophisticated linguistic conventions of later cultural developments with what is truly
basic to language. The whole argument is further confounded by the considerable social and cultural prestige which attaches to certain manifestations
of spoken language and to literacy.

What is basic in talking and listening is the forging of links between
thinking and language, the communication of ideas, feelings and messages
and the personal development which can come from having access, indirectly,
to other people's minds. Reading and writing extend these possibilities
dramatically, and necessarily put greater emphasis on the clear and unambiguous formulation of meaning and purpose in human communication.
Literacy overcomes the limitations of time and space and radically transforms
human thinking. No longer limited to the vagaries of memory and the distrac-
tions of face-to-face conversations we acquire a history and a literature and a
keen sense of the impossibility of ever catching up with the mounting backlog
of human knowledge (Goody and Watt 1963).

Seen in this perspective the so-called basics of standardized spelling and
punctuation are very recent phenomena, evolved to increase mutual understanding and facilitate better communication. They should be approached in
this spirit with children in school. Standardized spelling comes after the establishment of a real pleasure in writing to communicate and to explore thoughts
and feelings. Spelling is helped by constant exposure to the standardized forms

in books and other written materials and should be linked to the desire to take the intended audience for the writing into serious consideration. It should hardly need saying that regularly misspelled words should be collected from the children's own writing and not conjured out of the air as a last minute homework routine. Words which are 'wrong' are always interesting for they are indicative of the child's approach to representing the sounds of speech in writing and his use of analogies with known words. Geva Blenkin includes, in the preceding chapter, some vivid examples of young children's discoveries about print as they look closely at known words and names. Correcting spellings should be an integral part of exploring and understanding the language, not a humiliating punishment.

The use of punctuation is also a consequence of wishing to communicate more successfully and children are quick to see that it is a way of compensating for all the lost face-to-face feedback of the spoken dialogue. The meaningful units and crucial pauses are helpfully indicated if children try reading their work aloud. They soon seize on the conventions which they will need to replace the tune of the human voice in the work.

A misguided concern for 'basics' in the spoken language has bedevilled education for generations of non-standard dialect speakers. It has resulted, as has frequently been observed (Trudgill 1975), in the creation of the belief in a majority of the population that they cannot speak their mother tongue 'properly' and are unable to write any official communication with confidence. This impoverishment of people's lives is a sad reflection on an educational process which should be concerned with access, the opening of doors in society, and the enrichment of the individual's life. Too often in the past the monitoring of talk in school has been less concerned with meanings, purposes and ideas than with the social and aesthetic prejudices which filter our hearing of accent and dialect.

Similar dangers attend the assessing of language development with pre-specified aims and objectives. If we are listening for the required structures and words on our check-lists we may be quite deaf, or unreceptive, to the child's real linguistic negotiations and concerns.

Such thoughts as these must lead to a re-appraisal of much that has been said, and written, about linguistic deprivation and inequalities. Common experience and current research now seem to come together in suggesting that the inequalities of our society are not linguistic but, as they always were, social, material and economic (MacLure and French 1981).

Summary and conclusions

In this chapter I have indicated that current theoretical research emphasizes the central role of social interaction in the process of early language learning. I went on to consider the implications of the child's interaction with significant persons, the spoken language, the environment and the written language. This led to some important insights into language learning and development. The child plays an active, initiatory role in his learning; language learning is a creative process featuring innovation and exploration; the form this learning takes is conversation-like, involving significant human relationships and strong feelings. These considerations led me to propose three main aims for language policies in the Primary school. Firstly, schools must continue to enrich the language development of children. Secondly, the development of literacy should be seen as an important part of extending and enhancing children's language learning. Thirdly, schools should generate their own research projects as ways of evaluating their language policies.

I have argued that language development springs from the real-life concerns, activities and experiences of the individual. Central to this development is a concern to make sense of the world and narrative seems to play a crucial role in this process. Narrative form organizes and evaluates experience, like an on-going story, and is the primal activity from which all later skills of literacy evolve. Thus I have stressed the importance of the child's experiences of stories, his own and other people's, as the supportive framework for learning to read. Reading and writing are vital processes for shaping and sharing meanings and understanding experience. Literacy is seen as giving the individual independence and control over his life.

In a brief review of recent approaches to research I indicated the increasing interest in the daily interactions of teachers, children and parents. This emphasis on learning in ordinary classrooms and homes has highlighted the personal nature of the learning process and the significance of the supportive social context.

My final conclusion, in discussing 'the basics', was that what is truly basic to language is the role it plays in developing and extending human potential.

(I acknowledge a debt of gratitude to many of my students past and present whose classroom provision and practice are reflected in this chapter.)

CHAPTER 4

THE DEVELOPMENT OF A MATHEMATICS CURRICULUM
STUART ILSLEY

On the one hand the development of a mathematics curriculum can be thought of as a personal matter for teachers. The decision to change what we do and how we do it is taken in the light of children's reactions and understandings. The decision to change one particular way of organization for another is taken as a result of what it feels like for teacher and children working in the same room.

On the other hand it must be thought of as a joint or group development. The merging of individual teachers, each with their own ideas of what to do — their own personal curricula — into a group which shares these ideas and contributes to the development of a broader curriculum is essential. This can only come about by teachers working towards a common agreement on many important issues. This will mean an open discussion on the **what** and **how** of teaching mathematics. It may also mean discussion about children's attitudes towards mathematics, emotional reactions to mathematics and so on. Both types of development — thinking about what happens with one's own class, and discussion with others about broader issues in the teaching of mathematics — are essential.

Developing a mathematics curriculum that seems to meet the needs of children and has a relevance to their lives is a goal most of us have. However, that goal may appear to be a long way from where we are now, and the road to it beset with obstacles. Some of those obstacles may be personal ones. For example, it is hard for many teachers to get past their own emotional fear of mathematics. As Laurie Buxton says in *Do you panic about maths?* (1981, p.1) 'Anyone working in maths rapidly becomes aware, not only that few share their interest, but also that the subject is regarded with some distaste.' This distaste is for many of us a huge obstacle.

Many of the obstacles may be external. For example, the pressures of running a class successfully; of finding the time to contribute to all major curriculum discussions in the school; of liaising with other schools and teachers; of working towards increased parental involvement; and many more. All these can be very off-putting when contemplating the way ahead.

It may be easier to take the first step if it is not seen as a great and instant-aneous leap in understanding but as a series of smaller steps each of which we take when we are ready to, and which are well within our range. What follows is a description of what some of those steps might be.

Getting started

Mathematics is often described as being interesting but hard. Most teachers would agree with this, particularly the part about its being hard. Many will tell you that they found the maths they did at school, and later at college, threat-ening and hard to understand. Some will say that it was the quality of the teaching they received that made it so. Others will say that the difficulty is inherent in the subject itself. Whatever the reasons, there are many teachers who are trying daily to come to terms with the fact that maths is hard, both for them to understand and, consequently, for them to teach. In a situation like this it is natural to turn to various agencies for help.

In some cases it may be possible to turn to a post-holder for mathematics. In others it may be possible to turn to an advisory teacher. There are often a range of courses available, and it is possible to read and use books on mathem-atics. For the time being however I want to concentrate on books, because it is to these that we usually turn first. It is thus one of the first steps we take in the development of a personal curriculum.

Turning to books and mathematics schemes for help

There are books on the theory and practice of teaching mathematics. Here I am thinking of books like *Primary Mathematics Today* (Williams and Shuard 1976), *The Psychology of Learning Mathematics* (Skemp 1971) and the publi-cations in the series *The Nuffield Maths Project* (Matthews 1976). These can be quite useful. But, as many of us know, it is very difficult to find the time to do much background reading.

There are also maths schemes, which appear to be designed to bypass the teacher and 'teach' mathematics directly to the children. Most teachers would say that it is helpful, both for them and the children, to use a published maths scheme. There may be arguments about which of the schemes to use. But it is generally agreed that commercial schemes seem to make the teaching and the learning of maths less hard. It may be interesting for our purposes to see how they do this.

One way that such mathematical software tries to make mathematics less hard is by what I shall call 'compartmentalizing'. As you scan a book from a scheme you will see, for example, that pages 6 to 9 deal with 'telling the time'; that pages 9 to 11 deal with 'hundreds, tens, and ones'; and so on. As well as this, these bite-sized chunks of mathematics are arranged in order of supposed difficulty — that is, in a prespecified sequence of learning.

One of the first steps in the development, then, is to rely on a published scheme. There is also the tendency to use the scheme in the same way as textbooks were used in former times, especially in the teacher's own early education. We encourage children to start at the first page and work through to the last, before going on to the next, 'harder' book.

Relying on something which prescribes what you teach and when you teach it may appear initially to fill a gap. But, as has been stressed in the two previous chapters, relying on something imposed from the outside takes little or no account of the 'learner'. These schemes are written for children in Newcastle, London and Exeter. They cannot possibly begin to cater for the needs of each individual child in your class.

Imagine the view of mathematics a child is receiving by working through a scheme in a methodical way. He or she is jumping from one aspect of mathematics to another for no other reason than that it is on the next page. It is difficult to know what a child makes of it all, but it must be a very disjointed and haphazard experience, and one that has little bearing on his or her life. So, to work through a maths scheme in the hope that it has got the curriculum worked out for you, and that it will make mathematics less hard for you and the children, will probably have the opposite effect in the long run.

Published guidelines

But, I hear you say, you are not meant to work slavishly through a scheme like that. A teacher teaches, and having satisfied themself that the groundwork is adequately prepared, backs up that teaching by selecting an appropriate section from an appropriate scheme. This, of course, means more careful research and preparation than is needed when one is relying on one scheme for everything, and is certainly more in line with how the authors envisaged their books being used.

This, then, is the next step to take in the development of a personal curriculum — to move on from using one scheme rigidly, to using selected books from different schemes in a creative way. However, when you take this step more questions than answers seem to appear. For example, you have to ask yourself what piece of maths to teach. Or how do you know when to teach these pieces of mathematics? How do you organize for it all? And how do you know which children to work with at any one time?

Having started to think about these important questions it may be helpful if we look at various models of curriculum 'guidelines' to see what other people recommend as answers to some of these questions. Curriculum 'guidelines' are produced, for example, by LEAs in order to help teachers come to terms with what mathematics to teach. These 'guidelines' are produced by inspectors, advisers and, perhaps, groups of teachers and then distributed. In them can be found the bare bones of a progression — a washing line if you like, on which teachers are expected to pin the washing. It could be said that the hope of the producers of 'guidelines' is that they will make the teaching of mathematics less difficult. Again, it may be useful for our purposes to see how they go about this.

Some 'guidelines' do have a section where they try to describe mathematics as the fascinating web of interconnecting ideas and relationships that it is. But the sections which teachers at this stage in their development find most useful, and therefore the sections which make the most impression, are those where the authors try to isolate the various strands of the web and show a clear progression along them. This, for example, may include isolating the strand of 'Whole Numbers' and showing everything it might contain, from one-to-one correspondence to very large numbers. The sorts of suggestions you may find here are, say, that you first provide activities that focus on the idea of the relationship between two groups of objects so that, by comparing the objects from one group with the objects from another, the child can say whether there are 'more than', 'fewer than', or 'the same number as', before he has learnt to count. Then you go on to provide activities where children count objects in small groups and match one of the numerals from 0 to 9 to the groups. Then the children learn to say the number names in sequence before learning to write the symbols from 0 to 9. And so on. This is the sort of advice 'guidelines' give to help teachers to plan.

One problem we need to bear in mind here is that such 'guidelines' are completely 'content' orientated and have little or nothing to say about our attitudes to maths; about ways of talking to and questioning children, and so on. In particular, they do not cater for teachers who are seeking insight into what processes are involved; that is, both the processes involved for them as teachers in generating activities — thus being able to pin the washing on the line — and for children when coming to terms with particular mathematical activities and concepts.

The most useful example of published 'guidelines' I can think of is the ILEA's booklet called *Mathematical Content* (ILEA 1976). In this booklet the web of mathematics generally regarded as appropriate for Primary age children is isolated into four main strands: 'Sets'; 'Numbers'; 'Measures'; and 'Geometry'. Each of the four strands is further split into subsections with generalized age-level indicators. Doing this is undoubtedly useful, imposing as it does an intellectual organization on what for most of us is a forest obscuring the trees. It helps a teacher to come to terms with what to teach and when. Consequently, it can appear to help to make maths less hard both to under-stand and to teach. Thus, spending some time unravelling the web of mathe-matics and coming to terms with the strands is the next useful step for the teacher to take.

Up to this point in the development of a mathematics curriculum we have been concentrating more on the teacher's understanding of mathematics and how to teach it, than on the understanding of the children. To highlight the danger of this, I offer a personal example.

I started teaching by encouraging children to work through the scheme we had in school. As time went by it became increasingly apparent to me that things were not going as I wanted them to. There were always queues of children waiting to have their work checked, or, more to the point, waiting for me to decipher the book for them. There always seemed to be children who coped well with reading for action, and so moved through the scheme reason-ably fluently. But there were also those who spluttered their way through a few pages a term. And this didn't seem to have anything to do with their mathematical ability. As if these were not danger signals enough, I soon became aware that even though some children appeared to be successful, the success was only in being able to meet the demands of those maths books. When occasions arose where they had to apply mathematical thinking, they often could not. In other words they could not relate what they were doing in their books to the rest of their life in or out of school. This lack of ability to apply the abstract to the practical was the most worrying aspect of all, and the one most difficult for me to deal with.

It was somewhat easier to deal with the organizational aspects of the problem. For example, I could get rid of long queues by not having every child doing maths at the same time. I could keep track of the children better by grouping them according to the mathematical task in hand. But the business about the children being able to add, subtract, multiply and divide when faced with the pencil and paper method, but not being able to work out Geoff Boycott's batting average, to use an example from a recent APU report (DES 1979a), was a more worrying and time-consuming problem. At the time I was tempted to think that my new organization and less rigid approach would make maths more relevant to children because they would understand more of it. Yet I began to feel that this was not going to be the case. The atmosphere in the room improved but it did not seem to lead to a significant increase in mathematical understanding. I learnt a lot here and moved on a step in my development. I'm not convinced that the children did.

Much can be accomplished by rethinking classroom organization and re-organizing how the children work. The hard work is in deciding what activities to plan and what is involved in these activities for the children. It demands that you begin to develop an understanding of the strands that go to make up the web of mathematics. This is where published 'guidelines' are useful. It means that you have to take apart those strands and collect together activities to match the ideas in them. Both a teacher's understanding and the development of activities takes a very long time — in fact, it never seems to end. It is necessary therefore to have a realistic expectation of how long it will take, or frustration will be yet another obstacle along the way.

There is another danger that needs to be considered here. It is tempting to think that this is the end point and to remain at this safe and comfortable position. But to plan your teaching on the basis that the strands of mathe-matics are isolated from each other, and by implication from the rest of the curriculum, is to deny the fact that mathematics, and life, are just not like that. Mathematics is complex and life does not happen to any of us, least of all children, in nice separate compartments, or in clear developmental sequences. Indeed it could be argued that if we stayed at this point in our development, the work we prepared would be further misleading children as to the true nature of mathematics. It is the very complexity of mathematics and coming to an understanding of that complexity that on the one hand is so hard, and on the other is so interesting.

Discussions with other teachers

There is much to be said for thinking and talking about your personal curriculum with groups of other teachers. One way to do this is to look for relevant maths courses. These can be useful in deepening an understanding of maths; they may give many ideas for methodology and organization; and, most important of all, they offer the forum to talk informally with other teachers. It has to be said that the support to be gained from meetings with teachers to talk about mathematics and how best to teach it is invaluable. These meetings can take place at Teachers' Centres or in local schools. Better still, they could be between like-minded teachers in your own school. Such regular meetings tend to change and develop teachers' views of the curriculum.

We are all, as teachers, thinking about **what** to teach. Every day of the week we have to consider what the mathematical idea is that we are trying to get across. But it is only really in group discussions — in groups one feels comfortable in — that we can extend our thinking. For example, discussing things in a forum may lead to thinking about:

- the **how** of teaching mathematics - different ways to present the same idea; what processes are involved in it for the children; ways of questioning children without either leading or being too threatening; assessing, commercially available teaching aids, and so on;
- ways to **record** which activities each child has experienced and why - there are some ideas on how you might go about this in Chapter 7;
- how to **assess** realistically what each child has learnt from the activities, that is, checking to see how successful you have been;
- ways to **record** each child's achievements - how to use such information to plan future work.

Eventually what you do in the classroom and what you talk about in group discussions become part of the same process. A teacher's experiences in the classroom and his or her children's achievements are often the starting points. The deliberation then feeds back into classroom practice. This collaborative process ends with teachers knowing and understanding more than they would have done if they had developed their ideas in isolation.

Assessment as a basis for responding to children's understanding

One of the areas I outlined for discussion in the previous section was how to assess a child's particular achievements, and therefore to plan more productively. In thinking about assessment it is important we consider what form it should take. As is argued in the introduction to the ILEA's booklet *Checkpoints* (ILEA 1978, p.1) 'Mixed topic tests, whether standardized against national scores or not, are only useful when pupils are to be compared with each other for grouping purposes. To provide a profile of the achievements of the individual (which is needed for continuity) a record of item by item assessment is the most useful'. The type of assessment they have in mind is a specific piece of interaction between a teacher and a child, or group of children, using familiar pieces of apparatus in familiar situations. The difference is that the teacher is merely asking questions, having withdrawn all the support which is normally invested in such situations.

This model of 'informal' assessment is very useful when a group of teachers is developing the **what — how — to whom — record — assess — record** cycle. If the relationship between teacher and child is right, we may just get an inkling of what is going on inside a child's head. We should be trying to see the reality and meaning he or she attaches to mathematics. The information provided by such an assessment of each child's understanding will undoubtedly then be reflected in the preparation of future work, and should also lead to a re-evaluation of work already undertaken.

I offer two personal examples of how reflecting on what children do and say can lead to the development of a teacher's understanding.

I was providing activities for a group of first-year juniors in the mathematical strand of 'Measures'. (I was using the ILEA curriculum 'guidelines' already referred to in this chapter as the model for my planning.) The children were working on linear measurement and, using non-standard units, were measuring the length of a particular wall. As I had anticipated, they all came back with different numbers and I was set for the discussion of why each of their measurements was different, and thus for the emergence of an awareness of the need for a standard unit. I was waiting for a point in the discussion where I could intervene without seeming like an elephant in hobnail boots, when I was struck by a thought. The previous week, this same group had been counting and comparing large groups of objects. I knew from that that some of them still had trouble saying the number names past about 70. For example, a child would say '. . . 75, 76, 77, 78, 79, 70, . . .'. In the discussion about how long the wall was the children were using numbers in the range from 100 to 200. How could I trust the quantifications of linear measurement they were using when I knew they couldn't 'count' properly? I realized that the mathematical strands of 'Measures' and 'Numbers' had intersected. They were not separate after all.

At the time I felt that the task of measuring the wall had to be considered a learning point for me, and that to use it as a vehicle for getting to the need for a standard unit would be wrong. So I introduced a further measuring task later that week where the thing to be measured was shorter than the wall, and where I had checked that each child's measure would not fit into it more than about 50 times.

Later still it became a topic for discussion with a group of teachers. It led to our trying to get clear in our minds just how far to take the strand of 'Whole Numbers' in relation to the strand of 'Measures'. It also alerted us to the possibility that it might happen again in other areas.

The second example focuses on a different problem. It comes from the same group of children and from the same topic. While we were engaged in discussion, a child told us about his parents' market stall. They sold material, and he knew how much various materials cost. He quoted names of materials and prices per yard. This was at the time I was introducing the metre as the standard rule. I hadn't considered that by leaving out imperial measures the mathematics didn't quite match up to the child's picture of his world. I felt as if someone had muddied up the waters in my bucket of understanding.

I was fairly non-committal with the children because I wanted time to think things through. Eventually I decided to ask the child to bring in one of the brass yards his parents used, and we used it both as a comparison to the metre and as a measure in its own right. Later, in group discussion with other teachers, we began to feel that there may be a place for using the dual system of metric and imperial.

Development through relevant experiences

Children show us not only that we need to acknowledge the fact that mathematics is a complex and interconnecting web of ideas, but also that we must value their interests and understanding. We must reflect this in the experiences we give them. They also help us to see that we need to make mathematics more explicit in the rest of the things they do in the classroom, in fact in the whole of their lives. Both these points need to be borne in mind when we are thinking about the **what** and **how** of mathematics.

This latest step — the one required if you value a child's interests and understanding — is both difficult to take and can take a long time to consolidate. It is also, by its very nature, difficult to capture in words. For, at this

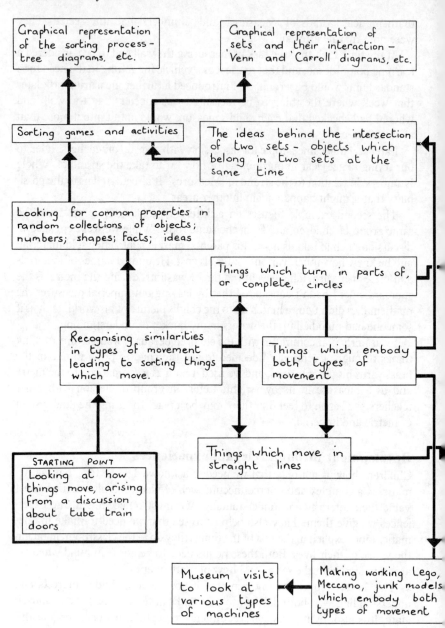

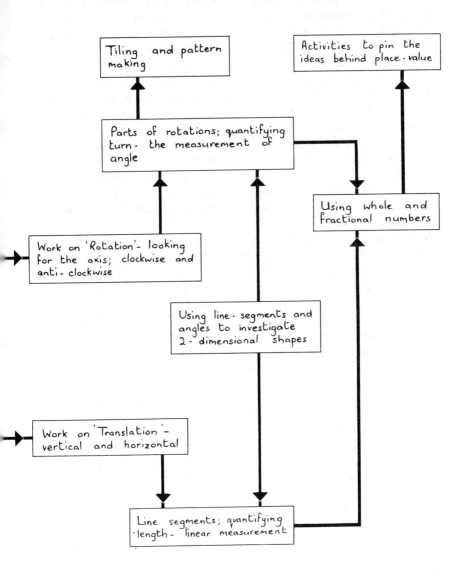

Figure 4.1   A teacher's record of how the maths. work of one class developed over the period of one term

stage, a teacher's planning attempts to respond to the interests his or her children show and what they say and do, so that this planning will be different for each child, or group of children. Perhaps I can offer an example of what I mean in the hope that it will be a useful discussion point.

The work illustrated here (Figure 4.1) evolved over a term. It was not possible to predict any of it at the beginning of the term because it was work which resulted from the teacher's perceptions of what the children were interested in, and could cope with. It is presented in the diagrammatic form we used to record it at the end of the term.

It would take more than the space permitted here to describe the activities generated to fit each of the boxes in the diagram. And in a way that is not what this chapter is about. My concern here is the process we go through as teachers in developing a curriculum for mathematics. So rather than concentrate on mathematical activities I will look more at the thought and organization that back them up.

All children in this class of fourth-year juniors were, at one time or another, involved in aspects of the work described. There were times when it was felt that the work was appropriate for the whole class. This was particularly so during the early stages while the teacher and children were feeling their way. At this time, when, for example, the teacher was concentrating on the idea of 'complete turns', it was possible for every child to bring something to the work. For instance, the following activity was designed during a discussion with other teachers to cater for the fact that all the children were having trouble with the idea of the axis of rotation.

Each child 'invented' two or three different two-dimensional shapes, drawing them on card and cutting them out. The types of shapes included: 'shapes with straight sides only'; 'shapes with curved sides only'; and 'shapes with straight and curved sides'. In turn, each child used the shapes as the basis of an investigation. (They were used again later in a sorting activity designed to highlight the ideas behind the intersection of two sets.) The investigation consisted of pushing a pin through the shape and through a piece of drawing paper, thus pinning the two together with the shape being able to rotate on the paper. Each child drew round the shape, rotated it slightly, drew round it again, rotated it slightly, drew round it again, and so on. They did this until the shape had done one complete turn and had fitted back on itself. This makes an interesting 'rotation picture' for all children. Having done this they removed the shape from the paper. The split pin was moved, pushed through another point on the surface of the shape and then through a clean piece of drawing paper. The shape stayed the same while the axis of rotation moved. Each child did this several times and compared each of the 'rotation pictures' they made. They were encouraged to record their thoughts about what they noticed of the relationship between the position of the axis and the shape of the 'rotation pictures'. All children could contribute something to this area of work. Following on from this, some children looked at regular and irregular shapes rotating while others consolidated their ideas about the axis of rotation.

At another time, some children would be working on the idea of rotation, while other children would be working with books reinforcing areas they were already familiar with; that is, areas where there was no real need for input from the teacher — thus relieving the pressure slightly. For example, a few might be engaged in an activity designed to pin the idea of addition and subtraction of equal groups, thus reinforcing their ideas of multiplication and division. This was work the teacher had predicted would not crop up from interests or environment — and which of course could be recorded by her at the beginning of term.

So, at one time or another in the week-by-week mathematics programme, there was a bit of everything going on. This was because of all the experience the teacher had accumulated in her development through stages similar to the ones outlined in this chapter. She had researched thoroughly and was using textbooks in a context that meant something to the children. She was clear in her mind about what the mathematical strands might be and had provided for a progression along them. She was reflecting on and planning her work alone, and with a group of friends. She was providing activities that focused on the processes involved in various mathematical ideas. She was beginning to come to terms with and make clear mathematics in other areas of the curriculum. And she was responding to the children's interests and needs.

Responding to the children's interests seemed easier when working in this informal way. For example, a small group of children showed an interest in the steering devices in the 'Technical Lego'. They built working models that embodied the ideas of rotation and translation. Their success and interest meant they were keen to explain to others what they had learnt. Later they were introduced to a book about various inventions. This book included some of Heath Robinson's drawings as well as some of Leonardo da Vinci's drawings for machines. This led to a long piece of work which included drawing, building and writing about working models they had made which embodied different types of movement.

It was clear that the work was relevant because the children kept on talking about things that moved in particular ways, challenging each other to say how they moved. The work, by being firmly based on things from the children's world, had led them to look more closely at it.

Of course, the classroom organization that supports this way of working and allows it to operate freely needs careful thought. It is important to recognize that many of the problems we think of as due to the mathematics are really to do with the inability of the organization to cope.

Summary and conclusions

One of the implications of this way of working that worries some people is that it is not possible to record what you intend to do before you do it. In other words, it is not possible to present a complete scheme of work at the beginning of each term. This, however, is the essence of planning a curriculum according to procedural principles rather than prespecified objectives. It requires that, instead of producing statements of goals, you prepare a scheme which outlines the principles which will underpin your work, the consolidation activities you intend to use and which pages in which books will be used as reinforcement. You can include also the things you think are not likely to crop up naturally.

This must also, as Maggie Bierley argues in Chapter 7, lead the teacher to thinking about different types of record-keeping. For keeping an on-going record of what happens in the room (this may be a flow-diagram of the types used here and in Chapter 7) and using such a record as the basis for group discussion and for planning future work is essential. The fact that this part of the overall record will not be completed until the end of the term provides an opportunity to reflect on the developing curriculum from the beginning of the term to the end.

For the development of the curriculum and of the children's work is a cumulative process. As I have tried to outline in this chapter, it may be easier to start such development if the process is broken down into easy steps and there is a realistic time expectation about each of those steps. But this kind of development must occur if we are to promote rather than to hinder children's mathematical education.

Is there an end to such development? The very nature of mathematics and the reasons for teaching it suggest that there is not. As each different group of children expresses different interests and abilities, the development that results will be different. For example, the next time it may all start from a remark made about different types of clock face and how confusing they can be. Mathematics is not a static thing. In practice it is a moving and growing thing, and our mathematical development and the development of a mathematics curriculum must also be continuous.

CHAPTER 5

LEARNING THROUGH SCIENCE
ROY RICHARDS

This chapter traces the recent history of the development of Primary science in Great Britain. It attempts to show what is meant by science with young children, taking a process approach to education. The benefits to be derived from science are enumerated and the work of the latest national project, the Schools Council Learning Through Science Project, is described in detail.

An historical perspective

Science is a study of nature and it is a commonly held viewpoint that 'nature study', as it was termed, has long held a place of esteem in British education. Yet as far back as 1913 Henry Armstrong was already bemoaning the fact that 'Nature too seldom comes into the work and too often study is the last thing thought of'. One of the besetting difficulties in establishing science in the Primary curriculum has been to get teachers to see that it is a 'hands-on', problem-solving activity involving a practical investigation of the environment.

Following post-World War II optimism, which culminated in the prosperity of the Swinging Sixties, a number of national projects were born. The first of these began in 1964 and was called the Nuffield Junior Science Project (Wastnedge 1967). Its first words were, 'The best of all cases can be made for the inclusion of science in the primary school curriculum, for it is essentially a practical investigation of the environment. It makes use of some of the young child's most outstanding characteristics, his natural curiosity and his love of questioning. What is more, science presents the teacher with a constant challenge to learn and discover for himself, a challenge which can only have a beneficial effect upon his teaching (op. cit., p.9).

Furthermore, this Nuffield Project team expressed a strong belief in children's natural powers of learning being closely related to scientific method, for they said, 'Children's practical problem solving is essentially a scientific way of working, so that the task in school is not one of teaching science to children, but rather of utilizing the children's own scientific way of working as a potent educational tool' (op. cit., p.22) and '. . . their own questions seem to be the most significant and to result most often in careful investigations' (op. cit., p. 28). Books from the project contained case studies showing how teachers had followed children's interests and describing the resources needed. The project did not concern itself either with the kinds of concepts that would be developed or with the content of what should be taught.

The year 1967 saw the advent of the Schools Council Science 5/13 Project (Ennever and Harlen 1972). This built on the work established by the Nuffield Project but now presented to teachers a substantial set of 'behavioural objectives'. The set was based on child development closely related to those stages delineated by Piaget and his followers. These 'behavioural objectives' in no way presented a course or syllabus. The Science 5/13 team, like their Nuffield predecessors, still saw the need to root experience in children's interests:

> In general children work best when trying to find answers to problems that they have themselves chosen to investigate. These problems are best drawn from their own environment and tackled largely by practical investigations.
> Teachers should be responsible for thinking out and putting into practice the work of their own classes. In order to do so they should find help where they need it (Ennever and Harlen 1972, p.4).

The project provided some 26 thematic books setting out possible experiences that might be developed in order to achieve the 'behavioural objectives' which the project team thought central to conducting science with young children.

Any study of these two projects will quickly show that, in spite of the frequent use of the term 'behavioural objectives', both lay emphasis on developing the processes of science. That is to say observation, questioning, proposing enquiries, problem-solving, perception of patterns and communication of findings were thought to be the most important attributes to develop in children. In actively pursuing these processes children would develop scientific concepts. However, no attempt was made to set up a concept model for teachers to follow because this would have taken them away from children's interests and would have created a stereotyped and restricted curriculum. The strongly held belief that children's thinking skills are best developed by direct practical experience in an integrated curriculum emerged clearly. An integrated curriculum was felt to be important because of young children's natural ability and inclination to cross subject boundaries, and because of the strength — and often the need — to utilize other areas of the curriculum to help develop science, and to use science to enhance language work, art and craft, mathematics and so on.

In 1972 the Schools Council Progress in Learning Science Project began (Harlen, Darwin and Murphy 1977). This examined ways in which individual children's scientific progress could be assessed by direct observation. In doing this the project team attempted to list the scientific attributes deemed worth developing in children. These related closely to the 'objectives' of the Science 5/13 Project.

With 1978 came the Schools Council Learning Through Science Project (Richards, Collis and Kincaid 1980), which again puts as much emphasis on developing the processes of science as its predecessors; it also strongly believes in interest-based work developed on an intercurricula basis. This project takes a strongly practical lead by producing twelve packs of pupil material each containing a set of teachers' notes. The twelve themes cover those areas of scientific knowledge commonly pursued by Primary schools when they present scientific experiences to children. In addition two separate texts discuss how to formulate a school science policy and the resources necessary for this, the nature of which is discussed in detail later.

It is now clear that a great deal of thought has gone into deciding what is meant by science for young children and into producing suitable materials to help teachers. Let us look at these in more detail.

What is science?

Science is often used as a term to signify the unified sum of all the separate sciences. That is to say it is the total of all our organized knowledge and understanding of the natural world. The more one could know of this, as of any other body of knowledge, the better. Yet it is obvious that no-one could assimilate or understand more than a tiny fraction of this corpus. However, science has certain ways of proceeding that allow us to attain scientific knowledge and it is to these that we should turn our attention when we teach young children.

It is best to begin looking at this by taking a case study of some first-school children working with their teacher (ASE 1981, p.2). The teacher begins: 'As I drove to school one morning I nearly ran into a child who was wearing a "snorkel" jacket with its hood fully extended. He had stepped off the footpath in front of my car. He appeared not to have seen or heard me. Later that morning I talked to Darren, the hooded walker, and his group about the incident. The children were keen to investigate. They suggested that they should find out how much the hood had really stopped Darren from seeing and hearing the car — or had he just been sleepy? Here are the tests the 7 and 8 year old children devised'. (Figure 5.1)

If we analyse what happened we can see that the work began from an initial *observation,* one that had an intrinsic interest for the children. It might not have gone any further if the teacher had not taken it up in the classroom by initiating a discussion. This led to *questioning* — had the hood really stopped Darren from seeing and hearing the car? This questioning led to *problem solving* — things were tested out. How far can we see around us with a hood up, and how far with a hood down? How far can we hear with a hood up, or with a hood down? *Tests* have to be devised. Children become better and better at thinking out how to test things the more they experiment. However, their discoveries need the guidance of the teacher. Here is a good example of a teacher and children working alongside one another. Conclusions were reached and records were made. Measurement, an important part of many scientific investigations, also played its part. Perhaps, over and above everything, one feels that the children are actively involved — and that involvement makes the usual approach to road safety exercises look a little sterile.

The example given shows how science is a way of finding answers — a method of thinking and doing. The way the answers are found is called the 'process' of science. Wynne Harlen, in the texts 'Match and Mismatch', has made a careful analysis of this process with special reference to the scientific education of young children. She delineates a number of attributes that characterize the process:

—Observing
—Proposing enquiries
—Experimenting/investigating
—Communicating verbally
—Communicating non-verbally
—Finding patterns in observations
—Critical reasoning
—Applying learning   (Harlen, Darwin and Murphy 1977)

How far could Darren see?

Darren stood in the middle of the front of the room, facing the wall. Other children walked up the sides of the room behind him, waving their arms. As soon as he saw movement they stopped and marked their position.

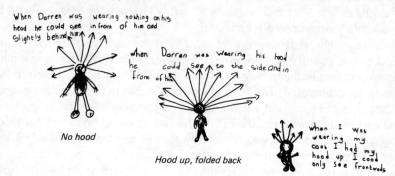

When Darren was wearing nothing on his head he could see in front of him and slightly behind him

No hood

when Darren was wearing his hood he could see to the side and in front of him

Hood up, folded back

when I was wearing my coat I had my hood up I coud only see frontweds

Hood fully extended

How far could he hear?

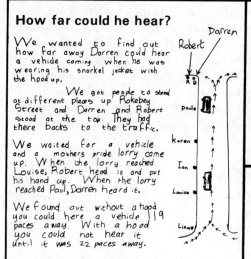

We wanted to find out how far away Darren could hear a vehicle coming when he was wearing his snorkel jacket with the hood up.

We got people to stand at different places up Rokeby Street and Darren and Robert stood at the top. They had there backs to the traffic.

We waited for a vehicle and a mothers pride lorry came up. When the lorry reached Louise, Robert heard it and put his hand up. When the lorry reached Paul, Darren heard it.

We found out without a hood you could here a vehicle 119 paces away. With a hood you could not hear it until it was 22 paces away.

Robert   Darren

R D

Paul

Karen

Ian

Louise

Lisa

What could he hear?

Darren and Robert stood at the front of the class room and we dropped a pin Robert heard but Darren didnt. Then we dropped a ping pongball. Robert heard Darran didnt. We banged some plastic Robert heard, Darren did it then we read words from a book getting louder and louder. Only when we read very loud did Darren hear it.

These "snorkel" hoods are popular, and the children were keen to tell the rest of the school about their experiments. They presented their work to an interested audience in an assembly.

This is a good starting point for more work on road safety.

Figure 5.1

It is a useful model. Science usually begins with some initial observation. Children will find things that interest them when they are encouraged to use all their senses in as many ways as possible in actively and practically exploring their environment. The teacher's task is to show them what is interesting about these things.

Using the senses

It is vital to develop the full use of the senses. Infant teachers are adept at this. A rich classroom environment, coupled with an active exploration of the world outdoors gives children many things to look at and handle. Blindfolded children can attempt to identify things by touch, lifting and generally handling things as well as simply feeling them. Can they distinguish between lemon peel, orange peel and grapefruit peel? Can they tell emery-paper from sand-paper? Tape-recording the children's speech as they do so is revealing. A play-back discloses their confidence, hesitation and search for the correct words and phrases. What about the texture of things? Are they rough, smooth, waxy, greasy, furry, sharp, prickly, crumbly, ridged, angled, moulded, carved? What shape is the object? Is it a cube, a pyramid or a sphere? Irregular shapes are fun! Looking at how easily they topple, trying to balance them, seeing how the weight is distributed, all add to the interest. Even the temperature of objects can be explored. Wool and expanded polystyrene will feel warmer than metals. Yet are they really warmer? Are the objects damp? Are they hard? Pressing, twisting or scratching objects such as plasticine, putty, rubber, balsa wood, beech, metals, chalk, limestone, granite, present further suitable experiences.

'Listening walks' are popular where the noises heard are noted down and then talked about. Often the use of a portable tape-recorder helps recall the sounds, and the odd emphasis of the sounds that the mechanical tape brings gives added effect and interest. Different places produce different sounds; the playground, the High Street, a supermarket, a wood, a church, a bedroom, a waterfall, all evoke different atmospheres. Can you hear a pin drop? This is the chance for a scientific test. Will it matter what the pin is dropped on? Does it matter what height it is dropped from? Does it matter how far away it is?

How many common bird songs can be recognized? The sounds of thrush, blackbird, sparrow, starling and a few other common birds should become part of the 'vocabulary' of any child. Sometimes just the listening is enough, for as Pestalozzi said, 'Lead your child out into nature. Teach him on the hill-tops and in the valleys, there he will listen better. But in these hours of freedom let him be taught by Nature rather than you. Let him fully realise that you with your art do nothing more than to walk quietly by his side. Should a bird sing or an insect hum on a leaf, at once stop your talk. Birds and insects are teaching him. You may be silent.' The primordial senses of smell and taste also bring their pleasures. Who can ever forget the smell of new-mown hay or kippers cooking? Pleasant and unpleasant smells, country smells and city smells, household and garden smells, all give cause for sorting and separating. Children often know the smells of dandelions, marigolds and pansies which we as adults have invariably forgotten.

Tasting things and smelling things need care. There are dangers to beware of, such as those that berries, seeds, tablets, medicines and cleaning fluids can bring. However, with proper supervision there is a whole world here for exploration. Can children distinguish the taste of apple, pear, banana, grape, onion, chocolate, coffee, tea, orange squash and so on when blindfolded? Can they group things into sweet, sour and salty tastes? Can they tell margarine from butter or saccharine from sugar? In all such cases fair tests will need to be thought out and tried.

Who can see best? Which colour combinations are good to use for signs and which are bad ones? Have you tried yellow symbols on white paper or black letters on purple? Each day brings new things to explore. Of course we normally use our senses in combination with one another and relate the sensations together in our memory. Children will do this well when school staffs produce the experiences and provide the materials and equipment to help the children employ their senses in every way.

Aids for the senses

Use of the senses results in an examination of our environment. Often we need to see things in greater detail, especially small things. We need to measure. We need aids to help us as we compare and sort things. Hand lenses open up a whole new world. Skin, newspaper, cloth, insect legs, nettle stings all take on new dimensions when magnified. Watch a child's face as she views the moon through binoculars for the first time. Craters and seas become real! Is Harry taller than Tom? What is the dimension of this oak tree? How wide is that mustard seed? Rulers, calipers and even micrometers begin to play their part.

How long does Jane take to run a hundred metres? How long does a snail take to cover one metre? Suddenly stop-clocks and stop-watches come into their own right. What is the temperature today? How much hotter are you after running for five minutes? In this case we need some thermometers.

All these things are aids to the senses — and vital aids at that! They let us compare things more accurately. They help us to look for similarities and differences in things. Often in the data we collect patterns and relationships appear. The world begins to emerge as ordered, often interestingly and intriguingly so. For example, in a graph showing the length of a collection of woodlice a few were about 5 mm and a few were as big as 20 mm, but most were about 12 mm in length; apparently diverse objects such as spiders' webs, electric light filaments, pea tendrils, bindweed, the floret arrangement of a dandelion, springs, screws, bolts, toilet-roll centres, and coiled ropes on closer examination are discovered to be spirals — some coil clockwise and some anti-clockwise; the springs of a piano also show a sequence — and pleasant sounds seem to repeat themselves in eights and a set of eight notes is called an octave.

The children begin to see pattern and order and at the same time they begin to appreciate that change and apparent disunity can also arise. The old adage says 'as like as two peas in a pod', yet two peas from the same pod might grow into two very different plants, one might be a dwarf plant with green seeds while the other might be tall with yellow seeds. Why does one pea give rise to tall plants and the other to short ones? This use of our senses, often combined with measuring and magnifying aids, results in a probing of our world that inevitably leads children to *questioning*.

Questioning

To answer the question about the peas demands some rudimentary knowledge of genetics. This may be too complex for young children, but they would have made an initial observation by growing peas that would have been stored in their body of experiences for answer at a later date. Much of science with young children consists of building up experiences in this way. However, very many of the questions that children ask *can* be answered by direct testing.

Will water go through cloth? Through wood? Through soil?
Why does the holding end of a spoon get hot?
Is John's toy car faster than Jim's?
Why is the bricklayer putting a dampcourse between the bricks?
Are all the tree leaves the same size?
Why is it cooler under a tree than in the open?
Why do roadmen wear orange jackets?
Do children hear better than adults?

The important thing is to pick out such questions in day-to-day living, to engineer situations where similar questions can occur or, sometimes even to pose such questions deliberately. Then teacher and children can sit down together and devise ways of finding answers to the questions. This is the heart of scientific method and one of the most difficult yet most rewarding aspects that children and adults have to indulge in. This problem-solving technique needs looking at in some detail.

Devising fair tests

Taking all the factors that can influence a situation and removing them so that each factor in turn can be examined on its own is what a scientist calls removing the variables from an experiment. For example, if you examine the swing of a pendulum consisting of a length of string with a bob of plasticine at one end, there are four variables that might affect the time of swing. These are the length of the string, the size of the bob, whether a push is given as the pendulum is started, and the size of the swing (the amplitude of oscillation). You would need to keep any three of these constant at any one time and just investigate the fourth variable by varying it on each occasion. As you do so you hold all the possible combinations of these variables in mind as you sort out how each influences the situation. This is quite a feat even for an adult mind and would be quite difficult for children in a Primary school. Yet this is the essence of a scientific approach to things and many children will approach, and some even understand, the sorting of variables before they leave Primary school.

To take another example of some of the other factors involved in devising a fair test, the TV advertisements claim that it is easy to tell a certain kind of margarine from butter. Is this really so? How can a fair test be devised? The children's initial reaction might be to get the margarine, get some butter and just get the class to taste them. It would probably be wise to let them do so but it would need an informed adult to make suggestions as the test proceeded. These suggestions usually entail sowing doubts by seemingly thinking aloud. For example, 'I wonder if it's wise to try just one butter and one margarine? Perhaps we should try two or three of each? Does it matter what we taste them on? Does it matter in what order we taste the butters and the margarines? Does it matter if some are salty and some are not? If this matters, what can we do about it?' In other words the children go on and on refining the test, removing the variables, until they make it as fair as possible.

We can often come to a definite conclusion based on the results that the tests yield. Yet interestingly, from a teaching point of view, what we are really interested in is inculcating a scientific way of thinking in our children's minds that they could apply to any situation. That is to say, given any problem could they think out a way to find an answer by practical testing that was as rigorous and fair as anyone could possibly make it. There are other 'spin-offs' too. The more the children go on testing things the more they realize that one test on its own is often not enough, and they begin to see that many scientific tests, especially when they apply to testing people, require large samples.

Recording and finding patterns
The results of testing things vary. For example, if a child compares the strength of one thread with another the result would be obvious. However, if a child wanted to compare the strengths of a range of threads then a table of results would need to be drawn up. Written records of this kind often yield further information. For example, all rayon threads tested might be stronger than cotton threads. Children tend not to be too keen on keeping records. They are much more interested in results. Yet it is very important to hit some happy balance because only with properly kept results can we begin to look for pattern and relationship. When such relationships occur it is often possible to research the work in greater depth as new questions and problems begin to pose themselves.

Recording results can be tricky. It is often easy to assume, having set the children on a viable and sound problem-solving path, that they can tabulate their results with ease. Sometimes they can, but it is surprising how often this art calls for close teacher involvement, an involvement that can prove quite taxing to the adult mind too.

Properly kept records are important in taking children from straight reporting of observations to the eventual ability to put 'two and two together' and attempt to find patterns in their observations.

Communication
In any busy classroom children will work together, sometimes as a class and sometimes in small groups. It is important that interaction and communication occur. When children are talking and writing together this happens. It can also happen in many other ways. Tape-recordings, charts, graphs, pictures, pieces of writing, stitched books or models, all displayed and used in the classroom help interpersonal communication. This is especially true when groups or individuals are given the opportunity to tell the class about a particular piece of work or bring a problem forward for communal discussion and approbation. This can also help individuals to express themselves clearly and

interact with others who possess different experiences or hold different points of view.

Knowledge

It is clear that the emphasis in science teaching placed here is on the scientific processes of observation, looking for pattern, questioning, testing and communicating. All these result in an acquisition of scientific knowledge. Such knowledge is extremely valuable, but the importance lies in the fact that it has been gained at first hand through active, practical exploration of the child's own world. Knowledge gained in this way is meaningful to children, and they retain it, providing a sure basis for building further knowledge. This is not to say that secondary sources of information such as books and charts, maps and graphs will not be important. These are just as vital to the development and understanding of a scientific approach to things. Children need identification books, and books which provide information such as the times of the phases of the moon, star maps, and biographies of famous scientists. In fact a library of knowledge is just as important a tool as the hand lenses, measuring devices and resource collections of specimens that every school should possess. Process and content must move hand-in-hand.

The nature of science with young children, together with something of its value, is now becoming clear. Let us look a little more closely at what it has to offer good Primary school practice and see what children gain.

What does science offer?

Someone once said that science is the discipline of applied curiosity. By watching children playing or pursuing some interest it becomes clear how curiosity leads them forward into new experiences where its satisfaction results in learning. Providing new stimuli or presenting familiar objects in an unfamiliar way and encouraging questioning help to develop such curiosity in children. It is a crucial attitude for any scientist of five or fifty to possess. Classroom activities that embody the processes of science already described help to develop this curiosity plus a host of other important attitudes. Science usually promotes interaction among children where *willingness to co-operate* with each other emerges in order to achieve a common goal. This often results in the development of higher mental abilities. It is impressive to note too the way children 'stick at' and *persevere* with a task in which they have become interested.

Problem solving, with its planning, sorting of variables, ironing out of simple design or technical problems, practical skills, analysis of results and conclusions to ponder, often leads to an ability to think independently, critically and objectively. Systematic reasoning, the ability to assess evidence, the making of one's own judgements coupled with an open-mindedness and a self-critical attitude are other attributes that can develop.

Not to put too fine a point on it, these are the extremely important attitudes that any Primary school teacher would wish to foster and science is one of the most crucial vehicles for their establishment.

So with due emphasis on the processes of science and on the attitudes that can be developed, what remains? The answer is *concept formation*. That is the ability to sort and separate things, an appreciation of what is meant by weight, length, area, time, volume, capacity; the understanding of a life-cycle and the relationship between cause and effect. Concepts of energy and of change must be developed in children. All these are major concepts and we could go on adding to the list. They are the concepts of the body of knowledge that we call science, and it is these concepts that we want to foster in children at the Primary stage of schooling.

So what are the major benefits of presenting scientific experience to children? Succinctly, they are to develop a certain way of thinking, one that uses the processes of science; to develop certain basic and fundamental attitudes; and to develop certain concepts that are mainly peculiar to scientific knowledge.

There are other benefits too. When children build a model suspension bridge or make cotton-reel tanks they are practising and developing manipu-lative skills. Often this kind of activity is coupled with thinking out and solving problems of design. The claim that science gives strong motivation for the growth and purposeful use of literary and mathematical skills speaks for itself. Looking at the transactional writing that children use to describe their scien-tific activities or viewing the different pictorial and graphical records prevalent in schools where science is pursued shows how true this is.

It now remains to look at how one particular project, the Schools Council's Learning Through Science Project, fosters the attitudes, skills and concepts of science in children and to examine the materials it provides to help children and teachers.

The Learning Through Science Project

One of the first things that interested the Schools Council's Learning Through Science project team when they began their work in 1978 was the enormous benefits that could be gained by schools forming their own science policy.

A school policy

It is true to say that one often finds individual teachers in individual schools pursuing work of a scientific nature. It is much less common to find a whole Primary school staff following a coherent and well laid out science plan. One of the main obstacles to this was identified by Her Majesty's Inspectors in a survey of 1978 where they say, 'The general impression given by head's statements was that only a small minority recognised the important contribution which science could make to children's intellectual development' (DES 1978a, p.58). Those in the minority understand how essential science is to a young child's development. They see their children improving in observational skills, asking questions, solving problems, discussing, arguing and putting to the test, perceiving patterns and relationships and communicating excitedly and vitally with others. They see their children developing in curiosity, prepared to listen and argue and yet maintain an open-mindedness, prepared to co-operate, show responsibility and persevere when things are difficult. The task of such headteachers is to convince their staffs of the value of science in the Primary curriculum and to show them its rightful context. Any headteacher, when planning the curriculum, needs to set a balance between the different subjects or areas of activity, whilst at the same time looking for a continuity between children at different stages of development within the school. He or she must also look at the professional strengths of the staff so that they can be utilized to the full. In so doing he must ensure that the school has adequate physical resources which are utilized effectively.

The Learning Through Science project team feel that the most important step forward to implement science nationally is for each headteacher to ensure that his or her school has a *science policy* and to make sure that it is implemented. In doing this it is very important for the school staff to write the policy collectively; this makes every teacher discuss the issues involved and helps crystallize their ideas. The result is a jointly drawn-up reference document, which each participant is eager to fulfil successfully.

In the book *Learning Through Science, Formulating a School Policy* there is a detailed but concise description of how a school staff can form such a policy. In essence it is 'an intention on the part of a school staff to agree areas of knowledge and experience, enumerate appropriate attitudes, skills and concepts, decide upon methods of evaluation and place these in an organizational framework which will give sufficient guidance to ensure effective and consistent teaching of science throughout the school (Richards, Collis and Kincaid 1980, p.29). The policy would need to be constantly revised and updated so that it retained its vitality and remained suited to the changing child population, its changing needs and its ever-changing environment.

Enough has already been said in this chapter to make clear what the aims of such a science policy might be, but what of the content? Regional groups of teachers reporting to the Learning Through Science Project felt that there were major underlying themes that should be looked at during a child's Primary school years, although these could not be organized into a tight four- or seven-year syllabus. For example, teachers seem concerned that children should know about *living things* and about the *cycle of plant and animal life*. They suggested that children should keep and look after living things and make comparisons, measurements and carry out simple testing procedures where these were appropriate and proper. Everyone seemed convinced that children should know about *themselves* and about ways in which parts of their bodies work — this would give many opportunities for discussion and questioning. The *immediate environment* together with its *weather* and *seasonal changes* was of intrinsic interest to children and was an important place in which to look for patterns and relationships. *Moving things*, in which the first fundamental experiences of *energy* and energy changes occur, were also thought worthy of study, as was an understanding of the nature and properties of *materials* beginning as it does in the Infant school with active exploration of sand and water, paint and clay.

How these were to be organized was seen as more problematic. A number of schools timetabled science separately but the majority seemed to favour integrating the science work with other disciplines. Frequently the science work was included in topics or thematic studies. Here the best work resulted where there was a balance between disciplines, so that the science did not get submerged by, or conversely overwhelm, other subjects. Although it is true to say that in any classroom at any one time there might be an upsurge in a particular area of knowledge, there is point in adjusting this from time to time so that children end up pursuing a balanced curriculum.

Evaluation of children's progress is essential. Any policy should not only lay down clear distinctions for recording the things that children have done, but should also attempt to show how each child is improving in basic skills, beginning to grasp concepts and developing attitudes. This is not the place to go into this in detail but Wynne Harlen, in the book *Match and Mismatch*, has written about it in some detail. She has listed the attributes which children might develop, each defined on a three-point scale and each adding up with the others to make a check-list for teachers to chart children's progress in science (Harlen, Darwin and Murphy 1977).

Resources
Any school policy would fall flat on its face at the outset without adequate resources. Elspeth Huxley writing in *Punch* presents a vivid picture of an Infant classroom.

> Providing things for small children to discover is the prime function of the nursery and infant school. A rich environment this is called. Rich it is indeed: a fantastic conglomeration of paints and brushes, plasticine and clay, old stockings, jars and tins; cartons that have once held cereals, detergents, cigarettes, sugar, almost anything under the sun; hammers and nails, scissors and paste, berries and nuts, teasels and twigs, shells and old birds' nests, spiders in jars, live guinea pigs, bottle tops, old sparking plugs, dolls, clothes pegs, wooden spoons — it would be totally impossible to list a tenth of all objects to be seen. The teacher must have eyes not merely in the back of her head, but all over, like spangles on a pearly queen. She must always be on hand, but never obtrusive; a sort of universal presence, like God, only more interfering; she does at least stop children battering each other on the head if necessary — if she does her job well it scarcely ever is. Small children doing something active seldom quarrel; it is boredom that makes bullies; every nursery teacher knows this and most mothers, but as yet few politicians.

What a lively classroom! Much of the success of work in an environment such as this lies in the variety of things with which children can interact. Science is essentially an interaction with things. They are not chosen at random for all have purpose. Yoghurt cartons, squeezy bottles, jam-jars, cereal cartons are all rich resource material for making anything from improvised plant pots and simple junk-models to water timers and boats. Careful planning is needed for buying, collecting, making, and storing and maintaining equipment and materials.

The book *Science Resources for Primary and Middle Schools* describes not only the material things that can be stored and used in the school but also looks at the use of the school buildings, its grounds, the local area and school visits as means of initiating and developing scientific activities with children (Richards, Collis, Kincaid and Bailey 1982). Within the school a *resource centre* with effective methods of organization and retrieval must be worked out. For example, resources could be grouped according to children's needs. There could be resources for arousing and maintaining children's curiosity which would include things that they can observe closely by watching, smelling, touching, listening and sometimes even tasting. Such things make the school a more interesting place to be. Resources will be needed for collecting specimens and data, and provision made to include those collections that children make themselves. Animal housing will cater for an interest that intrigues and interests many children. Resources that help develop enquiry skills are essential. For example, to find out if Jane's snail moves faster than David's snail children will need a timer and a ruler, while to find out which snail is the heavier they may need to improvise a balance. Materials may also be needed for recording and communication. Adequate reference sources must be provided as they give much valuable second-hand experience as well as generating further questions which may be answered by practical investigation.

Pupil material

As well as the national projects there are many commercial sources from which teachers can gather ideas about the kinds of scientific experience to present to children. Traditionally the materials from the national projects have been in the form of teachers' guides, the most notable of these being the Nuffield Junior Science Project, the Science 5/13 Project and the Teaching Primary Science Project. There was good reason for this. If these projects believed in an interest-based, process approach to child-centred science education they would need to express their philosophy in such a way as to leave teachers free to choose what they did with their children, and the way that they carried out the work. Commercial approaches ventured into the production of pupil material but invariably and inevitably this tended to be prescriptive. Yet pupil material can often be used more directly and hence can take children more quickly into scientific experience than ideas expressed in teacher guides. These were the thoughts that went through the minds of the Learning Through Science team as they began to write and try out pupil material in schools.

Was it possible to write pupil assignments that helped develop certain attitudes, concepts and abilities? Would children really be encouraged to show initiative, challenge ideas and interpretations with the purpose of reaching deeper understanding in this way? Could work cards be devised that encouraged children to develop an enquiring mind and a scientific approach to problems? It was immediately found that any one-sided card tended to be prescriptive. Taking a four-sided card allowed more room for manoeuvre. Each card could then be used to put problems in the paths of children in such a way as to develop a 'mini-topic'. Each page of a card tries to keep to one basic idea, but the aim of each four-sided card is to try and present a unit of work that allows children flexibility in the way that they develop the work in hand. Usually it allows children scope to bring forward their own ideas. An additional intention was to present each card in such a way that the work could be attempted at many levels and still leave scope for children at different stages of development to take things as far as they could. The cards are not presented in any set order nor has there been any intention that a child or a group of children should necessarily complete everything set out on an individual card. Investigations can be handed on to other individuals or groups and this entails informing the new experimenters of what has gone before. Work on a particular card can therefore be done by an individual, a group or by the whole class.

Of course the cards would need to be written to some form of content framework. The areas of experience listed by teachers as those commonly found in Primary schools were chosen (Richards and Kincaid 1981, 1982; Collis and Kincaid 1982; Kincaid and Richards 1983). The resultant themes became:

— Ourselves
— Colour
— Materials
— Sky and Space
— All Around ⎫
— Out of Doors ⎭   A study of animals, plants, soil and weather
— On the Move   Looks at animals moving, and at making models that move
— Moving Around   Looks at cars and lorries, wheels, machines and magnets
— The Earth
— Electricity
— Which and What   An identification pack
— Investigations   Looks at time, change and growth

Each theme has been presented as a series of twenty-four cards accompanied by a teachers' guide. The latter explains the aims of particular cards, discusses where children may find difficulty, tells how the tasks in hand may be taken further and gives additional background information.

The material has been written for those children who have reached Stage 2 of the developmental sequence set out in the Science 5/13 Project and are moving towards Stage 3. That is to say those who learn best through working with concrete things through to those who are, albeit tentatively, beginning to think in the abstract. The resultant body of material is not only comprehensive but is also sufficiently detailed to allow teachers to pursue studies in depth with their children if relevant.

Slow learners

The Warnock Committee proposed that all children with special educational needs, apart from the gifted, should be described as 'children with learning difficulties' (DES 1978b). Their difficulties include serious physical, mental and behavioural problems which need remedial help or special attention from a class teacher. The majority of children with learning difficulties are in ordinary classes and every teacher in Primary and Middle schools is likely to teach such children. Special help was needed for teachers of these children. It could not, because of the obvious literary problems faced by the majority of children with learning difficulties, be in the form of pupil material. Therefore the Learning Through Science project team framed a series of teachers' guides which were complementary to the pupil material already mentioned. The guides attempt to bring out the processes of science and are based on topics which arise from children's interests or everyday surroundings and integrate well with the rest of the curriculum. Short, practical investigations are suggested which often repeat the same experience in a number of ways to reinforce children's understanding. Simple and quick recording methods are suggested and some discussion points are put forward to help the teacher bring out pattern and relationship. The guides in no way constitute a course or syllabus and are merely set out as examples of a method of approach to science with children who have learning difficulties.

Slide/tape sequences

Much can be gained by presenting to teachers gathered together in a staff group, in a Teachers' Centre or at an in-service training meeting, material which will initiate and inform discussion. One last aspect of the project to mention is the production of slide/tape sequences intended for this purpose. Some six of these have been developed with titles such as 'Starting points for infants' and 'Science from the building site'. Each is accompanied by notes and questions for teacher discussion.

Summary and conclusions

In our excursion through the world of Primary school science we have touched on many things — on the nature of science, on its place in the curriculum, on interest-based learning, on the need for a school policy, on the gathering of resources, on the work of various projects — on many things. Ultimately an understanding of all these things helps us to help children develop enquiring minds and a scientific approach to problems. This central concern of Primary science was well summed up by Michael Faraday when he said, 'The scientist should be a man willing to listen to every suggestion, but determined to judge for himself. He should not be biased by appearances; have no favourite hypothesis; be of no school; in doctrine have no master. He should be no respecter of persons but of things. Truth should be his primary object. If to these qualities be added industry, he might indeed hope to walk within the veil of the temple of nature.'

CHAPTER 6

DEVELOPMENT THROUGH THE CREATIVE ARTS

HARRIET PROUDFOOT

The forms of education now needed to meet the profound changes in British society must take greater account than in the past of the capabilities, values and the processes of teaching and learning that the arts represent in schools . . . considerable significance should be attached to those activities which are concerned with the life of feeling and the development of creative powers. We maintain that a well-informed pursuit of all kinds of creativity will enable us not only to cope more positively with the economic necessities of the world, but also to increase the potential for discovery and progress on the many fronts of human interest and activity that they offer us.

We also emphasise that the arts are as much a part of the life and atmosphere of our society as, for example, science, technology, morals and religion. Due account should be taken, in the discussions now taking place at all levels on the school curriculum, of the important contributions of the arts in the following six areas of educational responsibility.

a. Developing the full variety of human intelligence.
b. Developing the capacity for creative thought and action.
c. The education of feelings and sensibility.
d. Developing physical and perceptual skills.
e. The exploration of values.
f. Understanding the changing social culture.

(*The Arts in Schools*, Calouste Gulbenkian Foundation 1982, p.141)

This chapter contains four case studies of children whose work seemed to show by the end of the year a greater command of their abilities than it did at the beginning. The case study seemed the only form that would actually demonstrate the action of the creative arts in a child's development, and also the interaction of the different arts in that development and in the wide curriculum that I think children should be offered.

We hope there is development in all our children over a year. I chose these children because in each case their development was more visible, because each child had one of the common difficulties that we meet, which need some individual attention (mainly from the child) before he or she can be working at their full power. As I hope to show, the creative work helped to solve the difficulties. It also undoubtedly fires new energy to the children's academic work, but my main intention is to give each child the best opportunity I can to develop all his or her gifts as fully as possible in the time we are working together.

In this chapter I shall attempt to show that the natural development of children as they get older, their increasing ability to use more of the potential of their minds, bodies and feelings with more direction and control and purpose, can be encouraged and strengthened by their experiences at school. This seems to be specially true if their work includes the opportunity to engage in the creative process.

Creative work as the starting-point for all learning

Creative work uses the whole person — mind, body, feelings and imagination. At its best it is a very alive and absorbing activity. Perhaps this welding together of the whole person is what makes it such a potent force in helping children — and adults too — to develop all their abilities as far as they can.

Any of the arts can achieve this, as long as the teacher enjoys it and feels at ease with it. It can work with music or drama, puppets, dance, drawing, painting, imaginative writing or making things. They are all forms of communication of ideas, feelings, visions or responses.

My second point is that as well as the children's whole development being furthered by including these subjects, far from being distracted, their school work will actually improve. They will find it easier to work, and when these subjects are learnt in a wide context of other work, the children will enjoy and work hard at the acquisition of the essential 'basic skills'. Further than that they will, in the creative process, be involved in work that necessitates decision-making at all stages, so that their judgement is being used and confirmed all the time. A child will have confidence when he knows he has the resources to make a work of art that will satisfy him.

As I am teaching children of nine to eleven, I am very aware that their next step is on to Secondary school. I therefore want the children to be competent and to feel confident in 'the basic skills', and to be interested in learning. I try to teach 'the basic skills' in such a way that they hold meaning for the learner , as Geva Blenkin suggested in Chapter 2 (page 31). I certainly believe that 'the effective application of skills, including their use in practical activities is important. The teaching of skills in isolation, whether in language or in maths, does not produce the best results' (DES 1978a, p.112), so that 'the basic skills are more successfully learnt when applied to other subjects' (op. cit., p.114).

The great value of creative work is that it offers the children the chance to find an immediate means of communicating their response to their own experience. I am always looking for quality in their response, for freshness, for something of their own. I find this (something all children are capable of in the creative arts) is most likely to come through if we are working from their own experience in the first place, and as much as we possibly can all the time.

I plan the work I am doing around the children's individual needs and within a project (or perhaps two). I like to work within a large project — one or two simultaneous ones for choice. In my first year at my present school in central London, we worked on 'Covent Garden and the Seventeenth Century', coupled with 'Creatures we have found'. The second-year themes were 'Soho and the Eighteenth Century' with 'Ourselves', which again included a lot of science work. This year our project is 'Change'.

A project like these can include many reasons for learning the skills the children need to acquire. It can include the information they should have mastered and the methods of study that I want them to have at their command by the time they leave. It can also be flexible enough to change direction and to incorporate new ideas, or the invitations and contributions that seem to crop up if you leave room for them. It can be flexible enough to follow the children's interest and energy as the subject develops. Such a project can be almost organic. If we as teachers can be adaptable, trying all the time to notice how we can match what is happening and what we are studying to the needs and gifts of individual children, we will get better work at the time and find that we also have interested children who almost carry themselves on to the next stage of their work.

Teacher: 'Can you help me? I've been asked to write something about the work we do. Can you remember things we've done that have been important, that have made you feel you could go forward?'
'Learning to swim.'
'That drama when Sarah wouldn't let Shaikh through her house to get in

his back window and while they were arguing, the burglars came in and had a cup of tea.'
'Prince Rama and the puppets.'
'When I learnt to play the recorder.'
'Roller-skating back stroke. I was scared at first.'
'Daniele swinging on the bars, being a gibbon when we got back from looking at the animals moving at the zoo.' 'Fatema was a tortoise.' 'Laura was a flamingo.'
'My embroidery on my cushion.'
'When I got the colour right for my pomegranate painting.'
'I took three weeks to finish my drawing of the flats at the back of the school.'
'Making those solid shapes in maths.'
'My owl picture.' 'And mine.' 'And mine, and my iris.'
'The first time I opened my eyes under water.'
'My cloth collage.' 'Yes.' 'Yes, and mine.'
'Being goalie.'
'My paper flower.' 'Doing clay.'
'My linocut of the tortoise.'
'My story, The Magic Mirror.' 'Mine called The Greedy Queen.'
'Putting my head under water.'
'My big model of a spider.'
'When I made my cardstrip skeleton twice lifesize.'
'My hornets' nest writing.'
'When we did that drama about the blood. I was the doctor.'
'Me and Ruhul were the blood soldiers.' 'I was a germ.' (Said with great relish)
'When we went to the Royal Banqueting House, and when we got back to school, we had a banquet in the hall, and Laura played Greensleeves on the piano, and we all danced round in twos and Taj cut Shaikh's head off.'
'The first time I hit a ball in rounders.'

The experiences the children are remembering have in common first, that they are their own experiences, and second, that they are memorable. They certainly remembered more than I did. Some were enjoyable; all were hard work; some include an achievement that makes overcoming a fear worth while. What they remember are the occasions when they broke through what they thought of as their limits; when they found they could do something they hadn't thought they could do.

Though sport and other areas of the curriculum provided some examples the children remembered, by far the greatest number came from different sorts of creative work. For the creative arts engage, educate and at the same time free the whole person to have fuller and more disciplined use of all his powers.

Art work

It isn't possible here to illustrate the full range of the art work the children do, but perhaps I can illustrate a little of their involvement in their work.

'I said to Miss, "Can I draw the milk lorry?" and Miss said, "Yes if you like it," I said, "I like it Miss," and I went to draw and I starts to draw, and the milk lorry went to the other side and I went to the other side and I draw the top of it. Then the milk lorry went away and I didn't finish my picture.'

Taj.

A happier occasion — the same boy:

'I painted a picture of a moss and I like the moss because it looks really lovely and I painted it nicely. Manikul said, you are mixing the wrong colour and I said sorry and I got the right colour. Ruhul [also from Bangladesh and an outstanding artist] said, "Your picture is really lovely", and Manikul said so too.'

'The Maidenhair fern'
I drew a plant with no flowers. First I drew it and got it wrong. Then the second time, I did it. It was perfect.   David

Children have a very strong response to beauty. They also have strong feelings. If we can give them interesting, attractive and challenging things to draw and if, within the discipline of having to do the piece of work, they can be given some choice, they will have the impetus of liking what they are looking at to help them finish what is often a demanding piece of work. What is important is not just producing a good picture, though when they do they can have great satisfaction and pride in that. I shall never forget the look on the faces of two very different children at very different times. One was a boy who could very seldom be persuaded to try and rarely succeeded when he did. He made a stone-age axe from a stick and some slate and strips of leather. He looked at what he'd made and he loved it. This, and a huge papier mâché model of Maiden Castle were the only things I ever remember his showing enthusiasm about. The other child was a girl who always works very hard, who is good at drama, and who writes very well. She had done a number of good pictures, but in general her art didn't have the edge and honesty of her acting. She made a cloth collage of some chickens she'd seen on the school journey. She took immense trouble and it was nearly finished, but we hadn't got the right net to represent the chicken wire of the coop. The next week our maths consultant brought us a piece from her garden. The girl stuck it carefully in place and gave a great sigh of pure content. She loves it and sees it as having been a milestone for her. Her art work has been more sensitive since.

Even more important is what they are learning while they are looking at what they are drawing. A fourteen-year-old (who hasn't done much art since Primary school) describes what is involved.

> 'When I'm doing a picture, I look incredibly hard. I get familiar with it. In my mind I take it apart as I draw different bits of it. To start with you may think it's pretty. When you start drawing you notice more in it. When you look closely, you see points of structure you haven't seen before. It's hard work. It takes a long time. When I've done a drawing I feel very drained. If it's a good drawing you should feel like that. You can put everything into it and carry on till you've finished. You've got to like something to want to draw it.'

The children do a great deal and a great variety of art work, black and white, colour, two- and three-dimensional. They draw things in school, and from the windows. They draw each other and they go out to investigate by drawing. As is clear from the passage above, the actual process is a learning experience involving looking, concentration, perseverance — both intellect and feelings. Each child's picture is so much their own that they have a very strong commitment to it.

The increased awareness and sensitivity do not only show in the children's response to their environment, in their classroom behaviour and in their work. They show also in their social development, their relations to the other children, and to the different cultures the other children may come from. As Andrew Fairbairn says:

> Possibly the greatest advantage of the arts is that they act as a catalyst in the general life of the school. So long as they are treated not as an academic exercise, but with vitality, they appear to release energy and add sparkle and inventiveness to the general life of the school.
> (*The Arts in Schools*, Calouste Gulbenkian Foundation 1982, Appendix part 4)

Writing

The children's art work is of a high quality, and they also learn a lot in the process of doing it. Practice in it works in other ways as well. Before he looked at a locust, this is what David wrote.

'Locusts are quite small insects that eat crops. They come from Africa and Australia. Sometimes swarms of them come to eat crops. Thousands and thousands of them (it is impossible to estimate the exact number). To get rid of locusts farmers use a spray called insecticide . . .'

After drawing one, he wrote:

'Its wings are transparent. At the front of their head they have little claws called mandibles. They pick up their food and put it in their mouths. At the end of each leg there are two claws. It has little hairs, situated under the body and on the legs. The legs are divided into three parts. There are little dots on the rear leg. Their mouths open up and down.'

This is very factual writing, but it is much more exact and interested.

Sometimes the contrast is even more marked. Dennis's diary every week went like this:

'I went house. I had my dinner I played with my friends. I went house. I had a cup of tea. I went to bed.'

When he made a cloth collage he wrote:

'I got some material and some cardboard and some silk, blue and red stripes and cardboard fingers and cardboard foot with stripes on his arm and fur hat and leather shoes, silver badge, white badge, cardboard whistle and truncheon and a chair and keys.'

When he went to see a demolition he said,

'He was smashing down the side of the building and it all fell down and he knocked the windows out and he smashed the wall. He hit the ceiling. You know when he was going to hit the wall he whacked down the ceiling and it all fell down. You know how that ball don't slide down? He's got this kind of button and it grips the chain. It locks onto the chain so it don't slide all the way down.
He bashed this side of the wall and it all come down, it crashed down, came crumbling. It went bang
          cr,
               cr,
                    cr,
                         cr,
down to the bottom.'

Here are some other examples where the children are able to find immediacy in their writing because of their first-hand experience of seeing what they are writing about, and because the sharpness of their perception and the accuracy of their training in looking and drawing lead to a desire to find a comparable accuracy in their response to words.

'The Badger's Skull'
I chose a skull of a badger. A Badger is a carnivore, it eats meat. When the badger is alive its head is bigger than the skull of a badger because when it's alive the head has fur all over. The Badger has canine teeth in the skull. They fell out and you can see where the canine teeth were. They were in a big hole on top of the Badger's lower jaw. It has a molar on both sides. In side the edge of the nose it has its nose cavity. The nose cavity looks like the brain but it isn't the brain. The Badger doesn't hibernate during winter. There is a big hole in the back of the Badger's skull. You can see what's inside. Inside it looks like two rooms and it looks like it has ribs in but it doesn't have any and I liked the badger's skull.
                                                                    Ruhul

'Jimmy's Winking Face' (to go with his portrait of his best friend)
When Jimmy winks you can see hundreds of lines, and his tongue sticks out. He has a flat sort of nose and looks funny. One eye closes and the other one is wide open and he gets a crease on one side of his face from his nose to mouth. He gets loads of lines on his nose and some coming from his eye. His lips are big and he has short curly hair. He looks a bit of a joker when he winks and a tooth sticks out.
                                                                    Nicky

The sense of touch can also help, as the next poem, the one on 'The Sheep's Heart' and the animal poems show.

'Snow Flakes Poem'
It is snowing to-day and it's going to be fun. They came twisting and turning in my balcony like cotton wool from the sky. When the wind blows it is like a group of hailstones. They fall on my arm slowly and lightly. I looked at it with my eyes and then I could see little little spikes that make the pattern.
We put some snow flakes under a microscope and it looked like the lights in Piccadilly in the night.
                                                                    Kwong Wah

'A snail'
It creeps along and leaves a mark exactly like a skid mark.

They have a twirly narrow winding slide on its protecting shell.
It wears no shoes but slimy silk.   Michael

'The Jersey'
The Jersey has two big eyes which are black. It has high butter fat
content in the milk. When the Jersey eats its mouth moves from side to
side. Its colours are golden yellow and golden brown. I chose the Jersey
because it looks nice. The Jersey looks like a square with four legs and a
head and a tail. When I went close to the Jersey the Jersey looked at me
with her big eyes. Her name is Cherry.   Wing Choi

'The Sheep's Heart'
The sheep's heart looks like some meat. When I smell it, it makes me feel
hungry and it makes me feel that I want to eat it. The shape is curly and
flexible. It feels smooth and bumpy. When I look at it, it makes me want
to feel it. The colours are brown, pink and creamy white. It looks lumpy.
The colours are all mixed together.   Daniele

'The Rabbit'
The rabbit is lovely soft and gentle
its ears are like velvet.
and the fur is cuddly like a baby cuddly toy
the eyes are like the teacher's owl's eye
but except its eyes are black, brown and a
bit of white on the edge.
The claws are sharp, a bit like a cat's claws
the body is long and fat and you could almost feel the bones.
I wish I had a cuddly rabbit.   Lung Yin

'The Ferret'
The ferret is long and thin.
When it curls up, it is like a spiral.
The ferret has short white fur.
It has short sharp legs.
Its eyes are like Snow White the rat
except it is smaller.
Its teeth are sharp and its mouth is small
the ears are thin like material.
When the teacher takes the ferret out of
the box it smells funny
And I quite like the ferret a bit.   Lung Yin

To get really fresh live writing, the experience they are writing from does not have to be visual,

'Sounds I like'
I like it when it's raining and I go out with an umbrella and when the rain pours on my umbrella, it makes a tip, tip, top, top noise. I like it when my mum makes little tiny cakes. When she rolls the rolling pin it makes a lovely sound it makes my mouth water. And I like it when I get a paper and write something if it's wrong. When you get the paper from the table and squash it, it makes a funny sound.   Fatema.

The experience does not even have to be real. Children are immensely alive in their imaginations. They will make up or write most lively stories if we can find the right starting button. 'Sometimes talk arising from literature has only the most tenuous connection with what has been read, but literature has this power to set us talking, just as real experiences have.' (Rosen 1973, p.78)

There are examples of stories and how they relate to other writing in the individual studies of chidren, particularly in imaginations that are at work in music and in dance. Here is just one:

'The Magic Ring'
One day as I was walking home from school I saw something small underneath a car it was shining. I went near it and I saw it was a lovely gold ring. I picked the ring up and I put the ring on my finger then suddenly I felt all funny. I couldn't see my own hands or my feet. Then I saw that I was invisible. I couldn't believe it. Then I took the ring off. I wasn't invisible. All the people in the street was very scared of me. They ran away. Then one day I went to school and my friends said 'What a lovely ring you got.' Then I wore the ring and Alma said 'Where has she gone?' and I said, 'Here I am!' Then Laura said, 'She has got a magic ring.' Then I took the ring off. When it was play time Alma, Laura, Maria, Laiyan, Joanne, Beth, Lungyin and Victoria they were all my friends had a plan to steal my ring. I put my ring on and I went near them and I heard what they had planned. Then when the school was finished all the girls were going home together. At night before I went to bed I put the ring on my finger and I went to bed. Then in the middle of the night I woke up. I heard something in my room, then I saw it was the girls. They were looking everywhere. Laura and Joanne were crawling on the floor like mice to see if they could find the ring. Alma and Beth were looking in the drawers. Alma found my watch inside the drawer

and they were fighting for the watch. Alma goes, 'I found it first.' Beth
goes, 'I found it.' They were arguing. Lai Yan, Maria and Victoria were
guarding the door to see if any one's coming. But they never looked at
the bed. Anyway I was wearing the ring so they couldn't see me. Then I
took the ring off and I said, 'Looking for the ring?' then everybody was
still and quiet and Laiyan said, 'am we am am sorry,' and they climbed
down the window and ran away. The next day all the girls said sorry. On
their birthday I gave them a golden ring but it wasn't magic like
mine.   Fatema

Nor does the starting experience have to be pleasant, as the next two pieces
show.

'When I went to the dentist'
Let me just tell you that I am terrified out of my wits of going to the
dentist and if I was not in school I would never dream of writing about
when I went to the dentist. This visit was some time in July. I had snakes
wriggling in my stomach. They got worse and began to turn into bats.
When I got into the building there was a sort of smell like powdery tooth-
paste. We told the receptionist which dentist we wanted but he was out.
There was a lady instead. I went with my mum down to the waiting
room. The bats had started to fly around my tummy. Soon someone
called our name. I went upstairs and into a room. The first thing I
noticed was the large black chair. I sat in it and a lady with curly hair and
glasses put a white thing on my chest. Dentist: open your mouth. Me:
Ahhhh. Dentist: wider. Me: Ahhgh. The dentist took a probe and
searched my teeth then she said I had to have a filling. My bats started
flying round faster and faster. While I had an injection I counted flowers
on the ceiling. Then came the filling. When they did it I thought about
my dad getting on a plane because my dad had flown to Ireland. Then
the Dentist said 'It's all over.' I washed my mouth out with pink water
which I loved. I got down off the chair. I passed all kinds of different
drills and needles. When I got out of the building I was relieved that my
bats had gone to sleep until the next 6 months.   Gabrielle

'When I was really scared'
One night in Italy I was lying in bed and I wanted to go to the toilet. In
Italy I sleep in the same bedroom as my parents on the top floor. The
toilet is on the ground floor. I slowly got up out of my bed and walked
slowly towards the door. OUCH! I said quietly. I had just banged my toe

against the wall. Oooh my poor toe. Limping I walked slowly to the door I held out my hand and felt for the key Click Click. I unlocked the door and pushed down the handle and went out and shut the door quietly. Just then I felt so scared I just leaned against the door took three deep breaths and when I tried to walk again I couldn't — my body had frozen. A few minutes later I had recovered. I started to move again but just when I started to move again I heard the stairs, the wooden stairs leading to the attic, creak. I stopped for a minute and then carried on walking. The stone stair cold against my feet, the loose banister moving when I touched it. At last I reached the first floor where my gran and my brother slept. This floor scared me in the daytime. The first floor always scared me because on the wall were all big photographs of all the old dead people. From then on I walked against the wall all the way. I felt the different type of stone. I went down through the living room into the kitchen and into the toilet.   Alma

As Alma and Gabrielle show, the experience does not even have to be in the present, but what I am always looking for is their *own* experience — things they do, things they have done, people they know, something they are looking at or something they remember.

I want now to turn to some examples which will support another of the points I made at the beginning of this chapter by demonstrating the carry-over effect that work in any of the creative arts can have for other aspects of the curriculum. For example, we spent most of a day doing experiments and talking about skin.

'Our Skin'
If I were a caterpillar I would once in a while I'd have to crack my skin all the way down my back and then I would have to step out of it. Then I would be bigger. Snakes and spiders also change their skin this way. Humans don't change their skin even though maybe when we have a bath little bits of skin may peel off. When you go to the beach and try to get a tan, it's the sun that cooks us and if you go just red that's because you haven't enough melanin. If you have a lot of melanin you can stay out in the sun and the sun wouldn't burn you because the melanin protects your skin. Our skin is very important because if we didn't have skin you could see muscles, fat, flesh, tendons and we would die because we would dry up and all the germs would get in. Sweat. In our skin there are sweat glands that keep our body our normal temperature. Our skin

is very sensitive and we can feel the heat, cold, pain and different textures so if we are near a fire our skin can warn us.   Alma.

Here the art work has been a necessary foundation for work in science which has been recorded as information writing. Each area of the curriculum can feed the others, once a creative impetus is on its way.

One may question whether this work is science or writing. What is clear is its relevance to other work. As Roy Richards says in Chapter 5 (page 97-8), 'Children's thinking skills are best developed by direct practical experience in an integrated curriculum . . . because of young children's natural ability and inclination to cross subject barriers, and because of the strength — and often the need — to utilize other areas of the curriculum to help develop science and to use science to enhance language work, art and craft, mathematics and so on.'

Constant practice of accuracy in art can only have a good result in the rest of the curriculum. It is also harnessing children's natural curiosity to their work. The accurate pursuit of the truth (which is what you are doing if you are trying to draw something) is an essential ingredient of maths, environmental studies, history and the sciences. The arts are of immense value in themselves, but they are also a training ground for the rest of the curriculum.

'Our visit to the zoo'
We saw a big snake and it was all curled up. We couldn't see its head. It was called reticulate python. The middle of the reticulate python was huge. The reticulate python doesn't sting. If it sees anybody it will curl around you and squash you. The reticulate python has lovely patterns on its skin.   Ruhul

During our visit, the children were asked to collect on paper notes for further work on skin; drawings therefore of fur or feathers or scales. It was a winter day, so we concentrated on reptiles and fish in the warm, with a quick visit to the owls. They were also asked to collect in their heads one or two ways an animal moved. We followed that up in the drama lesson and some of them had looked so carefully they were instantly recognizable. The drawings were converted into lino-cuts. We were studying skin, but I was also looking for a subject that would translate well into a print. This was because, in our parallel work on 'Soho and the Eighteenth Century', we were looking at local crafts, and printing was one of these. The class was invited to visit the shop of a print dealer, who had an antique etching press he let the children work. Work at a remove from the original, like a lino-cut done at school from work at the zoo, needs good observation to sustain it. I was very interested when one boy's drawing of 'Porter's blackish tortoise' at the zoo was very sketchy, but his lino-cut showed that he'd noticed very much more than he'd put in his note-drawing.

If you think about it, isn't it only for ten years at the most (11-21) that the natural way of learning — from everything we come across — is compart-mentalized into subjects? It is essential to the way I work for there to be a flow between all the different areas of the work we do. Drawing provokes writing, as you have seen. We will explore a story I've read them in a drama lesson. Music and dance will amplify a story or a puppet play. They can read for themselves stories I've read them in class — such as the Greek myths — and draw their own ideas of them. A project on 'Ourselves' will produce writing of all sorts, a great deal of science work, and estimates and tests, with the recorded results of 'Who is the fastest?' and 'Who is the strongest?' — which was what they wanted to find out. History will come alive in visits; in drawing things people lived with and clothes they wore; in noticing what's changed in a neighbourhood. But we need to know about the music and the paintings and the tastes of people in the past. Someone once said, 'If you want to know a person, you must learn his dance.' You could equally say, if you want to know about a time in history, the best way is to enter into that time through your imagination in the drama.

Drama

The most powerful freeing agent, the part of the mind that has the effect of pulling together all a child's abilities, is the imagination. It seems to free energy in mind and body. We need it to make up stories, for poems and other writing, for hypothesizing in science and maths, to compose music, to be able to move in harmony with an idea or feeling in dance, and, as I said, to be able to under-stand history. Its use is also necessary for growth towards social maturity, 'What if it was you ...' Perhaps the activity where it can have the freest exercise, and at the same time the best training in its use, is drama.

I think the following was Maria's best piece of writing:

'The Heart'
We started to do some heart work. Miss said that the heart pumps the blood to go all over our body. Then me and Lai Yan were the pumps that pumped Oscar, Daniele and Ruhul over to Wing Choi, Shu Hong and Lung Fai who were the window workers. Wing Choi, Shu Hong and Lung Fai got the oxygen and then they came back behind me and went

to Laura and Beth. They were the cleaners and then the blood messengers came back to me and Lai Yan, and me and Lai Yan were the heart pumping the blood. The blood messengers were Oscar, Daniele and Ruhul. Then they got the oxygen from Wing Choi, Shu Hong, Lung Fai. Then they went to Laura and Beth who cleaned the blood. Then we looked at a sheep's heart. I did not like the heart. It looked slimy. In some parts it looked like a spider's web. I feel a bit sick with the heart.

Is this essentially science, art, drama, information writing or expressive writing? And does it matter? What comes over in Maria's piece is the vigorous enjoyment of the movement in the drama lesson as the children took the parts of the lungs, the kidneys and the blood moving round. She has remembered that and her disquieted fascination with the organ we were studying. She has retained a simple version of the theory of the circulation of the blood. She's written more than two-thirds of a page — most rare — and taken a lot of trouble with a best copy too. We learnt about infection and inoculation in the same way. 'Jennifer was only a cold, but Valerie and I were tetanus germs and the body had had a taste of tetanus, so the blood soldiers were ready and they got us.'

Drama is enjoyable, drama is alive. It is one of the very best training grounds for the use of the imagination and in social awareness and sensitivity. There is performance drama (live or with puppets) and that has great value as we shall see later in the stories of Tom, Kwok Leung and Giovanni. There is also a kind of weekly practice drama that includes acting and mime games, explaining an idea (Persuasion is a good one), providing *The Wind in the Willows* with alternative endings, and acting out 'Prince Ivan', 'The Witch Baby' and 'The Little Sister of the Sun' from *Old Peter's Russian Tales*.

Playing with puppets and acting in another character can be most valuable opportunities to practise talking quite informally, especially for second-language learners or children who are shy or withdrawn. They can also have a potent effect on confidence, as we shall see later from the account of our Ramayana in the case study of Giovanni.

Drama can also include making your own small play. This involves organization, decision-making, selection, sharing and social responsibility (no real hitting in drama), as well as improvising characters, scenes and dialogue. It is perhaps the most valuable way of actively exploring 'What was it like when that happened?' 'What is it like if you are . . .?' 'What might happen if we . . .?' And, as always with the creative arts, there is the possibility of the child's discovering a special gift, or just having a day when his imagination is inspired and he is able to communicate something special. As we saw, drama is high on the list of the things that the children remembered.

Other arts

As you can see, I teach mainly through art, writing and drama. However, we do some three-dimensional work too, as you will see from the case study of Giovanni later in this chapter. We also do sewing. Once they have learnt stitches, I like the children to sew something they have seen and drawn themselves. They have the choice of what to draw in a given place, as for instance when we went to see eighteenth-century shop fronts, and the impetus from what they choose will carry them through the patient sewing. We have freer cloth work in the cloth collages.

No-one can do everything. We are very lucky that all the children have the chance to work with an excellent music specialist. This adds a whole dimension to their overall experience, and to events like our shadow puppet play, which was enormously enhanced by the music the children wrote for it with her help. The children have also had a valuable opportunity to work with clay with experienced teachers. We have had a very illuminating session with a dance teacher too. She was able to bring out unsuspected gifts in some of the children which were a real revelation to me. It seemed such a strong and important means of communication for some of the children that I am certain it is one they should be offered. In fact, we need to make available as wide a range of opportunities as possible, so that every child has a chance to find his or her strengths.

Four case studies

Now I would like to show you the arts at work in the development of four particular children.

Giovanni

This is an account of a boy with co-ordination difficulties who develops and progresses by means of puppets, models, art, drama, music and writing.

'Giovanni' is a boy who was born with difficulty in controlling his fine co-ordination. 'I remember the first time I was able to peel an orange, all my family clapped.' This has always been a great frustration to him especially as he is intelligent. His reading, up to a certain level, had not been impeded by it, and he is in other areas (such as football, maths. and general popularity) a front runner.

When I first met him, and during most of the year, his usual problem was intensified by the fact that there were difficulties at home which were so much on his mind that he really was not able to concentrate. It is apparently characteristic that intense anxiety will have a particularly disintegrating effect on a child whose co-ordination is already poor. It was necessary to sit beside him and support him, and almost literally hold his hand when the work demanded any degree of accuracy. The only solution was for him to work very large. He was then able to do the work. His written work was short and poor. His maths was numerically accurate, but hard to read because of poor figure formation, and recording geometrical work defeated him. His handwriting was, with difficulty, legible but extremely untidy and uncontrolled, and a mixture of upper and lower case.

He badly needed to do satisfactorily if not the best, then at least the same work as the others were doing. Drawing was hard. He found most satisfaction in painting and did some good pictures. A turning point was a wire and papier mâché model of a mosquito that he'd caught. He found it very hard, but he really wanted to do what the other boys were doing. (The girls were making a giant snail.) He tried hard, and did well, and was very pleased with it. It was important to him.

Soon after this, we read the story of Prince Rama, and explored a scene or two in our drama lesson. By common consent he took the leading part of Rama. When we came to making a shadow puppet play, he kept the part. To cut out his puppet, according to his own drawing, was a major challenge, but he managed it, and worked his puppet on the screen as well.

At about this time he began to master what was perhaps for him the most acute difficulty if he wanted to be equal with the others. All the children learn the recorder, and, of course, for him this was at least twice the struggle that it was for them. He had extra help and care from the music teacher, culminating in a special performance in assembly. That was I think the breakthrough for him, and he has continued to progress well. He needs no allowances made for him now. ('I play the recorder, and I like it a lot.')

All these pieces of work helped him very much. He won from them the realization that he could control his fingers. He now knew that he was not up against an insuperable difficulty. With courage, determination and work, he could win. By now his personal writing could be full of life. This piece is very characteristic of him in observation of detail, sensitivity, and sheer vigour.

'Sounds I like'
I like the sound when I wave a book and I like it when I run and the wind
goes past. I like it when someone breaks a bottle and I like it when someone in a car passes a motor bike. I like it when I'm in my uncle's lorry
and he stops with the brakes. I like it when I throw a dart at a board and I
like it when a wheel is punctured.

He began to be able to afford to be dissatisfied with things that had once
been a great achievement. Far from demanding support, he was taking on
challenges of his own.

We were working on 'Soho and the Eighteenth Century' and we were lent a
white lace fan. Absolute determination produced a really careful and excellent
drawing of the intricate pattern of the lace. Mrs Delaney is buried in the
school's patron church, St. James's Piccadilly. In her time she was renowned
for her cut-out paper portraits of botanical specimens. We decided to make
some paper flowers by cutting out. Giovanni insisted on doing one too. It was
four times the size of anyone else's, about 80 cm, but it was very carefully cut
out and neatly stuck together. I was not invited to help at all, I was just shown
the finished work. He is very proud of it, and his family asked for it to go on
their sitting room wall. He now says 'I like making things.'

Giovanni now has evidence that if he harnesses the courage, energy and
determination that make him one of the best footballers ('Football is so good,
I'd love to thank the person who invented it.') he can beat his difficulty. Now
he has good results before him, it is possible for him to make demands on himself about the content of his work. It is also possible for his teacher to do so,
instead of needing to be satisfied with his overcoming the immense physical
effort of getting work down on paper.

His handwriting, though idiosyncratic, is quite legible, and even, on its own
terms, neat. It is possible for me to return a piece and ask for a better copy. He
has become more interested in reading, enjoyed *Stig of the Dump*, and is at
present immersed in the *Labours of Hercules*. He is enthusiastic about writing
stories and often produces five pages. He enjoyed the school journey,

'The Gurnsey cow is big and furry. It hasn't got horns and it has big ears.
Her tail is bushy and her legs are very strong. You can see her bones
under her skin. Her neck is long and flexible. Her colours is brown,
orange, white and pink. She has four teats. She produces one of the
most milk in the world. And she is pregnant and has all mud over her.'

But, as he says, 'I *love* drama.' As he'd been Prince Rama, when we came to act our Nigerian creation myth, other boys had the leading parts. He chose himself for a very important small part by having a confident and musical voice (not to say loud). In fact, he was so good, a new part developed in the play expressly for him. This is his own praise poem at the crowning of the new king.

'The King'
The king is like a lion because the one who defeats him will be sorry because the king has got so much power. His crown is filled with a million diamonds and he is strong and brave. A king is so brave, that he could even go in a cave of devils. He could do war with a million men.

He was entirely happy and practised at home (as we heard from a neighbour). He looked splendid and performed excellently.
Soon after this he did some work in science.

'The Sheep's Heart'
The sheep's heart is quite big. There is a tube which is filled with blood and it feels like jelly and it is slimy. The colour of it is dark red and blueish black and pinky white and greyish blue and the strings feel like winegums and the fatness feels gooey.

'Ears'
Yesterday we looked at the school cat's ears. Their ears are very thin and they are dark pink inside and you can just about see the bones. Their ears are very interesting. When the cat didn't look at us we clicked our nails together and the cat turned towards us and thought it was a mouse.
    Even rabbits have long ears for when foxes come because when I was in Italy I saw a rabbit and I walked up to him. He heard me so he ran away. So that proves rabbits' ears are very good at hearing.

I don't think he will lose his impetus, because he has taken over. I did not know that what he needed was the amount of creative work that we have done together, but looking back and seeing the change in his work, this is what we have been doing and it has happened. And now, instead of a boy at a standstill, believing he could do nothing to help himself, and naturally enough uninterested in his school work because it offered, even with very great effort, no success or reward at all comparable to his football, we have a happy boy whose skills match his energy and ability sufficiently for him to be looking forward to

Secondary school, and who is improving his own performance every day.

Giovanni has had a physiotherapist's assessment. It was agreed that, for a boy of his character, with his particular gifts, the usual exercises might not meet his whole need. He has needed first to realize that he need not accept defeat. Then he needed to realize that he himself, with a consistent effort, could gain control of his fingers. Luckily he knows that hard practice does produce results. He's won his bronze medal at swimming and is training for the silver, and he jogs over London's bridges one night each week. He has needed to see that by his efforts he can produce work of the standard that he expects of himself.

To reach this point, he has had the support not only of his family, class and teachers, but also of all the strong heroes in his reading and of the knowledge of his success as a hero in our plays and in the shadow puppet show. He has had the practice of manual dexterity, but with and for a purpose. His jogging results in improved skill in sports. His written work, art, music and model-making give him practice while they give him results as well. I wonder if this method, and its simple logic, would work with other children with similar difficulties, or indeed generally. The experience Alan Goddard relates in Chapter 11 suggests that it can. Since for a child to be actively engaged in the learning process, the content of that process must have meaning for him. We can only ensure that it has by planning that content in terms of his choices, his enquiries, his interests:

Giovanni has reached the stage now where I no longer have to set the challenges. This week he came to school and his handwriting was enormously improved. It was consistent, it was on the line, it was well-formed and attractive. He and his elder brother, with whom he trains, have taken on the last area of difficulty, and they are going to win.

Joanna

This is an account of a girl who develops her concentration and her sensitivity through art, drama, music and writing.

When 'Joanna', with her long blonde hair, neat movements, her imposing personality and occasional tendency to drama, came to the school towards the end of a year, she seemed very keen to work. Gradually it became clear that she lost interest fairly quickly, so she would rush a piece of work and then ask for something else to do. She seldom became absorbed as the others did, or really did her best. In a way she joined in the class quite quickly. She was certainly thrown in at the deep end, since we were in the middle of getting our Indian puppet play together, and she didn't at all mind taking the part of the she-demon, sister of Ravana, king of all the demons. When we were making our tape she screamed splendidly.

In fact it took her a long time to settle down (after a number of family moves) and to find her place in the class. She enjoyed acting, but more as a performance than as a group activity. She did, as the whole class does, a lot of drawing, but was not completely satisfied with her work. Before she could really profit from the creative work the class was doing, she needed to be prepared to find hard work satisfying.

'My Map'
I started my map on the 4th Nov 1981. I have just finished it. The date today is 5 Dec 1981. I am very very happy that I have finished it. At first I thought that making a map would be boring but now I think it's great fun. When I started my map I first drew a rough plan of the class then I measured all of the walls and wrote them all down. Then I drew my measurements down on some squared paper. I wrote 1m down as 10cm then I got all the measurements of the furniture and I drew that down on my paper. On my first map I wasn't bothered to do it. Then on my second map I tried but my measurements were nearly all wrong. But now on my third map I thought 'I must finish it', and I did. I had my map at last. Then I checked my measurements and then I got a backing for my map and stuck my map on my backing paper. Then I trimmed my work and I had finished my map.

Building on this, she began to take more trouble with her work, and to put her energy into finishing it. Her talent for writing began to emerge:

'To-day I went outside to look at the snow. When I picked it up it first felt like a lovely soft feather but then it felt very very cold like a lollipop. When I looked up to the clouds all I could see was lots and lots of snow which looked like a pillow being shaken all over London.'

Soon she was settling in and enjoying the work, and, as she became more part of the class, her work became more sensitive. She did quite a lot of drawing and painting and it was better work, but she still did not seem fully behind it. It was after nearly a year, when we were doing cloth collages of animals the class had seen on the school journey, that she was really able to let go. Collage work is very slow, and a lot is involved in it. There is maths in the area work, in the proportion (the backing card was about 70 cm²), and in enlarging the drawing. There is delicate colour matching, careful drawing and then the chance to add texture.

She chose a Wyandotte cock (she was working from a photograph of the bird she had seen) and drew it well. She didn't take trouble with her first choice of materials but, when she was sent back, she ransacked the bags of cloth for a lumpy yellow brocade for his legs and worked out an equitable division of the bits of black velvet with the girls doing a picture of cats. These she cut into flowing feathers and stuck so they were loose like the real bird's moving tail. Another child had written about the same bird:

> 'The cockerel is a smart and elegant bird. It stands up straight and poses.
> Its feathers are neat and tidy. When another cockerel calls he answers
> with a very loud cry. Its tail feathers are a shiny blue with a bit of purple
> in them. Its body feathers are mainly brown and white. Its claws are
> sharp and dangerous. When the cockerel bends down to eat, all his neck
> feathers spruce up and look as if they're changing colour.'　　　Alma

Joanna really caught the elegance and pride of the bird in her picture. She also worked very hard at it and found that rewarding. Slowing down may have been a key, but she was very happy with her collage and considers it to have been an important step forward. She is aware she learnt a lot doing it.

Her increased sensitivity and application were coming through in her other work. She brought in something from home and asked to write about it.

'My Hornets' Nest'
> My hornets' nest is lighter than anything I have ever touched. The larva
> is soft and bouncy and gooey. The grub's mouth is very very small. You
> can see the grub's blood swerve and pulse around its delicate body. The
> cells are like hexagons. The outer shell is very delicate. The outer shell
> has different colours and textures.

The quality and sensitivity of observation and of language in this writing were suddenly far ahead of anything she had done before. She took a lot of trouble to make a very best copy of this work she was proud of. Since then, she has done a drawing she loved of an eighteenth-century soup tureen in the form of a swan, in the Victoria and Albert Museum. She seems launched now, as she was recently able to do a much larger than life-size drawing of a globe thistle with enormous care and pleasure.

Joanna is a powerful personality and has had difficulty finding acceptable uses for her full strength and for all her energy. She has needed to develop her sensitivity to be able to discover and practise her best gifts, notably her creative writing.

It must be clear by now that I believe there is a great deal more in art (or any creative work) than a pretty picture. If children can make pictures or models that they are pleased with, they will derive great satisfaction, enjoyment and confidence from the result. They can look back at that piece of work and say 'I made that and it's good. I like it. I can do good work. I had to work hard, but I enjoyed doing it. What can I do next that will make me feel as good again?'

So much the better, but, as was stressed in the Introduction, it is the processes of education that are most important. The process of making a picture (which is the creative work at which Joanna had most practice), like all creative work, uses your mind, your judgement and your feelings. It helps to develop a child precisely because, as has been emphasized throughout this section, the learner is actively engaged mentally and intellectually in the learning process.

You have to like what you are working on in order to want to work on it. Once you want to work on it, you have the impetus to overcome the difficulties that are involved in doing anything worthwhile. With a picture, you need to look very carefully and honestly at what is really there, how it really fits together. You have to consider the proportion of your picture in relation to itself and to the size of the paper. ('It's going over the edge. Can I have another piece of paper to stick on, Miss?') You have to appreciate the proportions of the thing you are drawing in relation to your own picture. You have, as you draw, all the time to consider the whole picture with all its parts in relation to each other, so you don't give more attention or more room to just one part of the object. You have to decide how big you will be working and keep seeing how the parts of the picture relate to each other. In order to undertake this process you do have to allow yourself to become sensitive to what is there. You have to be observant, decisive and patient when you mix colours. You also have to be sensitive to what will be the most appropriate material to represent the thing you are making a picture of.

These are the processes that Joanna has been engaged in. Drawing something beautiful can bring out a sensitive response in a child. Joanna needed to discover that she enjoyed hard work and finishing her work off well. But, even more, she needed to relax and to discover and develop her abilities. The process which has given her satisfaction has also been a training. She is now much more able to be sensitive in her work, and is becoming more aware of the feelings of the other children. She is therefore more able to manage her prodigious energy. Her increased control means she is more able to have reliable friendships, although she still finds it hard in drama to discover a balance between her desire to shine as a performer and the sensitive co-operation with other children that is the essence of drama work. She loves poetry and her other work — maths, music, science, history — is all reliably good in content and appearance. She is currently enjoying reading *The Phantom Tollbooth.*

'Well, Joanna, you do believe hard work is enjoyable now, don't you?'
'Sometimes, Miss.'

Kwok Leung

This is an account of a boy who grows in confidence and in his command of English through writing, art and drama.

'Kwok Leung' was quite big, but a very quiet boy who spoke Cantonese at home. He was shy and obedient and his work was not outstanding and was slow compared to the other boys. It was sometimes unfinished. He was unobtrusive, almost nervous. There was a sudden contrast in the playground and at games. Here he was dominant, loud, a leader, ruthless at football, highly skilled and brave. I've known him kick a football neatly in at a second-floor window. His playground reputation was one thing; back in the classroom he again shrank into insignificance and became a follower. He needed to do comprehension work with a friend, he found reading hard, and worried about his maths although it was good.

The clearest area of development is in Kwok Leung's writing. In order to illustrate the progress of his work, I need to quote several of his stories. This is an early one:

'My Lost Dog'
Once upon a time there was a dog called Philip. Now he had live with a family called Johnson. They were kind to Philip then one after the noon Philip hear a noise it sound like its come from outside so Philip went outside he could not see anyone but it went on and on then the noise move so Philip follow the noise it went on and on then the noise stop. Philip barked he was in the forest he was lost he walk for long time then he came to a city he never saw so many people in one city there was cats and dog he went in to the city went he touch he will fly and come back

then dog came up to him and said are you new to this city Yes said Philip. There was a man he was seting in a chair and the man said were do you come from USA said Philip, put him in prison all right sir said the dog so they him prison went was in prison he saw other dog and Philip said have I saw you befor no said the dog then the other dog said Yes I am your neighour next door Oh Yes Philip then there Fairy came and said do want to get out it please said Philip and other dog so shut eyes then will be in the forest again.

The story is quite long (this is a shortened version) and there is a touch of imagination in the 'moving noise', but it is incoherent structurally, and he is only just breaking-even in his struggle to write in a second language.

He drew and painted rather stiffly, if strongly, but came into his own in drama. He was a bear in our shadow-puppet play. Later, one short play, which he made up, had him as an orphan who finds treasure in the cellar. Next day in school, his head is entirely filled with dreams and when the teacher asks him what is 2 times 2, he answers with a beatific smile, 'Gold'. His imagination had found a personal and physical outlet, and we had a number of memorable drama lessons. He ended up with a leading part in the play we did from a Nigerian creation myth. He acted and spoke this confidently and extremely well.

During this year he was pleased with several pieces of art work, a very sensitive water-colour of a fish, a painting of a cow he saw on the school journey, and a watchful oil-pastel owl. When the children did self-portraits, his was very strong, and he did a second miniature one when most children were painting a friend's face. He began to find himself in his self-portraits, and with a lino-cut of an owl done at about the same time. Something of the power of his personality, his sensitivity, his physical enjoyment, and his feeling for language (in his second language) are beginning to emerge in his writing, in spite of some mistakes.

'The Snow Poem'   11th December 1981
Snow snow falling fast falling like a feather. The wind swept by and the feather snow won't come my way. The snow is light. It falls on my face, then it melts slowly down my face. When it fall a long time, I will love to jump into the snow.

In 'My Report' (which the children write at the end of the year) he put,

'I enjoy writing. My drawing has improved this year and I have written

more than last year. I am pleased that I have written more. I like writing
stories very much. I think I have got better in stories.'

'It Started off all right'
Once there was a boy called Victor he was a poor boy he live any way he
could and he was poor. One day he was walking through the forest to
look for somewhere to live, when he saw this house and he saw a light
coming from the window. So he knock on the door. There came an old
man. He asked Victor what did he want? So Victor asked him could he
stay for the night. The old man said "All right". So he went in. When he
went in, he saw lots of gold. He said to himself I could get the gold when
the old man is asleep. But in night he went downstairs and saw the old
man and the old man saw Victor. What did he want? Victor said "A glass
of water, please." So the old man gave him the glass of water. Then he
finished and went back to bed. He was very angry to himself. Victor
said to himself in the morning, before I leave, I will get the gold. In the
morning he woke up, went down to get the gold and leave. So he did.
After he left the house he saw a lion he was chasing him. When he ran he
came to a river. He knew that he could not swim across. Then he
dropped the gold and swam across the river. When he got to the other
side of the river he ran and ran but he never got the gold back but the old
man did.

Here we can see that he is clear what he wants to say, and he is managing to
make quite subtle points, such as the boy's excuse for being up and 'He was
very angry to himself', and to produce a consistent narrative. He is also
beginning to make a shape for his moral tale.

'The strange way Home'
Once upon a time there was a king called Michael he was a wise man and
he had a son called William. He was good at hunting. One day his son
William went fishing to catch a food and fish for the cook to fry it for
supper so he started to walk through the wood. While he was walking he
heard a bird sing. Then the bird stopped and it started to talk and it said
'Come! Come! There is lots of food. Look! Fishes!' and William said to
himself, 'Good, there are good fishes there'. When he got there he saw
only one beautiful fish. So he caught it. Then the beautiful fish started to
grow and grow. It started to eat William up but William was not scared.
So the fish ate him so then he went back to the river. When William was

inside he could see some people, they were his friends. The friends said
'help us, please.' Then William felt himself being pulled. He came out,
then he was led to a castle. The fish took William to the King of the
fishes. He was very angry. He ordered William had to be killed.
William's father didn't know. After a long time some people came. It
was William's friends and he hadn't seen them for a long time. 'You
must come. William is go to be killed by the King of the Fish.' but King
Michael did not go and save his son. He told the God. The God said you
must let the beautiful fish get you. So he did let the beautiful fish get him.
There inside, he saw William's friends they said 'Help! Help!' but then
he was brought to the King of the Fish. Then the King of the Fish said
'He will die too.' Then the king was put in prison. There he saw his son.
In the night the King and his son break out of prison. When they were
nearly out of the dungeon they saw this beautiful woman. The king said
'Come, beautiful woman.' So she did. While they were running, William
was behind. He saw the beautiful woman's tail. It was a monster. She
was eating his father up. It was lucky that William had a sword. He
killed the monster. Then the God gave William some gold for saving his
father.

This has quite a good shape, and a strong relationship. It has more imagination coming through clearly. The narrative has good pace. It has clear and
lively details — like the cook who was going to fry the fish, a beautiful fish that
grows and eats him, and the beautiful woman's monster tail. By now he is not
at all just struggling with the language, but trying to do something altogether
more ambitious.

In February we spent a day at the zoo, collecting information in detailed
drawings of scales, fur and feathers for some work on skin. Kwok Leung had,
as most children seem to, found information writing difficult. But by now his
story writing was flowing more freely. We spent a whole day talking about skin
and did some experiments. Then he wrote:

'Our Skin'
To-day we talk about our skin. We talk about how our skin is related to
our body. Some animals and insects take off their skin by itself. Take the
caterpillar. The caterpillar zips its skin and come out. Some part of body
are very sensitive some are not. Our hands are sensitive because our
hands need to feel and to touch. Our skin is elastic and very strong. At
the top layer of our skin is dead and when you put a pin through the

dead skin the blood don't come out. When we cut ourself a liquid called
lymph protects us from the germs coming in. Some people have a different colour skin that mean some people have melanin. Melanin is
kind, it protects you from a sun burn. When we sweat and run a lot and
get hot the sweat help us to keep a normal temperature.

His English is already much improved, and his meaning comes across
clearly. As part of the work on the skin, and in order to give them a strong
fresh experience to write about, a friend had brought in two of his animals.

'The Rabbit'   February '82
Rabbit Rabbit soft and gentle. The long legs run run. See its ear sharp to
hear. Watch its nose twitched to smell. See its body smooth like a
feather. See its tail small and furry. See its head warm and soft. See its
colour black and grey.

'The Ferret'
Ferret Ferret long and thin. See its legs short to run. See its claws fast to
attack. Feel its teeth sharp to bite. See its eye sharp to look. Feel its ears
short and furry. See its nose sharp to smell. See its colour just white.

Here Kwok Leung has had the certainty and courage to find his own form
for his writing — the only child in the class to do this. His sharp imagination is
apparent in each line as he sees the reason why each part of the animals is
shaped the way it is. He gives us the picture and the character of each animal
strongly by the precision of his choice of detail and words.

'The Great Emergency'   7th April 1982
Once there were two boys. They were great friends. They always like
playing but they didn't like school. One day the school had a play. The
two boys love this. They were very good at it. So the school play started
when the two boys were in a boat. They were sailing down the sea when
they saw a light gleaming so they sail down to where the light came
from. When they got there, they found three big trees of gold. The two
boys were greedy. One of the boys was very greedy and he wanted the
third tree. The other did not want him to have it, so they fight for it.
When they were fighting they saw some policemen they took the boys
and took the tree too and then it was the end of the play. Everyone was
very pleased with the school play. Then it was half term, so everyone
went home. In the holidays the two boys and their mother and father

were in the country. When they had been in the country for two days, one of the fathers bought a boat. But the boys must not sail without their father and mother's permission. On Thursday morning the two boys took the boat and sailed away. The two boys thought they might find a treasure. Then there it was, a gleaming light was coming. They did not believe it. While they were getting near the gleaming light they felt something being pulled. Then two long arms came and got one of the boys. The other one tried to kick the two arms. Then three arms came and caught the other boy. The other was going to drown and the other one was going to drown too. Then a fisherman came and he saw what was going on. So he called for help. Then the two boys' father and mother got the police and they tried to get the two boys free. It took them a long time till everything was happy again. The two boys did not play about again.

Another moral tale, but this story is longer and more detailed. It has the very sophisticated idea of the school play's being reflected in real life. The boys are energetic and the monster is powerfully imagined. The command of English is also greater.

The starting point for 'The Great Emergency' had been a Victorian children's story of that name by Mrs Ewing. It is an exciting domestic tale of the brave eldest boy leading his younger brothers and sisters to safety in a fire. I told them the outline of the story, and this was what Kwok Leung wanted to write for that title.

The next piece of writing is the character he invented after I read the children the Gollum chapter from *The Hobbit.*

'A Character'   21st May 1982

Once there was an evil person he was half human and half monster, he live in a dark cave. His eye is green and yellow and his eye could burn a thousand things. His breath is like the wind. Its claw is like a knife. It runs like an animal with the wind. It hunts very hard. The human monster is 3 metres tall. One day human monster was on the hunt of food. Creatures hide then it got its prey and it ate it. Then he was on the move again. Then human monster kill it second prey then the third. Then went to its cave and went to sleep. An old owl sat on its tree, and said to his friend the dog 'We must stop this creature before it's too late.' The dog said, 'How?' but the old owl said 'Nonsense.' The dog had an idea he will stand out and bark and then let it catch him, and then he will run to the river and the human monster will get drowned. It did not work. Then the old owl said, 'We will play tricks on him.' They would act like him, so that he will go mad and then all of them will start attacking him. So they did. It worked and everyone was happy in the end.

Kwok Leung's 'character' is powerfully imagined. His fearful qualities are brought before us in detail and they have a mythical quality. His solution is quite original. The strength of this writing is parallel to Kwok Leung's physical strength.

I've mentioned how good Kwok Leung was as Orishanla, eldest son of the God of Gods, in the Yoruba creation myth that we acted for our Open Day, with the African Arts in Education Project. As part of the work we were doing, each of the children wrote a praise poem in honour of the coronation of the first king of the Yoruba people. You can see how his imagination had responded to the Nigerian praise poems I had read to the children, with their mixture of honour and awe.

'The King'   25th June 1982
The king is like the lion. He is the wonder of the world. People greet him and pray to him. His clothes are like a shield. His palace is like a wonder of a dream. His crown is like a bowl of diamonds. He fights with strength and power.

During the year, Kwok Leung found his own way of responding through his imagination in powerful language full of evocative images, and with a strong sense of rhythm. It seems to me that it not only does not matter that his English is not perfect, it is all the more remarkable that these lively and atmospheric narratives and rich poems are written by an eleven-year-old in his second language.

It is clear from Kwok Leung's first story about the dog, Philip, that he has a strong imagination. He has not yet found a way of letting it out or any confidence in the use of it. His story line is not coherent, and there are only glimmerings of the power of his later work. His difficulties with English are very evident in the simple sentence structure. He hasn't yet discovered his feeling for language which in the later stories outweighs the fact that he is still improving his English.

And yet I was sure that English exercises alone would cramp and not help him. As the 1978 DES report puts it:

It should not . . . be assumed that increasing the practice in relation to one particular activity necessarily improves the children's performance. The indications are rather that giving reasonable attention to a range of different activities is more likely to be effective (DES 1978, p.91).

For his development it was essential to encourage a flow of thought and unity before insisting on total correctness. Edward Storey mentions a boy who was very reluctant to write.

The fear of spelling paralyzed his imagination until he could see that imagination has to come first. His imagination and his natural curiosity, when liberated, inspired him in the rest of his school lessons. Consequently the other subjects improved as well (*The Arts in Schools*, Calouste Gulbenkian Foundation 1982, Appendix part 5).

With a boy as uncertain as Kwok Leung and as anxious to do well, I think those attitudes would have been perpetuated and not overcome by concentrating too much on accuracy first. Children need to want to write; and therefore they need to be free to write about what interests them. If we can free their imaginations, they will have a large supply of material. They will enjoy writing stories well for other people to hear or read and enjoy. They will wish to keep improving their stories, in vitality of speech, choice of lively vocabulary, atmosphere and action and in planning and sharing their material. As part of this they will also want to make their work more correct. As Marian Whitehead says in Chapter 3 (page 78), 'standardized spelling comes after the establishment of a real pleasure in writing to communicate and to explore thoughts and feelings'.

All of Kwok Leung's work improved steadily and consistently, including his maths, once he realized he could count on his own gifts in drama and writing. As with the other children, it was necessary for his whole development to find an area of growth, something he liked doing and had the potential to do very well. When a child has found his full strength in any area of his work, all the rest of it will improve as well.

Tom

This is an account of a boy who gains command of his high intelligence and develops his sensitivity and social awareness through art, drama and writing.

'Tom' is a tall, strong, good-looking boy, energetic and active; a boy of very high intelligence, uncertain of his limits, eager to have the answer and anxious to be the best. He seemed almost inexperienced socially, with not much idea of how to make friends, and was continually dissatisfied with his work. He had two areas of reliable achievement, his physical strength and a fluency at drawing. He did very careful sophisticated black and white shaded drawings of a striking sort. His method of shading began to be sincerely flattered all round the class.

He felt he should be achieving more in his work: 'Before I came to this school I was not reading very hard books.' He was well-grounded in maths but somehow not enough to be able to make full use of his knowledge. He had to make a real effort to keep up with the fastest children. He was so often dissatisfied with his written work that it was inclined to be unfinished. I did not realize how uncertain he was until we were doing some art work other than drawing with a soft pencil. He had not met 2B and 4B pencils and had been revelling in them.

His first attempt at water colour (the elderberry twig, Figure 6.1) was very stiff and unnatural, and the first time he came with us when we all went out to draw with felt tips (eighteenth-century shop fronts) he became almost paralysed. He restricted himself to just one lamp, and produced, with quite vocal anxiety, another stiff picture, as you see (Figure 6.2). He was so very good at drawing I was surprised, and felt he had to overcome the very narrow limits he was imposing on his gift.

In the end the result seems to have been a draw between us:

'My Report'
I like pastels and chalk, charcoal etc., because you can make them smudge to do shading. I also like pencil and different paints. Before I came to this school I only used pencil for art. Mrs Proudfoot didn't like this so she made me change and now I use all kinds of art facilities.

Once he overcame his initial anxiety, of course, he made excellent use of each new medium. His next water colour (no pencil allowed) was of a red gurnet (we were working on breathing) seen head on and painted flowingly, full of movement and colour.

He enjoyed drama lessons, though he had a lot to learn about working with a group. He began to learn the recorder. He really began to tackle his reading and persevered with *The Indian in the Cupboard*, *The Ogre Downstairs* and *The Third Class Genie*. In fact, when he left he was in the middle of *Watership Down*. History does not relate whether he finished it.

The area that seemed to worry him most was writing. 'I like writing stories very much but when I cannot think of a story to write I cannot write a story at all.' I read a lot of stories to the class which (I hope) feed their imagination. We

Figure 6.1

Figure 6.2

work on some of them in the drama lessons and all the time there is art work from observation on the projects we are doing. A direct fresh response in art stimulates the same in words. This began to work with Tom, and there were occasional fresh, live phrases in his writing.

'Snow'
When the snow falls it looks like feathers falling from the sky, or swarms of flies falling to the ground. If you look at it, it looks like diamonds glittering. When you try to catch snow it just melts in your hand and gets very cold then all that's left is water. I put some snow under the microscope. I could see different patterns. When the wood is underneath the snow it makes a lovely pattern.

The excitement that comes through is about looking closely and seeing something unexpected.

It was somehow characteristic that this got lost the next time we were doing this kind of writing, in an ambitious attempt to scan, if not exactly to rhyme.

'The Rabbit and the Ferret'
Rabbits have very soft fur,
And very big eyes.
And very small fluffy tails.
They have very big ears,
And very long nails.
They have very long legs,
And very long sharp teeth
Their eyes are for seeing danger,
The legs are for running,
The teeth for eating,
And the fur is to keep them warm.

He was, as usual, dissatisfied with his work and I suggested that he should just try to look, as he did for his good pictures, and say what he saw and what he felt.

'The Ferret'
The ferret is long and thin. When I first saw the ferret I thought it was a rat that had been stretched. It had red eyes that glittered like rubies. I didn't really want to hold it because of its sharp teeth and Mr Steward had lots of cuts on his hand so I thought the ferret had done it. But Mr

Steward reassured me that he did the cuts on a bramble bush and the
ferret had never bitten anyone before. After Mr Steward said that, I
decided to pick it up. It felt long and rubbery and quite furry. When Mr
Steward took it off me the ferret folded itself in two. I wondered whether
it had a spine or not, the way it folded in half.

He has used looking and his feelings, and the result is fresh and interesting.

He found his full power in writing two weeks later, after hearing in
Assembly the story of Epimetheus and Pandora's box. He has only used
directly the element of the forbidden box full of something horrible, and has
made entirely his own story.

'Black Sunday'
The house was in a derelict part of town and all the windows were
smashed and the door was hanging on its top hinge.
'Come on, Chuc Wu. Let's go in that old dump', I said.
'No. I don't like it. There's something strange about that house. And
anyway it's not right going in other people's houses.'
'Well I don't care if you're coming or not. I'm going in', I said angrily.
    Chuc Wu waited outside the house. The house was musty and old.
'Huh, who'd want to live in a house like this,' I said.
    'Oh come on Tom, let's go,' Chuc Wu shouted from outside.
    'No. I'm going upstairs', I said.
    At the end of the corridor there was a strange wooden door. Feeling a
bit scared I opened the door. To my amazement the room was painted
black . . . 'Cor,' I said, 'Chuc Wu's got to see this.' I ran down stairs.
'Chuc Wu come and look at this. It's really weird.' 'No', said Chuc Wu ,
'I'd rather not.' 'If you don't I'll tell everyone at school that you're a
little coward.'
    'Oh, all right then,' we went back to the room . . . 'I wonder who'd
want to paint the room black,' Chuc Wu said. 'I don't know, maybe a
witch lived here. Hey — just a minute there's an old chest over there I
didn't see before' I said, 'I'm going to see what's in it.' 'Well I'm not
going to stay and find out,' said Chuc Wu. As he walked he brushed
against the wall . . . 'Hay — Tom, the wall's not painted black at all . . .
it's warm . . . and furry . . . ALIVE arrrrgh. The room's covered in flies.'
Chuc Wu ran as fast as he could. I was still in the room by the chest . . .
The room became lighter as the flies came buzzing off the walls and they
came down to the chest. They had been waiting for the chest to be

opened. At that moment outside . . . Chuc Wu grabbed a policeman and said 'Come quickly! My friend's still in there with those flies.' 'All right, all right, calm down', said the policeman. Meanwhile upstairs in the room of flies a giant fly had come out of the chest . . . 'No, no — get away from me! Get away!' The fly bit me on my hand. A few minutes later I walked out the house wearing dark glasses. 'Are you all right' said Chuc Wu. 'Yes, sure why not?' 'But what about those flies?' said Chuc Wu. 'Oh they've gone, flew away,' I said.

'Now young man,' the policeman said to Chuc Wu, 'If you try another hoax like that I'll — I'm sorry but it wasn't a hoax,' Chuc Wu said to the policeman. 'No, not a hoax, most definitely not,' I said. I took off the glasses I was wearing and my eyes were those of a fly, big, black and horrible.

The visual gift, and the practice he'd had show in the detail of the writing, and the headmaster's story, very graphically told, touched his imagination, and on this day, at least, allowed him to 'think of a story to write'.

In 'What do you expect', he is in fact writing about a real visit he had made to his prospective school. He did not go to that school, but only because there was no room; not at all because of his feelings about it which entirely preponderate over the observation this time.

'What do you expect'
This is what my secondary school was like when I went to see it when it was dark . . . it was very big and old like a haunted house, eery and cold with the leaves blowing across the playground and the trees swaying to and fro making dark twisting shadows on the floor. The branches of the trees were like arms and long bony fingers ready to reach out and grab me. I walked up to the windows and peered in. I could hear a muffled sweeping sound of the caretaker clearing up. Then suddenly all around me echoed the sound of a bell, then about twenty boys came barging out the door which I was standing next to and then another twenty and another and another until the playground was filled with shouting and laughter of all the boys who were going home. Then they all disappeared and it was quiet again, but one thing didn't go and that was the cold eery feeling I had before.

He did not write such powerful pieces of work again, but he was writing well, finding it less of an effort to start and being able to finish. He began to be able to start a drawing by completing the outline, instead of shading in from one corner, and risking not finishing something over ambitious. This is what happened with the drawing of the head (Figure 6.3), which was part of a whole wooden statue. He became gradually more relaxed, as his sensitive iris drawing shows (Figure 6.4).

A little later we were working on the brain and this is what he chose to write about:

'Inside my head'
Inside my head is like a tape recorder. It tapes all my memories and thoughts, imaginations and all the things that I have done. And when I think back its like pressing the rewind button on the tape recorder, but when I die it's like recording over my memories, thoughts, imagination and all the things that have happened in my life to leave the tape blank.

All his work was better by now. He seemed content to be less competitive, and this was making it a bit easier for him to make friends. The close friendship in Black Sunday was wishful thinking, the boy in that being the boy whose art work he most wished to emulate and whom in fact he'd been trying to beat. At about this time we were working on the Nigerian creation myth and Tom was chosen to be the king. He wrote a warm and imaginative poem of acceptance about the responsibility of being a king.

'Poem of Acceptance'
I thank you my people.
Out of all the thousands of people, rich and poor, you choose me to be your king.
I hope that I prove your choice to be a wise one.
I shall take from the rich and give to the poor.
I shall treat you justly and lead you to victory against all enemies.
Once again my people I thank you and may your crops prosper and your goats produce much milk.

This responsibility, both in the dramatic imagination of the play and towards the other children, by having the most important part, made an impression on him. He relaxed and became much more part of the group than he had ever been. They were able to be warmer with him and he was very happy.

Can one ever say whether any change or apparent progress is permanent? One of his contemporaries dropped in recently and said, 'I've seen Tom. He

Figure 6.3

hasn't changed. He's still the same.' But when Chuc Wu wrote about 'The best day of my holidays', what he wrote about was, 'The day I went to Tom's house'.

Summary and Conclusions

I chose these four children because, although they were in no sense slow learners, I think it is possible to see development in each one's work. Personal and academic development are very closely interlinked. In a time of unemployment it is especially clear that work affords a source of strength and confidence, a sense of progress and therefore a hopeful outlook. It is as much true for children as for adults, and is more true if the work done is good work and is enjoyed.

To find real satisfaction in their work, children need to be putting into it something comparable to the energy with which they throw themselves into games. As D.H. Lawrence says in *Work*,

There's no point in work
Unless it absorbs you like an absorbing game.
If it doesn't absorb you,

Figure 6.4

If it's never any fun,
Don't do it.
When a man goes out into his work
He is alive like a tree in spring.
He is living not merely working.
(Lawrence 1964, p.145)

Put more mundanely, if it's not used, as every teacher knows, the energy will find alternative outlets.

The work of all the children in the class has developed. The class has been the support and the audience to the individual children all the year. In a whole class of children, it is a small minority who are always able to do their best. Most of us need some encouragement, discipline, help or elucidation at times. In some areas we may need a more sustained support.

I've chosen to write in detail about children whose reasons for not being able to put their full energy into their work (over-anxiousness, working in a second language, a need to settle down and concentrate, a physical difficulty) were different, but ones we come across very often. I've also tried to show that each child developed (in the sense of bringing from a latent to an active state) a gift (or more than one) with the help of the variety of creative work we do, which they can see is their own and in which they can have confidence. (Tom has his art and drama and his stories; Kwok Leung his poetry and drama; Giovanni models, drama, music and art; and Joanna acting, art and writing.) I've also tried to show that this affects and improves their whole academic performance.

I hope I have been able to illustrate the value of our work in the creative arts. They offer the children a choice and a variety of means of expression. This is valuable to all the children, but some of them will also discover that they have an outstanding gift for one of the arts, which could be an enrichment for all their lives. Beyond that, it can be of inestimable value to a child who, for any reason, finds it very hard to communicate through academic work — in, for instance, a new language, or because of particular learning difficulties. This point is made very clearly in the Appendix to *The Arts in Schools* (Calouste Gulbenkian Foundation 1982). The area of struggle is bypassed and the child can communicate freely, and will often do sensitive, interesting and beautiful work. This, of course also helps the teacher to gain a truer estimate of the ability and quality of that child. Seeing or knowing he has done a good piece of creative work is bound to have a good effect on a child's confidence, which can then be fed back to the area of difficulty. A different, more successful attitude to his whole achievement will often make possible progress with the academic work as well.

The processes of creative work demand an active involvement. You have actually to *do* them — to look ('Till your eyes ache', one child said) and use the pencil or paintbrush; to move in response to the music and the feelings it calls up; to *be* someone else and think and talk and move like them, and in response to the other characters. Unlike learning bare facts, you can't escape participating, and the demand is on the whole self — mind, body, sensitivity, intellect and feelings. While they make this demand, the arts are at the same time training these faculties, so that they offer something like a total education.

Because of the need to use the whole person, the creative arts have the effect of integrating the gifts and faculties of a child. As these work together, a great deal of energy is freed which can be put into all the children's activities, including their academic work. Starting from the children's own experience and offering different creative opportunities mean that *their* interest and *their* energy are motivating their work. No-one has to make them do it. The children will take on their own pursuit of learning with gusto and with energetic enquiry. They will wish to do their work well and to present it well. They will develop a secure confidence and will enjoy learning. In Margaret Donaldson's phrase, they will become 'people who rejoice in the exercise of creative intelligence' (Donaldson 1978, p.14). And, with luck, that's what they'll continue to be.

PART THREE

STRATEGIES FOR IMPLEMENTATION AND CHANGE

INTRODUCTION TO PART THREE

Any form of curriculum will need supporting structures. Without these it will be unable to develop. What is crucial is that these structures should actually support — often they have the opposite effect — and to do this they must match the curriculum they are designed for. In short, the structures need to be based on the same principles as the curriculum itself.

Nowhere is the truth of this more apparent — if only from contrary instances — than in the systems of record-keeping which are currently to be seen in use, or abuse, in Primary schools. For it is clear that those simplistic systems which many teachers and schools are currently being required to use, particularly in order to meet demands for increased accountability, not only fail to support the teachers' work but often have the effect of distorting and placing limitations on it. And this is due not only to their simplicity but also to the fact that they are often based on similarly unsophisticated, and often un-recognized, assumptions about the essentials of curriculum planning. Again, the obsession with prestated objectives rears its far from handsome head and we begin to see elements appearing in our Primary schools which are having the same inhibiting effects as the 11+ once had and as the public examination system still has too often on the curriculum of the Secondary school.

Part Three, then, begins with an examination of what may be the most essential supporting structure careful curriculum planning requires, and what is certainly the first concern we must face when considering strategies for the implementation of the kind of curriculum we are concerned with here — the development of a suitable system of record-keeping.

This, however, is only one aspect of the supporting structures which need to be developed in every school, whether our concern is merely with the implementation of what must be seen as a continuously developing activity or with something which might be seen rather as a form of innovation, in short, whether we wish merely to develop or positively to change the curriculum. That curriculum development must be school-centred is now regarded by many people as almost self-evident, for whether this is seen as the continuing implementation of agreed principles or as the adoption of new ones, it is clear that it must begin and end with the teacher in the classroom. A lot more work needs to be done, however, to explore questions of what are the most effective strategies for achieving this. It is not enough to will the end; we must devise the means too. And it is clear that there has been rather more optimistic talk than effective action in this field, that rhetoric has often been allowed to take the place of practice (Hargreaves 1982).

We turn next in this section, then, to an exploration of some of the issues which need to be faced if teachers are to be supported by the general structure of the school in developing their work in this way. And then we consider the kinds of support they may be given from outside, by offering an account of an experiment by one local authority in the creation of curriculum support teams. For the question of providing adequate support for teachers must be approached from both of these directions.

Finally, the third major factor in the task of supporting teachers in developing their work is the quality of their professional preparation. There is little point in encouraging teachers to adopt particular approaches to their task if the courses by which they became qualified have not prepared them to do this or, worse, if they have had the effect of pointing them in a completely different direction. Furthermore, one of the major effects of that move towards school-centred development and innovation we have just referred to is that it makes it essential that we look more closely than ever at the methods by which we prepare teachers for the responsibilities we are placing on them and that we maintain and develop their levels of professionality. Close attention must be focused, then, on both initial courses and, perhaps more importantly, on the provision for the continuing in-service education of teachers. For the quality of the teacher will be crucial for the quality of the educational experiences he or she is able to offer pupils.

It is to this question, then, that we turn in the final chapter of this section. Our concern there is to elucidate, again with some concrete examples, how teachers can be prepared for this kind of teaching and to argue the case both for planning courses of initial preparation along these lines and for increasing the scope and quality of induction programmes and in-service education. Our discussion is tempered, however, by an account of some recent and current developments in the field of teacher education which seem to us to make it unlikely that much can be expected, at least in the immediate future, in the way of improved provision in that area.

CHAPTER 7

THE DEVELOPMENT OF A RECORD-KEEPING SYSTEM

MAGGIE BIERLEY

It is clearly important for teachers to keep records, and the more the individual nature of children's learning is acknowledged and catered for the more necessary the keeping of detailed records becomes. Such records are required primarily for the teacher's own guidance; a detailed knowledge of each child's work, interests, progress and possible development is crucial for proper planning. They are also important for other teachers in the school and the Headteacher in particular. They need to be kept too so that parents can be regularly informed of their children's development. And they form a basis for responding to accountability demands from other interested agencies outside the school.

However, to argue for the importance of record-keeping is not enough. It is far more important that we look to the form and the design of our record-keeping systems, since there is no doubt that these can either assist the development of the work of the teacher and her pupils or inhibit that development. In particular, the simplistic 'check-list' system of record-keeping, so often foisted on teachers these days, is clearly based on assumptions about the need to plan by prestated objectives and thus will have the effect of distorting rather than promoting the work of any teacher whose approach to educational planning is based on an adherence to principles rather than to 'aims and objectives'. In short, that form of record-keeping will prove quite inappropriate for any teacher who is endeavouring to develop his or her work along the lines described in Part Two of this book.

Thus the development of a system which will support this kind of approach becomes an essential consideration, both in the positive sense of being an important strategy for the implementation of such an approach and in the negative sense of providing a defence against attempts to impose incompatible systems. What follows is an account of the development of such a system.

The evolution of a record-keeping system

Early stages

The development described here began in college as a device to assist students during their school practice in Infant classrooms.

The students' college course was designed to prepare them to teach in schools which were following an integrated-day approach in a resource-based classroom. The diversity of schools, however, provided problems for college supervisors, students and teachers. Students could be expected to be teaching in a wide range of classroom situations. Consequently, the expectations of students varied from situation to situation.

The college required students to develop children's interests and experiences in different aspects of the curriculum from the activities provided in the classroom. An essential part of the college course was that the students should become skilled in making careful and detailed observations of children's development. Therefore, the problem seemed to be one of communication and accountability between college, the student and the school. It was felt that communication could be improved by using a different method of processing and presenting essential information, and checking that action of a kind that was most likely to lead to successful learning followed.

The School Practice Journal at that time was detailed and comprehensive but, because it was largely in narrative form, was time-consuming and proved to be a difficult format from which to extract essential information. Therefore, the first part of the development work was to begin to produce a new form of record of the school practice to include flow plan diagrams and tabulated summaries of the development work coming from them.

On final school practice, the college required detailed flow plans of possible development arising from each resource area of the classroom. Many students felt this failed to accommodate their understanding of a child-centred approach to teaching, in that it seemed to require them to forecast what was to happen, rather than to capitalize on children's interests, where learning investment would be at its greatest. However, in restrospect, it perhaps gave the student a feeling of security and a framework within which she could become increasingly more flexible as the practice developed. Although it now seems a crude method of recording, it was certainly invaluable as a means of organizing thoughts and it indicated the range of provision that would be needed. The tabulation at this stage was made under the headings — provision, storage, display, possible development and actual development. The tabulation summaries were kept under area- or interest-based headings and not under a child's name. An example of that type of tabulation on final school practice can be seen in Figure 7.1.

Provision	Storage	Display	Possible development	Actual development
13th Various sized boxes, odds and ends, glue, newspaper, brushes, scissors, paint 16th Reference books on transport and streets	In labelled boxes according to size or shape	Close to painting area and near brick play 18th Display area created on flat surface boarded on two sides for shops, etc.	14th Ian interested in building car, may lead to garage/house, street system, extend into shape or transport	15th Car built, picture drawn and parts labelled Ian, Danny, Mark 17th Beginning to plan road system — traffic lights, roundabouts, etc.

Figure 7.1   Junk modelling — the initial stages of the tabulation

As a probationary teacher my immediate concerns were the organization of the classroom, the provision of resources and keeping records of children's experiences and development. The approach to record-keeping, already practised in college, proved to be invaluable as a means of provision and long-term planning for areas of interest and enquiry as they arose in the classroom. For example, having sketched out a flow diagram for Autumn and collected the necessary provision for display and identification, when a child showed interest in, perhaps, berries, I could immediately capitalize on that interest, in the security of knowing the subsequent experiences appropriate for that child's development, and indeed for other children too. The flow diagram was and still is sufficiently open-ended to allow for the direction of enquiry to be changed or modified by the teacher's structure or the child's comment.

By the end of that year all the teaching staff were asked to keep, in a separate book, a record of flow diagrams, showing interests that had arisen in the classroom, and they were read each half-term. These diagrams were not intended to be forecasts but rather summaries of interests and the resulting development work for an individual child, group of children, or maybe the whole class. A more experienced colleague, having read them, could indicate strengths, weaknesses or areas that could have been developed more fully. This was a great support and a feedback into my own teaching and enhanced my observations of children's stages of development and learning.

Extending the scope

During my second year of teaching, my record-keeping improved in detail, but not in the scope it should have covered. There were slight modifications made, largely of a practical nature. The first was to use two coloured pens; one for possible development and one for actual development taking place. The second was to list very simply the reasons and educational justification for developing a particular interest and its relevance to an individual or group of children. Parallel to this method of recording, there was and still is the notebook for teachers issued by the Inner London Education Authority.

It was towards the end of my second year of teaching that there seemed to be a need to link these two patterns of record-keeping. It was felt that they should not be separate but should complement each other. Therefore the third modification was to record the development work from the flow plan (kept in a green book) in green pen in a separate section under each child's profile at the back of the ILEA notebook.

Shown below (Figures 7.2 to 7.5) is an example of this system of record-keeping for one child, although a group of children at a similar stage of development worked alongside her.

Connie (a reception child)

Situation: Class of 35 children, vertically grouped.

Teaching method: Integrated day.

Educational content: Connie's interest in her model of the Post Office Tower.

Possible lines of development:

1. To give the child the experience of the comparison of a paired relationship in height, and relevant language.

2. To introduce the ideas of grouping objects and counting how many, and to extend the notion of ordering and ordinal language.

3. To begin estimation of height in improvised units.

4. To begin measurement in improvised units.

Figure 7.2

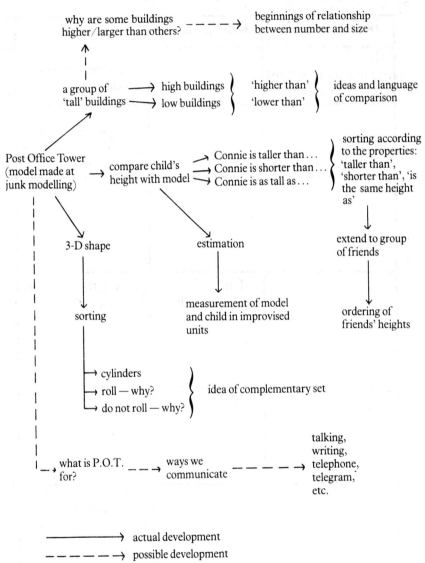

Figure 7.3 Flow diagram

Display and storage	Added provision	Practical work	
5th Floor display against covered pegboard		Making boxwork model	Why
		6th Using room to find things she is taller or shorter than	U la
	11th Measuring box	Finding things she is 'as tall as'	
			1st,
			12th Discus of wor high, l people
		14th Estimated how many of her hands high the model was and then Yvonne, Paula, Mark measured with their hands	

Figure 7.4

	Reading	Writing	Mathematics
ade it	Wrote and read own caption for the model		
ect			Putting objects into sets according to the properties: 'Is taller than', etc
	8th Began to make a book with captions 'Connie is taller than —, but shorter than —'		
d, 4th			Put into sets. Beginning to order and wanted to compare heights of friends. Ordered heights with ribbons
out use hort, n ildings			
			Connie, Paula, Mark, Yvonne recorded by side of model

Connie.   5 years 3 months

1. (a) Attitude to Self
       Connie has made a lively and confident entry into school. She shows great interest in materials around her and uses them well.

   (b) Attitude to Others
       She makes friends easily and co-operates well in a group situation. Her attitude to adults is one of interest and she enjoys their company, sharing her experience with them, but is not dependent on them.

   (c) Attitude to Work
       She concentrates well and tries hard to achieve a good standard. Sometimes the fun and enthusiasm for her work seem masked by her determination to succeed.

2. No entry

3. No entry

	Flow Diagram Tabulation
4. (a) Reading Approaches early reading activities with confidence. Can read simple caption book back.	Post Office Tower: Caption book made has increased her confidence with extended sentence material and beginning to recognize words.
(b) Written and Oral Able to express herself well — needs more support in group situation. Good letter formation. Stories imaginative.	Post Office Tower: Some confusion with taller, higher, etc. — will need reinforcement. Beginning to look for words she needs.
5. Mathematics Makes a thoughtful use of apparatus and is able to explain her reasons and actions in sorting.	Post Office Tower: Can make groups of objects and order them with good use of language. Needs lots of practice with estimation with one improvised unit.

Figure 7.5   Profile in ILEA Notebook

This stage in the development of record-keeping was reached after two years of teaching and was consolidated over the following two years.

During that time, the staff, because of their own professional development and growing expertise in their observations of children, began to feel the need for a more detailed record of a child's reading and mathematical experiences. We began with an experimental zigzag book for each child. For the reading record each page was divided into the following headings: date; task or book; comment; suggestions (Figure 7.6).

Date	Task or Book	Comment	Suggestions
September 17th	I Can Jump	Confident 'reading'. One-to-one correspondence. Used pictures well; said 'That begins my name' (j — Joanne)	Begin collecting words beginning with 'j'.
September 20th	I Can Fly	Wanted to read book twice.	Read set of books to another child to reinforce confidence to make book for herself — caption book 'I can…'

Figure 7.6

The mathematics zigzag record took the same format, and the stages of development were based on the school's extension of the Guidelines for Teachers produced by the ILEA.

Reappraisal

There then followed a period of approximately four years during which I was out of the classroom, on secondment and as a floating teacher at my present school. Although I was not keeping records for my own class, I began, together with colleagues, to implement the record-keeping format. This proved to be a valuable and supportive experience, because an entirely different set of people were using the system. As a group we began to reappraise the design and several thoughts and questions were raised. It should be noted that, just prior to this stage, the teachers concerned had gradually changed their teaching methodology to an integrated approach.

The flow diagram was readily assimilated into the teaching style with some feelings of security and excitement at seeing ideas develop and link. There were some teething problems, in particular feelings of constraint from having to operate rigidly within the flow diagram. These were soon solved with discussion and growing understanding. We were then able to branch out in another direction of the flow or to prepare another diagram for a child or group of children who had stronger interests elsewhere in the classroom.

It is perhaps worth quoting two teachers. They had both been teaching for about four years but for only half that time using an integrated approach. Teacher 1 said:

I think I made a mistake when I first started using the flow in that I wasn't flexible enough. Therefore I got a little bored and so did the children, but I feel once you realise the flow's flexibility and that you don't have to stick to it rigidly, it becomes a more exciting possibility.

Teacher 2 agreed:

Yes, it does help me to look ahead and know with some certainty what I am going to need to prepare. The children seem to assimilate more if activities are related to a certain idea. Before, I felt that any 'topic' I did with children I was just scratching the surface and now when you really start to think about the possibilities of an interest, make a flow diagram and explore it in depth, it gives me more security to give children relevant experiences.

The teaching style had changed with this group of teachers and they began to see that the more flexible the teaching style, where the content is less clearly defined, objectives are not predetermined and the messages between teacher and child are more implicit, the more necessary it is to devise an efficient system of record-keeping to identify what is happening to each child and to support that child in an approach to successful enquiry and problem solving.

Therefore one of the questions to be raised was, 'How and where do I record how the child operated in a particular situation?' Another was, 'Am I to some degree duplicating information?' At that time the child's name was indicated on the tabulation at his or her point of involvement. The statement of how the child operated was made under the flow-diagram section of the ILEA Notebook. This was felt to be something of a duplication but at that time remained an unsolved problem. The tabulation headings were changed to include two new headings and clarify others (Figure 7.7). It was felt that the reason the child was being involved in a particular experience needed to be accounted for, whether on social, emotional or educational grounds.

Interest Provision Date	Children and reason for involvement	Practical activites	Numeracy		Literacy		
			Language and practical	Recorded work	Language	Reading	Writing

Figure 7.7   Revised tabulation headings

Within the last two years, during which I returned to classroom teaching, there has been growing frustration and dissatisfaction, arising from the feeling that the flow diagram, tabulation and qualitative statement about the child's performance were not coming together and the record did not seem a coherent whole. Moreover, the feedback for ourselves was fragmentary and we felt we needed to be able to look at a child's record of development and extract information at a glance.

Therefore, after discussion, it was decided that each child in the class should have a printed tabulation spanning three sheets and that they should be arranged alphabetically in a ring file. On the front sheet the interest areas in which the child had been involved were listed and dated. The actual tabulation headings were now altered to include a column for observations and suggestions for further development.

Figures 7.8 and 7.9 show examples of the flow diagram and the tabulation as they are at the time of writing.

The ILEA notebook was sectioned for each child into areas that we felt were not sufficiently covered by the tabulation. The headings included:

General personality sketch

Spoken language

Written language

Handwriting

Two-dimensional work

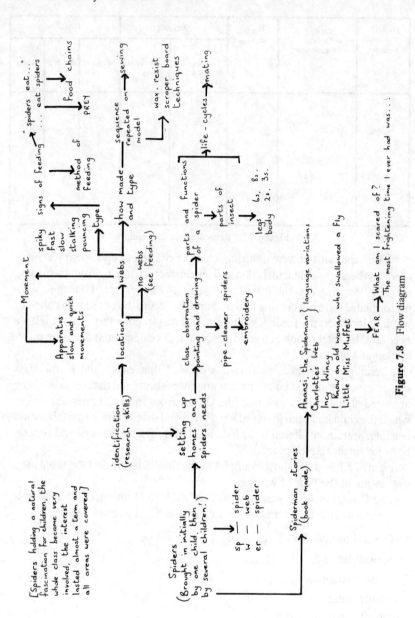

Figure 7.8 Flow diagram

Three-dimensional work

Gross motor skills

Fine motor skills

Music and dance.

While all these modifications were taking place, it was felt that more detailed reading records needed to be kept as our observations of a child's reading improved. After much reading and discussion, we devised a system of reading-record sheets according to a child's developmental stage. Figure 7.10 shows some examples of these.

The observations are written with the child by one's side so that the child is involved in his or her progress, and it becomes an obvious feedback into the teaching of reading.

Although the records have been in operation for about three years, there are now some plans to modify parts of them. As with all record-keeping, with continual use one looks for refinements to make it more efficient as a feedback system. At present, a group of teachers has based its mathematics record-keeping system on the authority's *Primary School Mathematics Guidelines* and *Checkpoints*. However, with changes in the school over the past year, the mathematical curriculum and our method of recording it are at present under review.

General issues and principles

It is evident that over a period of time, this particular system of record-keeping has had periods of inactivity and consolidation, but it has also had periods of real activity in its shaping and modification. This only happened when what are perhaps the basic questions were repeatedly being asked. 'Are my records meeting my needs as a teacher?' 'Are they helpful or cumbersome and time-wasting?' There seems little point in writing down information that cannot be extracted efficiently and used for future development either for the child or the teacher.

Throughout the years other questions and thoughts that have been offered seem to fall into two categories: 'Why keep records anyway?' and 'Who am I keeping records for?'

To look at the first question, discussion showed that if the teacher is to be the initiator of a learning situation, or the person who capitalizes on and nurtures the children's interests, then he or she is central to the planning and evaluation of that process. Furthermore, it was considered that there needed to be

Interest provision	Reason for involvement	Practical activity / play	NUMERACY	
			PRACTICAL LANGUAGE	RECORDING
September 14th. Spider	He brought in large spider to school	Setting up a 'home' for spider		
Sept. 16th. Selection of books about spiders	To identify his spider			
Sept. 19th. Webs	Began drawing webs and his observations of webs in playground	Tried to collect webs on paper		
Sept. 21st. Web / book of how a web is made / string / branches	To give sequence of construction	Making web construction	Sequence ordinal numbers spokes / spiral	List of instruct 1st..... 2nd..... ordering spid movements
Sept. 23rd. Webs / card / wax crayon / clay tools	Introduction of new technique	Scrape board picture of a web		
Sept 24th. Spider's legs ↓ Sept. 25th.	Work on 2s and 8s		Number sentences within 8 Grouping and sharing Words meaning same as 2 Counting in 2s on number line	Recording in sent and x, y — Book on-goi piece of w Find the mis number
Sept. 28th. On-going through ↓ the week. interested in differences	Had been browsing through books	Close drawings of cobweb and spitting spiders		
Oct. 6th. Another spider brought in	His spider / not able to identify / later found to be pregnant	Close drawing		
Oct. 7th. Web and material (silver thread)	Asked to sew a web	On-going piece sewing		

Figure 7.9 Tabulation for Joseph (6yrs 2mths)

LITERACY			Observations and Suggestions
Language	Reading	Written	
Diagrammatic representation with labelling and functions	Research in books for needs of a spider	Account of how and where it was found	Can now be used to direct others. Understands exactly what is needed
Discussion about difficulties of identification because of size and similarity of markings	Beginning to look at contents and index	Written account about provisional identification beginning of a book	Comments about level of information in books frustrated Needs better, if more complex books with support
			To try and reproduce a web with branches and string
			Enjoyed experience, good fine motor skills, monitored his own difficulties
			Comments on relationship between 2 and 4 in grouping and sharing. Already anticipating
Language of description catching food, how spiders eat	Continued experience with research skills.	Written account for class book	Simple guidance on how to extract information needed. Comments on how little some books tell you!
		Began a diary of the development and laying of eggs.	
			Bigger job than he anticipated difficulty with spiral - with support completed good standard of representation.

Class teacher	No. of terms in Infant department Nursery ☐ 2 yr ☐ 2.2 yr ☐ 2.1 yr ☐ 3 yr ☐			Any difficulties observed 1 (a) speech .... (b) vision .... (c) hearing .... First language of child	
Date	Talk, story, picture, own story, book	Directional rules	Cueing system, picture, meaning, language	Visual attention to print	Generalisations, Suggestions

Class teacher	No. of terms in Infant department Nursery ☐ 2 yr ☐ 2.2 yr ☐ 2.1 yr ☐ 3 yr ☐			Any difficulties observed 2 (a) speech .... (b) vision .... (c) hearing .... First language of child	
Date	Reading context	Cueing system	Evidence of self-correction	Visual attention to print	Generalisations, Suggestions

Class teacher	No. of terms in Infant department Nursery ☐ 2 yr ☐ 2.2 yr ☐ 2.1 yr ☐ 3 yr ☐				Any difficulties observed 3 (a) speech .... (b) vision .... (c) hearing .... First language of child	
Date	Reading context	Cueing system	Evidence of self-correction	Visual attention to print	Reading preference	Reading application

7.10 Reading-record sheets

structured links between experiences and processes necessary for successful learning and teaching to take place. It was strongly felt that the progress of teacher and child alike was being checked.

Who am I keeping records for? If it is for myself, do they capture what I have done, do they begin to answer some of the questions I have about myself as a teacher and about the children's development, do they make a positive contribution to my thinking, planning and methodology? If it is for the child, do they record both what the child has done and how it was done, do they give me the feedback I need into my teaching approach with that child? If it is for the head or another colleague, do they indicate my teaching style and appoach, do they give any helpful insight to a particular child and do they indicate curriculum areas covered and the reasons why? If it is for a supply teacher (in case of my absence) do the records provide the aforesaid information and give the teacher clear guidelines for development of the children, so that their experiences and learning are not disrupted?

Why do we need to evaluate our pupils anyway, and do we need to record it? Perhaps we should ask ourselves, 'Am I carrying information in my head, and indeed can I carry that information with clarity?' All teachers are faced at the end of each academic year with an annual report on a child, and often find too little evidence of recorded development to base this on. There is the possibility of then relying on generalizations and platitudes, that say little to succeeding colleagues or to the head or, perhaps more importantly, to the parents.

Is it then to tell the children how they are doing or to judge how effective our teaching is or to communicate to children what our concerns are? I believe that the asking of these questions is the crux of designing and initiating a record-keeping system. This chapter is not the place to attempt to answer them; its intention is rather to stress that these and other questions should be asked continuously, of oneself and in discussion with colleagues.

I should like to believe too that as children develop they can themselves take part in the record-keeping system; that they can themselves share in the design of flow diagrams and thus extend their logical thinking; and that they can thus participate in the assessment and evaluation of their work. Then and only then will they have a real chance to be a force in their own learning and development.

Summary and conclusions

This chapter has offered an account of how one teacher designed and developed a system of record-keeping of a kind which would support her in a process-based approach to her planning and her teaching. It has revealed, first, that the development of such a system is possible and, second, how it can be achieved. It has also demonstrated the additional advantages of extending such a system throughout the school or at least throughout groups of teachers working in similar areas. It thus shows that it is possible, with some ingenuity, to keep records which are more than check-lists, which go far beyond the largely quantitive assessments of many systems and which thus provide for all interested parties — the teacher herself, the Headteacher, other colleagues, parents, governors and anyone else who has a right to it — information that is more extensive and more revealing than that which is often available.

In doing this, I hope the chapter has demonstrated not only that such systems are possible but also that they are eminently desirable.

CHAPTER 8

AN APPROACH TO SCHOOL-BASED CURRICULUM DEVELOPMENT

ELAINE BALL

Curriculum development is about change. We can call it improvement or development but it will inevitably involve change in some degree or form. The change may not only be concerned with what has been described as the content of the curriculum, it will also be concerned with its processes, the principles underlying what the school sets out to do. It will be concerned, in effect, with all aspects of our pedagogy.

Chapter 1 gave an overview of the current educational scene and offered some reasons why a process of rethinking should begin. It noted how the changes anticipated in the Plowden Report have not yet become established in our schools. Certainly much good work has been done. Increasing attention has been focused on the teacher's role in curriculum development and his or her potential as a researcher (Stenhouse 1975; Elliott and Adelman 1973). But for many of us the Plowden recommendation that all class teachers be encouraged to look critically at their day-to-day work and draw up a statement of their aims, relating them to guiding principles instead of short term objectives (DES 1967, p.187), could still be usefully heeded. Certainly, if attempts are to be made to give education a sounder basis and the child is to be at the centre of our curriculum planning — if, in effect, we are attempting to implement the principles of a process model of the curriculum as outlined in the earlier chapters of this book — then the ability to change and critically to appraise and review our activities needs to be built into our teaching. Furthermore, it is not enough that individuals have this capacity. If change is to be sustained and of permanent benefit to the children we teach, then schools as a whole must work together to this end.

This chapter sets out to do two things; first, it attempts to offer a possible framework to help innovating teachers in planning and implementing school-based curriculum development. Through this, various important factors can be considered which highlight some of the constraints and possibilities of this form of development. Second, it considers the support which is needed for school-based projects and attempts to indicate where this might be found.

Preparing for school-based curriculum development

In this first section dealing with a school-based model, it is assumed that an individual or group in a school wish to bring about some improvement or, at least, to begin to raise questions about the work of the school. Anyone who has ever returned from a course brimming with enthusiasm for some new idea or approach will know of the variety of responses which can be received from other staff. These may vary from supportive to cynical — and this indicates the first problem for the innovating teacher in a school, and the first of several factors which need careful consideration.

Recognizing the need for curriculum development

Undoubtedly the most vital precondition which must exist for curriculum development is an awareness of the need for change or improvement in the work of schools. This places the teacher firmly in the centre of the curriculum development process, for, if teachers have no desire to change their methods, no amount of excellent planning or attractive curriculum packages will have any lasting impact. This has been borne out by several Schools Council projects including the Schools Council's 'Integrated Studies' project. Evaluator David Jenkins (1975) highlights the problem of assessing and interpreting correctly the feedback from teachers of varying backgrounds, experience and qualifications. The meticulous field trials carried out on most Schools Council projects become a purposeless activity if the principles adopted by the project are not those of the teacher. John Pearce (1975), concerned with the Schools Council's 'Linguistics and English Teaching' project, concludes that 'material gains purpose according to how far it matches the aims of those who are to use it. If the match is not a close one, the teachers concerned need re-training as several projects have found' (op. cit., p.126). (Alternatively, it may be that the methodology of the project needs closer scrutiny.)

How then do teachers become aware of the need for change? Certainly some teachers reach this point more quickly and easily than others. Hoyle (1980) makes a distinction between two kinds of teacher, the restricted and the extended professional. He describes restricted professionality as 'intuitive, classroom focused and based on experience rather than theory' (op. cit., p.49). He makes the point that the good restricted professional is sensitive to the development of individual children and can be a skilful class manager. He also suggests that such a teacher is not encumbered with theory or prone to comparing his or her work with others, and tends to value his or her classroom autonomy. The extended professional, however, attempts to locate his or her class in a wider educational context, is more likely to compare his or her work with other teachers and is inclined to collaborate with them. He or she also reads educational books or journals, becomes involved in various professional activities and is inclined to extend his or her own professional development through courses.

It would appear that the extended professional would be aware of the need for curriculum development and would value the opportunity to collaborate with others to improve the work of the school.

The restricted professional category of teacher, however, would pose some problems for the innovating school. These problems may relate to:

1 teachers' lack of awareness of new research, reports, surveys etc. and the implications which these may have for classroom practice,

2 a knowledge of the above, but an inability to change because the discrepancy between theory and classroom practice is not recognized or the difficulty of adjusting methodology to new approaches is too great,

3 a deliberate rejection of the contribution of theory to practice.

Of these three categories, the first is the simplest to deal with as deliberate strategies can be adopted which will reduce, if not resolve, the problem. First the local education authority should have responsibility for increasing this knowledge as an important aspect of its INSET programme. Courses should also be aimed at postholders and Headteachers with an emphasis on their responsibility as disseminators. If the authority does advocate this, then it follows that it should have repercussions on the staffing of schools, as postholders should be released from part of their teaching load to deal with development issues.

Second, the role of advisers and inspectors as disseminators of new information and its implications for schools is extremely important here. Nevertheless, this does not absolve teachers themselves from the necessity to keep up to date with reading and to adopt an increasingly professional attitude to their work. It must be emphasized that the initial training which qualifies us as teachers is precisely that, and further training and certainly further reading are necessary to maintain and improve the standard of our work.

These strategies in themselves, however, will not provide an instant solution to the problem of improving practice. Indeed, a study by P.H. Taylor (1974) of teachers' perceptions revealed their opinions that research findings or developments in educational sociology and psychology are unlikely to produce improvements in teaching.

This leads to the second category defined; that of teachers who are aware of new research but fail to match it to their practice. Teaching is a very demanding occupation. There is little time for the reflection that is needed. Philip Jackson (1968) has noted the dynamic nature of life in classrooms. He differentiates between pre-active and inter-active aspects of teaching. In the former, the lone teacher reflects and plans activities and perhaps at the end of the day rationalizes the causes for success or failure or the specific behaviour of particular children. Interactive teaching describes the intuitive nature of a teacher's activities in the lively arena of the classroom. Reaction must be immediate. There is no time to deliberate consciously over choices, to weigh evidence, evaluate potential outcomes and make the appropriate pedagogical choice. The teacher more often reacts intuitively, drawing upon the strategies proven by time and personal experience. The teacher, therefore, may not have time or opportunity to note discrepancies between his theory and practice. This has been evident through various classroom observation procedures (Delamont and Stubbs 1976).

Of particular relevance here, however, is the type of self-evaluation technique evolved by the Ford Teaching Project (Elliott 1976). The project grew out of the work of the Humanities Curriculum Project and was based on the premise that the problems of implementing discussion-based enquiry were caused by teachers' unconscious behaviour patterns; for example, the ways in which teachers may invite consensus or promote their own views would inhibit students' involvement. The project encouraged teachers to invite observers in to monitor their work and use this as a basis for discussion. A further strategy was the introduction of triangulation techniques, where a teacher's, observer's and pupil's perceptions of a class lesson would be compared. It would appear that the findings of such projects have contributed to the thinking behind the Open University course, 'Curriculum in Action'. For this focuses firmly on the reality of what happens in classrooms and provides the teacher with a set of questions as a format for classroom observation and, consequently, self-evaluation.

Such a course, with the support of local study groups, could be very influential in heightening awareness of any shortfall between teachers' theory and practice. However, there is some evidence to show that classroom observation techniques do not work equally well for every teacher. John Elliott concluded at the end of the Ford Teaching project (op. cit., p.9) that the teachers involved fell into three categories:

— Teachers who are adopting an objective stance to their practice, but require support in collecting and analysing more sufficient data as a basis for constructing accurate accounts,

— Teachers who are not adopting an objective stance, but inasmuch as they sense or feel their situation to be problematic, are ready to do so,

— Teachers who are neither ready or able to adopt an objective stance to their practice.

Teachers in the first two groups may recognize the shortfall between their theory and practice and be aware of a need for curriculum development. The support of fellow staff members and possibly outside agencies plus good planning and time for reflective thinking would enable this to take place. Elliott's final category above is of more concern. It would seem to link with the third category outlined on page 185; that of those teachers who deliberately reject the contribution of theory to practice. Teachers in this situation pose a substantial constraint on a school's ability to develop its curriculum, so the possible reasons for such resistance to change should be understood in order to develop strategies for its resolution.

One psychological theory which would seem to have relevance is that devised by George Kelly. He attempted to explain, through his personal construct theory, how individuals assimilate and/or reject new learning. A basic postulate of the theory is that a person's processes of assimilation are determined by the way in which he anticipates events, which is in turn influenced by the personal constructs which he has built through past experiences. New learning or change occurs by the process of absorbing experiences into this system and, upon meeting confirming or disconfirming data, the existing constructs are modified, reinforced or revised. Bannister and Fransella (1971) describe the feelings of 'threat' which occur when major beliefs about 'our social, practical situation are invalidated and the world about us appears to become chaotic' (op. cit., p.37). Hence there are times for some individuals, when, if their construct system is to be preserved, they cannot afford to be wrong.

The relative isolation of teachers in classrooms might be regarded as a factor in reinforcing such personally evolved constructs. Teachers involved in the Ford Teaching Project have referred to the uncertainty which the experience has produced. 'Like children, we hanker after the finiteness of things and, like children, we are disturbed when there is frequent reassessment and modification' (Rowe 1973, p.54). Is it surprising, therefore, that, in the dynamic classroom context which has been described, the teacher should seek to maintain an unchanging, permanent personal ideology? Could it be that the difficulties and frequent failure of teachers attempting new methods, such as those of the Humanities Curriculum Project, are related to such a threat to fundamental constructs? It is certainly significant that such cognitive dissonance is thought by some to be a necessary precondition of change (Geortsina and Mackie 1969).

Ryle (1975) has drawn attention to the fact that any system of personal constructs is to some degree shared by others as well as being to some extent unique to the individual. This may be reflected in schools among staff who have some similar background and daily concerns. Therefore, it is obviously important to find, through discussion, as much common ground as possible to make the idea of change less threatening. It will obviously help if attention is focused away from the teacher concerned and possibly placed on the work children are doing. This will give a basis for discussion which does not overtly threaten the teacher. Creating a situation where other teachers can discuss their doubts, concerns and even failures may encourage the reluctant teacher to take part. It can be clearly seen also that the social situation in the staffroom can be extemely important. It would be very easy for a teacher who feels threatened to retire into his or her classroom until the whole thing blows over.

The OU Reading Development Course has an interesting booklet entitled *The Extended Professional Role* (OU 1979). One section makes some very salient points about relationships with colleagues and offers advice to teachers attempting to develop their school's language curriculum:

> You will be asking your colleagues, both individually and collectively to discuss their attitudes, their problems and their proposals for change with you and each other. In many schools this will be the first time that teachers will have participated in discussions of this kind and you must take this into account from the beginning. . . . You are in effect creating a new situation and at the same time introducing new ideas, and you must not be surprised if there is resistance, suspicion and even hostility at the beginning. You must be prepared for this and you must also realize that any attack is not directed at you personally, but springs from a normal reaction to change (op. cit., p.20).

Although the booklet is devoted to the language postholder/curriculum developer it has equal relevance for anyone attempting some form of innovation in schools.

Defining the task

The previous section outlined the centrality of the teacher to the curriculum development process. Assuming that the first hurdle, that of recognizing a need for change and improvement, is passed, then the next problem which needs to be faced is that of task definition. What is the task to be and who defines it? Obviously the staff must be involved if the problems of previous projects based on a Research, Development and Diffusion model (Havelock 1971) are not to be repeated. But it is often extremely difficult for a school to assess its own needs, as the very closeness which is being regarded as a positive feature may result in a myopic or distorted view of the school. This has been one criticism levelled at the advocates of school-based curriculum development. Similarly, doubts have been expressed about the teacher as developer (Stenhouse 1975) and the strategy has been criticized as likely to lead merely to a pooling of ignorance. Therefore an outside perspective may be useful.

Much interest has been shown in another curriculum diffusion model defined by Havelock (op. cit.), the Problem Solving Model. MacDonald and Walker (1976) have described this perspective where the receiver or school initiates the process of change by identifying an area of concern or by sensing a need for change. 'Once the problem area is identified, the receiver undertakes to alter the situation either through his own efforts or by recruiting suitable outside assistance' (op. cit., p.10).

Thus, although this school-based model allows for some outside help and advice, the problem of identifying an 'area of concern' is left with the school. But does this mean that key figures in the school make such a decision? This raises a number of issues about the school's patterns of communication and decision-making. Nevertheless, it has been suggested that curriculum change should be viewed as a species of socio-cultural change (Reid 1978). If this is so then the focus should be broadened from individual teachers to groups of teachers and to the culture of the school as a whole. Such a culture deeply affects and should therefore be shaped by all who are included in it. If this reasoning is followed, then as many members of staff as possible should be involved in defining the scope of the task to be undertaken. This, in fact, can be a difficult and sophisticated problem to set a school. For example, if good communication patterns (vertical and horizontal) do not exist and regular staff meetings do not take place, then a school will find such a task extremely difficult. It also makes many assumptions about the decision-making ability and organizational health of the school.

Matthew Miles (1965) has suggested that the organizational health of the school must be the real target of change, not short-term innovations. A school which achieved the ten dimensions of organizational health which he defines would have the capacity for self-renewal, could be described as an autonomous *(Times Educational Supplement,* 7 December 1979) or 'creative' school and would have the capacity to sustain innovation. Some schools may need to look closely at their organizational health, particularly on matters relating to communication, before embarking on a curriculum development project. Work on such development might be described as process development, as it is concerned with less obvious but fundamental problems such as the school's underlying decision-making and problem-solving procedures. (See page 208 for Bolam's (1978) definition of process and task consultancy.) The more usual project such as the implementation of a language policy, or extending science work in the school, could then be described as task development. Task development has, in fact, a less threatening image. It is much easier to focus on an area of the curriculum than to make inroads into established patterns of operation which will relate to the distribution of power in the school. It may be that drawing staff together to work jointly on a task may set up new patterns of communication and the experience of working collaboratively could strengthen relationships to the extent that more delicate areas could eventually be handled.

Whatever task is decided upon, it is extremely important that the aims and scope of the task be very clearly stated and recorded. This provides the focus of the work which has been agreed. This does not mean that the aims cannot be altered by mutual consent. Indeed, regular review sessions should be incorporated into the plan and formative evaluation should be established as a feature of the project.

Implementing curriculum development

Having recognized the need and defined the task, the school is now in a position to implement the development. Regardless of the task or process involved, successful implementation will depend on the existence of the following factors:

1 good patterns of communication throughout the school,

2 someone to take responsibility for the project on behalf of the staff,

3 sufficient time to allow release for involved teachers during school time

(larger meetings, workshops and courses will take up much after-school time),
4 good planning and organization.

Communication

The importance of good communication has already been emphasized. Many
assumptions are made about communication. It is often taken for granted that
teachers share values and meanings (Gray 1979). However, it would appear
that considerable divergence exists. Even when there is verbal agreement, the
actual meanings may be at variance with each other (Elliott 1976). Therefore
it is important that discussions take place which will give an opportunity for
such meanings to be clarified.

There is another particular way in which communication is important for
the implementation of a project. Not all members of the school will be equally
involved in the development, and if their interest is to be maintained and they
are still to feel a part of the project — essential points if the innovation is to be
sustained — then means have to be found of involving people in certain areas,
of keeping them informed of progress and involving them at important stages
in the project. (It should also be remembered that schoolkeepers, cleaners and
ancillaries should be involved along the way as there is rarely an aspect of
school life which does not affect them in some way.)

For teaching staff, the provision of in-service training must be considered,
as the innovation may require visits or workshops run by visiting advisers or
lecturers. Apart from this there will need to be meetings between working
parties or smaller groups more directly involved in the innovation. The communication needs must be very clearly thought out and planned, as the consequences of not informing participants efficiently can easily result in bad feeling, misinterpretation and consequently a negative attitude to the project.
Another problem can be presented by too many additional meetings. A tired
staff with many other commitments will not work together well, so communication priorities must be carefully established and various means of sharing
information considered. It may be that a centrally positioned notice board
could be used with staff informed briefly at usual staff meetings of the new
information which is detailed on the board. A book (signed when seen) may
also be used, but it should be remembered that only brief messages (reminders
of meetings etc.) can be passed on in this way. A clearly worked out flow diagram coloured or ticked at various points can also be useful as it can express,
in a visual and linear form, the stage the project has reached.

Finally the social aspect of communication should not be overlooked. A maths adviser, once asked what he regarded as the thing most needed to develop a maths curriculum, replied, 'a kettle'. The point is a valid one. Times need to be available when staff can chat informally over a cup of coffee or tea and exchange ideas.

Responsibility

The importance of involving as many staff members as possible in the work of the project has been stated at length. In this sense it is hoped that a mutual sense of responsibility will exist. However, it would seem to be necessary to have an overseer or coordinator to take overall responsibility, to spur things along and keep the aims and interests of the project in the forefront of staff's minds. This should be seen as a management and administrative post — a person, in fact, appointed by the staff to maintain the project under staff direction. This is a very important appointment, as the coordinator should possess some management and organizing skills and have some knowledge of the area to be developed. He or she should also know where help and support can be obtained. But, possibly most importantly, the coordinator should have particular personal qualities of tact, empathy and good judgement. A coordinator who creates unreasonable pressure or generates discord among staff can easily jeopardize the project.

The person appointed may and should vary according to the task definition. If a maths development is envisaged then it may be natural that the maths postholder should coordinate the project. Alternatively, responsibility may be taken by the deputy or Headteacher.

Time

The coordinator will obviously need time to carry out his responsibility. It may be that a school has a floating teacher or deputy head who could allocate some of their time to the coordinator if he or she has a teaching commitment. A major problem arises for the small school with no extra staff. It may be possible in this case to call upon the Head to take on some teaching load to release the coordinator, but this is often a poor solution as emergencies may crop up and the Head may be called away.

Alternative possibilities should be explored with the local education authority. One authority (ILEA 1981) has listed its priorities for in-service training during 1981/2. The first two are:

(i) the development of the ability of teachers to review critically their own professional performance and that of the school as a whole.

(ii) the extension of opportunities which teachers have of observing and learning from the work of their colleagues in other schools (op. cit., p.12).

Funds need, therefore, to be channelled from the INSET budget to support school-based curriculum development. Obviously the confidence with which authorities will underwrite such projects relates to the credibility of school-based curriculum development as a legitimate form of INSET. Writers like Henderson (1978) have indicated doubt about the efficacy and efficiency of standard course-based INSET techniques, but highlight the problem of evaluating school-based work. Indeed Bradley (1978) notes in his survey of INSET expenditure in the UK that there is almost no evidence of the effect of INSET for teachers on schools or children, and that it would be useful to have more information about the comparative effectiveness of courses run within a school for its staff and those offered outside schools for groups involving teachers from different schools.

More evidence of the success of school-based curriculum developments seems to come from abroad, particularly from Sweden, Australia and the USA. Certainly there is a wide consensus among those in education, research and administration that the school-based or school-focused model is more effective than the traditional course-based model (Bolam 1980, p.95).

Thus local authority funds should increasingly become available to support such work. If this is the case then schools may be able to employ additional staff for a given time to allow the release of the coordinator or teacher most in need of time for the project.

Having found a means of making time available for the project, careful consideration should be given to how it is spent. Obviously, it will have to be used in a variety of ways. Time will need to be available for:

1 administrative tasks, perhaps undertaken by the coordinator, organizing the project, arranging visits, making agenda for meetings etc.,

2 organizational work, particularly on a task-based project, such as ordering and storing new materials, making inventories of old, arranging for storage, access and retrieval etc.,

3 INSET work — specifically geared towards the staff's professional development. According to need and relevance, this may involve visits to other schools, arranging or attending workshops, exhibitions, lectures arranged by

advisers or outside authorities.

A recurring theme in this chapter has been the principle of maximum staff involvement. It is important that, whenever possible, members of staff be given time out of class to take part in work in both categories 2 and 3 above. Also, whenever possible, visits should be arranged for two or three teachers to attend at a time, perhaps with a specific brief to make observations on a particular aspect to share with other staff on their return. There is some evidence that such a shared experience has more value. Certainly, it generates and provides a focus for discussions — an important factor if such patterns of communication between staff are weak.

On occasion there will be a need for the whole school staff to attend meetings. Obviously these will have to take place out of school time. Staff, however, who have benefited from release for specific activities during school time should be better disposed to attend meetings and workshops after school.

A final but important point concerning the release of class teachers is that one should be aware of the potential disruption that this can cause to classes. However, certain simple strategies will minimize this possibility, such as

— release being made by the same person — possibly the coordinator or the additional teacher 'bought' for the project;

— where sustained and regular release is necessary, arranging this for the same days every week;

— carefully planning work to be undertaken by the children with the class teacher.

Organization

Much has been stated tangentially about organization on previous pages but it must be emphasized that good planning and organization are necessary for the project to succeed. The coordinator has a responsibility for four main organizational aspects:

1. Direction: The sequencing of work and balancing of activities should be carefully planned.

2. Pace: Some kind of time allocation for phases of the project will be necessary, particularly if an additional staff member is being employed.

3. Communication: The coordinator has a responsibility to ensure that all participants are informed and involved wherever possible in discussion, planning

and decision-making.

4. Evaluation: Review sessions need to be set for formative evaluation. Evaluation in this sense, should not be presecriptive, but should be regarded as an aid to planning the project. It should not be undertaken by an outsider or authority but by the staff themselves. One aspect of this type of participatory evaluation model has been described by Eklund (1978) as an information service to the participants about the characteristics of the school's whole development programme, and thus a basis for participatory planning and decision-making.

Support for school-based curriculum development

An attempt has been made to outline some factors which seem to highlight critical stages in the development of a school-based project. There is no universal panacea to the problem of curriculum development. There are too many variables involved in the process. It is for this reason that school-based methods would appear to have a better chance of success. For here at least some of the factors are known.

The analysis given has drawn upon several disciplines and related them to some commonsense issues drawn from experience in the facilitating role of a member of a curriculum development team. An attempt has been made to extract some principles from that experience and combine them with my current concern with curriculum development in my own school. It would be interesting to see if these principles drawn from practice are generalizable to other situations. To this end, a flow diagram of questions and remedial strategies based on the foregoing discussion has been drawn up (Figure 8.1). It is hoped that this draws attention to some stages which could be potential stumbling blocks to a project's success. Undoubtedly there are others which have been omitted. (It should also be noted that the simplicity with which remedial action is stated does not reflect the ease with which it could be carried out.)

The flow diagram and the foregoing discussion also seem to indicate where various forms of support are needed. Undoubtedly the support of the school's staff and Headteacher are fundamentally important. If they have been involved at all stages prior to implementation it would seem that concentration must be focused on sustaining that support through good communication and by providing a forum for any negative feedback, which should be taken seriously and dealt with as quickly as possible.

You want to initiate a school-based curriculum development project:

Start here

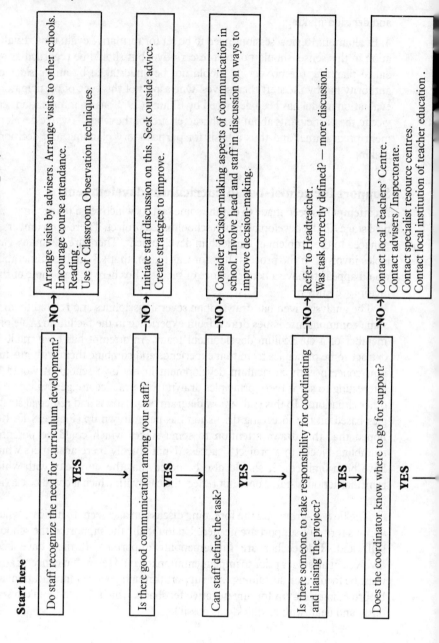

Do staff recognize the need for curriculum development? —NO→ Arrange visits by advisers. Arrange visits to other schools.
Encourage course attendance.
Reading.
Use of Classroom Observation techniques.

YES ↓

Is there good communication among your staff? —NO→ Initiate staff discussion on this. Seek outside advice.
Create strategies to improve.

YES →

Can staff define the task? —NO→ Consider decision-making aspects of communication in school. Involve head and staff in discussion on ways to improve decision-making.

YES →

Is there someone to take responsibility for coordinating and liaising the project? —NO→ Refer to Headteacher.
Was task correctly defined? — more discussion.

YES ↓

Does the coordinator know where to go for support? —NO→ Contact local Teachers' Centre.
Contact advisers/Inspectorate.
Contact specialist resource centres.
Contact local institution of teacher education.

YES ↓

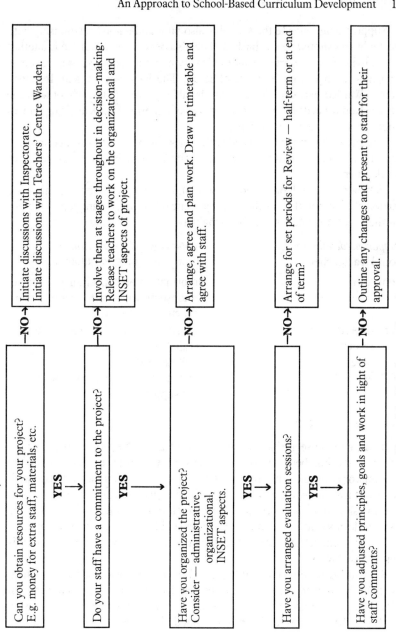

Figure 8.1 Flow diagram of questions and remedial strategies

Support from outside the school is also vital and a good relationship with local advisers should be established. The Teachers' Centre Warden is another key individual whose brief includes identifying and planning in-service developments, both centre- and school-based. The local adviser and Teachers' Centre Warden between them should be able to provide the school with the information it needs on resources, sources of expertise and schools or centres where good practice is in evidence.

It is also to be hoped that local authorities will be able to respond in practical terms and increasingly to make funds available for this form of development.

However, if one looks more closely at the kinds of support which are needed, it becomes obvious that there are one or two important gaps. One can list the support needed in the following way:

Support needed for project	*Support needed for coordinator*
from Headteacher	information on curriculum area
from staff	information on consultancy skills (relationships with staff, group dynamics, etc.)
from LEA, in terms of — resources — time	information on what resources are available to schools and how one applies for them
from Advisers	an outside reference point for advice and support

from Teachers' Centre

It can now be seen that the support needed for the project itself is quite clear-cut and has been thoroughly discussed. However the support for the coordinator is certainly not formalized. If he or she knows the authority well, the coordinator will know where to go for help with curriculum matters and who to ask about resources etc. However, this takes time. It also makes the task a little more difficult. Local authorities could easily organize and publicize the services which they already provide in order to be more responsive to this school-based work.

But it is highly unlikely that there will be any provision or courses which will help the coordinator with advice on relationships or group dynamics — in effect, the process side of his or her work. There does not appear to be any way in which advice of this kind can be obtained. Similarly, there is no reference point for the coordinator outside his or her school. It should be possible for the Teachers' Centre to organize a local support group for schools working on the development of their own curricula.

In fact, it may be that the role and work of Teachers' Centre Wardens should be reconsidered. For there appears to be a grass-roots movement in favour of school-based curriculum development and a corresponding bias in researchers and administrators. If school-based projects are not to founder as so many others have, it is vital that sound support systems are set up between these two layers and the Teachers' Centre would appear to be strategically placed to meet this need.

Summary and conclusions

This chapter has attempted to analyse many of the elements involved in school-based curriculum development, to focus thinking on some particular aspects of this process and to organize these into a framework which might offer support to the innovating teacher or school.

'Support' appears to be a key concept in school-based curriculum development and the provision of support from outside the school was considered, with the conclusion that support for a school-based project can often be found within the services already provided by the local authority.

A fundamental gap in the provision is evident, however, when the professional, managerial needs of the coordinator are considered. If school-based curriculum development is to be successful in enabling schools continuously to review and modify their practice, then facilities are needed to support this 'process' aspect of curriculum development.

It is obvious that the responsibility for providing this kind of support rests with LEAs. However, if innovating schools create pressure for such support through their requests for assistance, then it may become more readily available.

Certainly the Inner London Education Authority has adopted an imaginative approach to this problem in one of its divisions. The following chapter outlines the school-focused support which it has made available to some of its schools.

CHAPTER 9

SUPPORTING CURRICULUM DEVELOPMENT — CASE STUDY OF A SCHOOL-FOCUSED SUPPORT SCHEME

ELAINE BALL

The previous chapter outlined a framework for school-based curriculum development and suggested that support was needed for such initiatives. This chapter describes a school-focused support scheme established in one division of the Inner London Education Authority.

The distinction between school-based and school-focused curriculum development needs to be clarified. The important distinguishing characteristic might be considered to be the source of the initiative. For it would seem that school-based development begins from and is located in the school, following the lines of Havelock's Problem-Solving model (1971). Outsiders may be invited in to help resolve a problem, but, if the initiative has arisen from the school itself, then the project might be described as school-based. On the other hand, a school-focused approach has been described as 'targeted on the needs of a particular school or group within a school' (Bolam 1978, p.25), and this seems to imply that the initiative here has sprung from an outside agency. The actual activity may take place on site or off site and, equally importantly, may be internally provided by certain school staff or externally provided by an outside agency such as a college or a university (Bolam and Baker 1978).

On this definition the Curriculum Support Team project should be described as school-focused. The teams are responsible to the Inspectorate, but their curiculum development services are made available to schools. The task to be undertaken is negotiated with the school and from then on the work, for the period of the project, is based at the school.

The following case study is one team member's perception of the project at the end of a two-year period.

Background to the establishment of three support teams in one ILEA Division

Within the ILEA, an annual review of the work of each division used to take place, at which reports were made by the Inspectors to the Schools Sub-Committee of the Education Committee. During the 1978 review, it was apparent that once again one particular division appeared to be faring worse than others, with children attaining below average results on comparability tests in maths, English and verbal reasoning. The problems faced by schools in an area of multi-deprivation with a high proportion of children for whom English is a second language were outlined. The Divisional Inspector was then asked what might be done to help schools in his division and invited to submit proposals to the Schools Sub-Committee.

The Divisional and Primary Inspectors felt strongly that any additional input in terms of extra teachers may have been lost because of the high incidence of teacher absenteeism in the division. The extra teachers may have been used in a supply capacity instead of providing opportunities to improve the work of the schools. If a system could be devised whereby the teachers worked for the Inspectorate, this problem could be circumvented. Thus it was formerly proposed to the committee (ILEA Report 8693, 1978) that 'three teams of three experienced and successful teachers be established so that each team can work for a period of one term in an individual school using their expertise to help in overcoming the particular problems faced there' (op. cit., item 7).

When questioned about how this suggestion had been arrived at, the Inspectors indicated that their proposal had been more intuitive than built upon any particular theory of curriculum development. They admitted, however, that their response may well have been influenced by the then current groundswell of interest in school-based and school-focused development.

The proposal was accepted and funds were granted for one year. It was hoped that the teachers in each team would provide a balance of curricular interests and experience across the Primary age range. It was envisaged that each team would spend one term in a school 'working closely alongside teachers to enhance the quality of children's learning' (ILEA 1979). It was also agreed that some form of evaluation should be built into the project. This was undertaken by the Research and Statistics branch of the ILEA who decided to adopt an illuminative case-study approach. The project was launched in spring 1979 with one team operating a pilot scheme in an open-plan school.

The subsequent Research and Statistics study (Jayne 1979) indicated that the strategy of using a team to work with the staff of a school to improve its curriculum was 'viable and productive' (op. cit., p.8), but drew attention to the following points:

(i) the difficulties of undertaking this innovatory work under such constraints of time;

(ii) the need for the clarification of the objectives of the exercise and a definition of what constitutes successful practice;

(iii) the need for the preparation of the host school;

(iv) the need for preparation and support of the team.

The last three points would seem to be contributory factors to some of the problems posed by the first.

Strategies have been continually evolving in an attempt to cope with the problems arising from points two and three, but steps were taken to deal with the fourth point as soon as the project became fully operational in September 1979. For, following initial induction activities and visits to specialist centres and resource bases within the ILEA, the teams arranged to meet one afternoon a week at the Teachers' Centre, spending part of the time on (a) discussing and planning for the work of their individual schools, and (b) providing mutual support and sharing ideas with the rest of the nine team members. In addition, it was agreed that a joint meeting would take place every three weeks for a half-day training session when teams would meet to discuss matters of mutual concern, review literature and reports on other INSET projects, hear outside speakers and consult with the Divisional Inspector and Teachers' Centre staff. Also the Research and Statistics officers were available in a consultancy capacity during the first year of the project. These strategies were an attempt to deal with the team's need for preparation and support.

Points (ii) and (iii) were more difficult to deal with at this stage as the new team members were most concerned to clarify their roles and were somewhat apprehensive of the open-ended nature of the work which they were undertaking. Extended preparation time for the school was obviously not possible as the term had begun and schools had expectations of tasks being undertaken as soon as possible.

This then outlines the background to the establishment of Primary Curriculum Support teams in one ILEA Division. It has explained what the teams were and indicated what they set out to do. What it has not touched upon is how the work was undertaken. This has been concisely indicated in a recent article prepared for the National Association of Primary Education Journal.

After eighteen months' working together, the teams further defined their work as follows:

> The Curriculum Support Team do not attempt to produce learning packages for a school, but are more concerned to observe, discuss and participate in the curriculum development process with the teachers involved. The support given by a team during their term in school varies according to the particular circumstances of the school. They may work with individual teachers, groups of teachers, the whole staff or any combination of these the school decides upon. (NAPE 1982)

In short, it is not the content of the curriculum area which is important but rather the processes which are involved, and Stenhouse has drawn attention to the importance of the teacher in this approach, stating that 'curriculum development is about teachers' self-development' (1980, p.255). This was, therefore, a key feature in the evolution of a team philosophy which could underpin their work, and a clear understanding of this was extremely important as the strategies adopted would be constructed on this foundation.

However, it must be pointed out that the following discussion is a subjective account and represents the views and perceptions of one team member. An attempt has been made to balance this with comments from the Research and Statistics reports and by attempting to provide practical evidence for some of the statements made.

Towards a philosophy for Curriculum Support teams

It is significant that the team members were not given a detailed job specification at the outset of the project. No clear principles of procedure for their work were set out. The Inspectorate's philosophy, though implicit in their expectations, was not clearly stated. Their influence must have been reflected to an extent in the team members they appointed. Beyond this, the Research and Statistics officers arranged for the team members to have copies of several articles from recent journals on innovation, consultancy and school-focused curriculum development — articles by Bolam (1978), Agyris (1970), Eraut (1977) and Hooton (1977). The choice of articles is interesting in that they highlighted the process aspect of the work in schools and illustrated a concern with the organizational well-being of the school. The Inspectorate's stance encouraged the team members to become actively involved in evolving their own philosophy — which was built upon the continuous self-evaluation and reflection which would take place within the teams of three and the larger group of nine.

Thus the points which will be considered below were not necessarily formulated within the first term or indeed within the first year. When they did emerge, principles were not always unanimously accepted by all team members. The development of the teams' philosophy can best be understood through their relationships with the schools, the Headteachers and the Inspectorate and its link to practice can be clearly seen if one considers the teams' roles with regard to each of these groups.

The role of the support teams in relation to the staff of schools

The problem of defining and clarifying the team's role became a major concern of members. During the first term's work, they were at great pains to indicate that theirs was not an advisory or inspectorial role. A local newspaper article in November 1979 highlighted the misinterpretation which was possible. The article (*Hackney Gazette*, 13 November 1979) stated that ' a team of troubleshooters had been set up to enforce better standards and a common teaching programme'. The paper was asked to print a retraction and the Curriculum Support team and staff in one school jointly produced a letter which was circulated to all schools in the Division.

The letter indicated a concern to develop a supportive relationship with teachers — one which emphasizes collaborative professional development rather than a deficit theory of teachers (Elliott 1977). Thus the teams see themselves operating as equals with teachers in the curriculum development work and sharing with teachers the practical realities of teaching practice.

The role of the support teams in relation to Headteachers

The team's role in relation to the Head is an important one and often presents teams with problems. Bearing in mind the last paragraph, where do the team's loyalties lie? Research and Statistics (Jayne 1981a) have reported on the importance of involving the Head, who often leads curriculum initiatives in the school. This point is also made by Golby, Crane and Tann (1981), who consider the potential of school-focused work with consultants as a threat to his traditional authority. They suggest that consultants need to be aware of this issue and also of how subtly a Head can manipulate the consultant's role. Thus it must be clear that the team members need to work closely with the Head but that they do not report to him on the capacities or abilities of his staff. The implications of a supportive agency, in this case the Curriculum Support team, adopting an authoritative role would be disastrous for the generation of an atmosphere of mutual trust, which might be considered as a consultant's primary task.

This issue sparked off a long and heated debate amongst team members when one team, following an unsatisfactory term in a difficult school, attempted a written analysis of why and how things had gone wrong. This they wished to discuss with the Head and the Inspectorate. Some members in other teams felt that such action would be a breach of the trust which so much of their work depended upon. The discussion had three important results:

(i) It confirmed and clarified the teams' relationship to the staff and the Heads of schools, providing a precedent which could be referred to on other occasions.

(ii) Secondly, it marked a turning point in the relationship between the teams. It revealed at once how the three teams were evolving their own philosophies and work style.

(iii) Conversely, it demonstrated their interdependence by highlighting how the actions of one team could affect the work of others. (For example, had it become generally known that teams were producing reports for Heads and Inspectors to which staff had no access, then the consequences for the project as a whole could have been considerable.)

Generally, however, teams have tended to assume a democratic stance and have attempted to involve Heads, senior staff and teachers jointly in the project. This has often led to a shift in the decision-making style of the school while the team has been there. Certainly the incorporation into the staff of three extra individuals, often with an organizing role and power of agenda at meetings, can result in considerable changes.

Argyris (1970) has written of intervention activities in other settings, and claimed that three primary tasks exist for consultants:

(i) to generate valid information;

(ii) to enable the client to make free and informed choices about the nature of the intervention;

(iii) to enable a high degree of commitment to the change and its implementation.

In order for genuinely free and informed choices to be generated, it would appear that (a) the whole staff must be viewed as the client and (b) that staff must have the political muscle within the school to make the reality of free and informed choice a possibility. Moves have been made in this direction in many of the schools which have worked with a support team. It would sometimes appear that the style which is established at meetings carries over after the team has left. This certainly emphasizes the incidental 'process' nature of the team's impact and would seem to reinforce a point made by Keast and Carr (1979) that in 'school-focused work the nature of the consultancy always becomes a process type at some stage'.

However, it has also been observed, when the Curriculum Support team has returned to a school for follow-up meetings, that the Head appears to be adopting a tighter control than previously on the decision-making. It may be that the teams have taken too strong a role previously and have left a 'power vacuum' in the school which is filled by the Head. Teams are concerned to support the postholders in adopting a stronger role and work alongside them to plan their contribution at working party sessions and staff meetings, but it must be apparent that, within the space of one term, such major changes in work style may not be possible. The teams, too, are often under great pressure to 'get through' a considerable task and it is possible that they too often find it simpler and more efficient to hold on to the reins of the project themselves.

A matter for concern, however, is that staff expectations of decisional participation may be raised and not fulfilled (Belasco and Alutto 1972). The extent and the significance of such developments will only be revealed by a longitudinal review.

The role of the support teams in relation to the Inspectorate

It has been stated that the Inspectorate did not lay down any 'ground rules' for the curriculum support teams and that these evolved gradually as the project progressed. However, the Inspectorate's overall responsibility for the project involved them in attendance and discussion at the joint meetings which were held among the nine members. It became very apparent early on that team members modified their behaviour when the inspectors were present. Meetings between the members, particularly early on in the project, were often sessions when the team could talk very frankly about their problems and frustrations. Schools and often teachers were mentioned by name. These were relaxed and often therapeutic sessions where other teams could be used as a sounding board and their advice sought.

This issue became critical during a debriefing meeting at the end of a term when Headteachers representing the local Headteachers' consultative body and a senior inspector were invited along. Team members felt inhibited and reluctant to talk freely about their term's work in schools. The meeting was an awkward one and was followed by a team discussion on confidentiality and the potential power which teams had to colour opinions about schools and teachers in the division.

Thereafter, a distinction appeared at meetings. Formal joint team meetings were held where agendas were prepared and minutes taken. Discussion of a more confidential nature took place at weekly informal meetings of the nine members, plus the Research and Statistics officers. (It was felt that the R. and S. joint role as both evaluators and consultants to the team granted them a neutral status.)

Nevertheless it was clear that the teams were accountable to the Inspectorate. Therefore, although it was not requested, some teams began producing half-term and/or end of term accounts of their work in the schools. One team during their first term produced a subjective report on the work which was going on at the school. Although it was unintentional, these necessarily included evaluative comments and it was realized that school staff would have to be involved to balance such subjective judgements. This precipitated lengthy discussion on evaluative reports and the teams' accountability, not only to the Inspectorate, but also to the schools.

It also raised questions about the purpose of evaluation. Ultimately four principles were agreed by this team which indicated a shift to a more democratic form of evaluation (MacDonald 1978):

(i) that accounts could only be produced which could be first presented to the schools;

(ii) that the purpose of such accounts should be that of formative evaluation;

(iii) that schools should be invited to comment on the accounts or submit a parallel one;

(iv) that accounts could only be released to go to the Inspectorate with the school's permission.

Thus it can be seen that the philosophy, or at least one team member's version of it, evolved through the practice of the support teams' work. In essence, the threads of that philosophy centre on attitudes to teachers' professional development, a respect for confidentiality, a democratic approach to both decision-making and evaluation and an awareness of the value of the organizational processes which the teams have been involved in. These points would seem to focus largely on the creation of an atmosphere of mutual trust between team members and school and would, therefore, seem to suggest that the creation of such a climate may well be regarded as a primary task for consultants in schools.

Strategies for supporting schools

Task definition

It would appear that the work of curriculum support teams comprises a form of consultancy and most kinds of consultancy can be assigned to one of two categories — task consultancy and process consultancy. Bolam (1978) has suggested that the 'task consultant will in all probability find himself working on fairly concrete and recognizable problems such as the teaching of reading, the evaluation of pupil performance or curriculum development. The process consultant on the other hand will be involved in helping the school with less obvious problems like its underlying decision-making and problem-solving procedures; he would thus be considering things like the departmental and school staff meetings, the way in which communication took place in the school and, ultimately, the nature and allocation of power and authority in the school' (op. cit., p.28).

Process consultancy embodies an organization and development tradition which is more familiar in countries such as the USA. It may be that schools in this country may respond more readily to a form of task consultancy, although it has also been noted (Keast and Carr 1979) that all forms of consultancy become a process type at some stage.

Thus the work of the teams normally centres around a specific task such as the establishment of a science or maths curriculum for a school. The school defines the task before the team begins work in the school. This can present major problems as Havelock (1971) and Keast and Carr (1979) have noted. Accurate perception of a problem and diagnosis of a need would presuppose that a school is at quite a sophisticated stage of organizational development. However, often the task or area which is defined reflects only a superficial concern which is a manifestation of a much more fundamental issue which needs closer consideration. For example, a desire to set up a resource centre in a school may reflect a need to consider how resource-based or teacher-directed the children's work is. Therefore, in spite of the fact that the school defines the task before the team arrives, some form of review, reinterpretation or flexibility must be woven into the project. On the other hand, it would be foolhardy for the team to take a highhanded approach and suggest that they really know what is best. It is extremely important that the school's contribution is valued and that the team handles this delicate stage of the project with great tact. There was a case in which a team refused one brief and renegotiated another, and it may be significant that this proved one of the more 'difficult' schools in which the teams have worked.

Another important issue arising from this style of task definition is the need for clarification of meanings and expectations of the task. The team has an organizing responsibility in this respect and should be able to indicate clearly what the scope of the task might be and reveal the alternative strategies for implementation which staff might like to consider.

Models for the team's work in a school

The evolution of 'models' of ways of implementing a task in a school has been an important development in the work of one support team. This represents one of the organizing functions of the teams which is so difficult to define and explain. Such models usually represent to the staff a view of what the work of the team might look like and are normally drawn up following lengthy discussions with the staff and Head of a school. An important aspect of the exercise is that of communication. It should describe how the Curriculum Support team views the possibilities and scope of the work, and staff should be invited to challenge or reinterpret this where necessary. Such a model will often comprise the following:

(i) a clear statement of the 'task';

(ii) a list of the staff who are to be involved in the work;

(iii) alternative strategies showing how the team can arrange and timetable its work with teachers.

Examples are given below of task descriptions which were drawn up for two schools. (School A is an Infant school and B is Junior.)

School A
1. The team should concern itself primarily with scientific enquiry and measurement in maths.

2. An attempt should be made to integrate science and maths with other areas of the curriculum.

3. An attempt should be made to involve all teachers.

4. The work should take into account the realities of classroom organization.

5. Where possible, an attempt should be made to extend interest in the work developed beyond the school.

School B
1. The team should concern itself with topic/project work.

2. An attempt should be made to determine the range of skills, concepts and experiences which might be developed through project work.

3. An attempt should be made to examine how curriculum areas relate to one another.

4. An attempt should be made to explore the possibilities of a structure/framework/system which seeks to avoid repetition of activities in project work.

5. The team should work initially alongside the following teachers: Mrs L., Mrs D., Mr N., Mr P.

In these two examples, it was indicated which staff would be involved. How this is decided varies from school to school. In some the Head makes a choice. This is often a cause of concern as there may well be a 'hidden agenda' or purpose to such selection. However, in most cases it is much more open and staff are invited to become a part of the project. The extent of involvement has varied from a total staff commitment to the team working more intensively with a small number of teachers.

The actual strategies for working with teachers obviously vary greatly according to the task, the number of teachers involved and the style of the support team. But an example of such strategies can be given by representing the two models which were chosen by Schools A and B above (Figures 9.1 and 9.2).

It can be seen that in the first model (Figure 9.1), the whole school, including the Head, took an active part in the term's work and, in the second example (Figure 9.2), the team worked initially with four key postholders who then intended to work themselves with the remainder of the staff in their school.

Both these examples demanded that detailed timetables be produced as the team needs to balance the time it spends releasing teachers with that which each team member will spend working alongside teachers on both planning and practical classroom activities.

Such models produce a clear indication for all concerned of the overall

School A

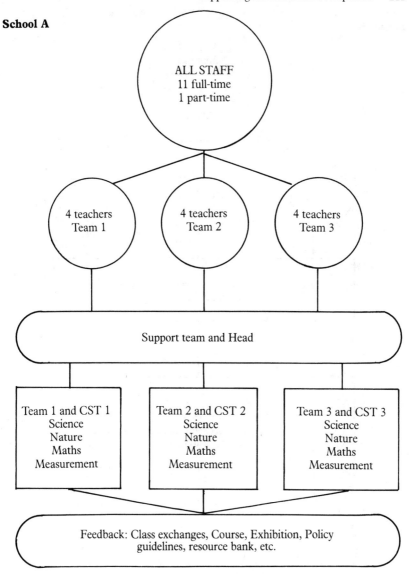

Figure 9.1

School B

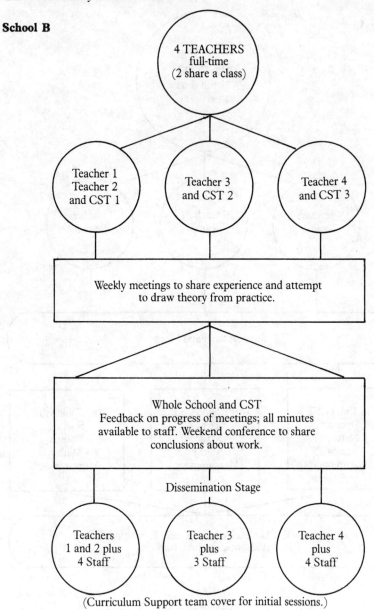

Figure 9.2

structure of the project in the school and the Curriculum Support team's responsibility. However, it does not clarify the contribution of other partners (teachers, Head, etc.). This is probably understandable, as the teams had to clarify their own roles before they could look closely at others. Much of the discussion which follows was precipitated by a one-day conference, held for teachers and Headteacher who had worked with the Curriculum Support teams, to reflect on and evaluate their contribution to the schools. At the conference it became clear that the schools were sometimes critical of the teams' attitudes and work or were not clear about their real emphasis, and, conversely, that teams were occasionally critical of schools where after-school meetings were poorly attended, of classes which never had sufficient materials (e.g. pencils etc.), and of a lack of support from teachers whose classes they would be called upon to cover. Thus the idea of a 'contract' which would go further in clarifying the work and spelling out all the partners' responsibilities began to evolve.

Towards a contract for schools and support teams

Golby and Fish (1980) have produced a very clear analysis of some of the problems which consultants in schools face and they suggest the drawing up of a formal contract.

> We believe that it is desirable to put the operation on a slightly more formal basis, both because consultancy is a new departure involving new rules for all to learn and, most particularly, because consultancy necessarily implies a two-way traffic of information and response not present in traditional theory-led courses . . . (op. cit., p.86).

They suggest that a list be drawn up of the rights and responsibilities of both clients and consultants. For the consultant, responsibilities would include listening to the client's views, respecting the client's confidences and allowing clients to come into the relationship only on a voluntary basis. His rights would include insisting on feedback and the right to challenge unconvincing statements, to serious consideration of any reports and the right to be informed at the time and directly of any dissatisfaction. The client, on the other hand, has a responsibility to keep the consultant fully informed, to be present at meetings and to be committed to ultimate group decisions on action. His rights, however, would include such things as being fully informed of all the consultant's enquiries and activities affecting him, the right to enter minority or dissenting views and to have them formally registered, and the right to inform consultants of any dissatisfaction with meetings.

It has already been stated that the teams found that a statement of the task and of a programme for completing it was of great value. They also found, following a report on Heads' and teachers' views of the project (Jayne 1981b) that schools were nevertheless not always clear what the focus of the project was. Similarly they were critical of how the team members spent their time early in the term. They felt things got off to a slow start and obviously had little appreciation of the preparation, planning and organization which the team often found it necessary to concentrate on at this stage.

These two points of clarity and accountability seemed to reinforce the need for some form of contract along the lines suggested by Golby and Fish (1980). The Research and Statistics group in the above report made a similar recommendation. 'Perhaps a clearer identity of purpose and method would be helpful. A more explicit contract could be negotiated, stating objectives and strategies or methods to be used as well as clarifying the roles and responsibilities of the teams and the resident school staff' (op.cit., p.7). They made the further important point that, if, as is the case, teams view their work as a three-stage activity;

1 preparatory stage when school staff collectively review practice and establish needs, priorities and working strategies,

2 the work with the team as agreed by negotiation,

3 continuation, dissemination and other follow-through activities (after the team has gone),

then it can be seen that the role of the teachers is paramount, as they are the 'prime actors in the first and third stage with a shared responsibility in the second stage' (op. cit., p.6).

Therefore, the support teams evolved a discussion document which could form the basis for the negotiation of a contract with schools. Many of the topics and questions raised in that document imply that the school should have a much more active role than has often been the case. Also some deliberately raise 'process' aspects, such as the section on decision-making. This would have the effect of making much more explicit the process tasks which tend to be implicit in most cases.

The support teams felt keenly that the idea of a contract was valuable but that it should not become an end in itself. Teams should use the sections or ideas from the discussion document which they felt were most suitable to them, the school and the nature of the task. It was felt that this should be especially emphasized as most of the team members, following two years of secondment, were due to return to schools and new teams were being formed. These new teams should not feel bound by a style of work which they had no hand in evolving. Thus the discussion document stands for them to use or not. However, if used wisely, it might help them to avoid many of the difficulties which teams often experience, such as the pressures placed upon them by conflicting demands and expectations from different people in a school. For it illustrates the shared nature of responsibility for the project and thereby strengthens commitment to it. Also it provides a good foundation for review and formative evaluation. However, the full potential of such contracts remains to be explored.

Summary and conclusions

It is significant that the 1979—80 ILEA *Review of In-Service Education and Training for Teachers* concluded with the Education Officer's comments that he would ask the Central Advisory Committee to advise him on the 'development of school-focused in-service training in the authority' (para. 10.4). From a nil expenditure during that year on this aspect of INSET, the 1981—82 estimate allowed £255,000 for school-focused development. This would appear to be a small amount compared with the £2,195,000 which has been budgeted for secondments to serving teachers. However, in March 1981, the Education Officer outlined priorities in in-service education for 1981/82. In stating the aims and methods of INSET he commented that 'the development of school-focused INSET has encouraged schools to reflect upon their INSET needs and to become more involved in the planning and implementation of INSET strategies' (ILEA 1981, para.4). He went on to note that the proposed annual and quinquennial reviews (DES 1981) would encourage schools to review regularly their INSET policy and to develop and assess their INSET programmes. He also suggested that the revised doocument *Keeping the School Under Review* (ILEA 1981) would have a greater emphasis on the importance of INSET.

It was also suggested in the above report that the emphasis of the authority's INSET programme should be shifted:

> The existing pattern of INSET provision within the Authority has developed over a period of time and the balance between its various components has been the result of an evolutionary process. If the INSET programme is to achieve its aim of improving the quality of learning by pupils, and if this in turn depends upon meeting the specific needs of teachers then it is desirable that some changes

in the existing balance of provision should occur. School-focused INSET has operated successfully in a variety of curriculum areas for some time and in 1980/81 resources were made available to support further school-focused projects in primary, secondary and special schools. These projects will be evaluated at the end of the current school year. The Central Advisory Committee on Induction and In-Service Training (CAC) has set up a working party to make recommendations about the future development of school-focused INSET (op. cit:, para. 5).

School-focused in-service education has obviously been followed with interest by the Schools Sub-Committee and it is significant that resources have again been made available for a third year and are now a part of the authority's 'rolling programme'. Thus it would appear in the short term that this work is regarded by many as successful.

But it is doubtful whether evidence will be rapidly available that standards in the schools in this particular division have risen dramatically. The area may continue to experience a high incidence of economic and social deprivation coupled with large numbers of pupils for whom English is a second language.

However, it is in the nature of school-focused curriculum development that the needs of specific children and specific teachers be taken into consideration. Teachers have often been encouraged and given time to observe their children closely and consider the match which is being made between the child's level of development and the task which he is set. Also emphasis on more stimulating materials or ways of working in schools may result in more interest and motivation in children. But perhaps the most important result (albeit indirect) might be in the attitudes of teachers. Teacher turnover had appeared to be high in the division and Primary school staffs often had low expectations of the children. How can teacher morale be measured? If it can be indicated even in part by attendance at courses, conferences or lectures, or the development of self-help groups for postholders in particular curriculum areas, then the good support which these activities currently receive may be significant. The teams have tried whenever possible to link teachers with other schools — often schools in which the teams had worked previously, where some interesting curriculum development has gone on. Some of these schools seemed to have acquired recognition within the division with the result that the teachers have gained in confidence and extended their contacts with other schools.

Thus tangible results of the teams' work are unlikely to be reflected in psychometric terms, but perhaps the long-term value of their work may rest in the impact which has been made on teachers and the schools. Ultimately this should be apparent in the quality of work which the children achieve. Another result of this project is the in-service experience which team members have had. This has provided them with a unique opportunity for professional development and it is significant that most team members, having completed their period of secondment, are returning to or taking up senior posts in schools in the division.

Research and Statistics Branch have suggested that, from having an overall aim of improving the quality of the children's learning, a subsidiary aim of the teams' work might be to enhance the school's ability to facilitate teacher-learning through co-operative and collaborative processes. They conclude that 'ultimately staff should be able to maintain the dynamic for self-renewal and change. In such schools there may well be a greater likelihood of sustained change affecting the educational experiences afforded the children at the school' (Jayne 1981b, p.7).

CHAPTER 10

THE EDUCATION OF TEACHERS
GEVA BLENKIN AND VIC KELLY

It will be clear from all of the foregoing chapters, but perhaps particularly from Chapters 8 and 9, that, if we are to promote the kind of education we have been concerned to describe and analyse, a crucial factor will be the quality of the teachers. Education, as opposed to teaching, is a highly sophisticated activity. To teach someone something can be a relatively straightforward matter; hence many people in many different contexts do it more or less successfully all the time. Our view of education, however, is of a much more complex process or set of processes. To educate, that is to attend to and promote the development of immature minds and persons, requires far more than mere teaching. It thus calls for qualities of a special kind and for a more sophisticated form of preparation than the term 'teacher training' would suggest.

This, as we shall see, has been too seldom appreciated and there are many both within and outside the teaching profession who are still happy to settle for a simplistic concept of teaching and for simple, not to say naive, forms of teacher training. Recent years have seen some, unfortunately all too rare, developments of a kind likely to produce the teachers our notion of education requires but there have also been, and still are, many trends in the opposite direction and our concern is that, if these continue, any progress that has been made towards our ideal will be not merely halted but even reversed.

Furthermore, it will not be sufficient merely to get our initial courses of teacher education right. The continued development of education depends upon the continued development of teachers so that, as the last two chapters in particular have demonstrated, if we wish to forward curriculum development, we must do this by promoting the professional development of teachers. And, if we are to do that, we must provide them with many different kinds of support, pre-eminent among which will be appropriate forms of in-service education.

This chapter will, therefore, attempt to do three things. First, it will attempt to show what is being done, and thus what can be done, in some places to provide aspiring teachers with the kind of preparation that will assist them to develop the qualities we believe the educator needs. Secondly, it will attempt to describe some of the recent and current developments in teacher education in the UK and to pick out their implications for the development of more sophisticated approaches to schooling. And thirdly, it will look at the field of in-service education, to explore not only what is being done there but also what might be done to assist teachers to develop a more adequate range of responses to the complex demands of education.

A 'process' approach to teacher education

It will be clear to those who have read the earlier chapters of this book what kinds of qualities teachers will need if they are to meet the demands of this kind of education. It will be equally clear that they will need a wide range of skills which will be professional skills in the full sense of that term, that is they will need skills not of a kind that will enable them to carry out their tasks like tradesmen but of a kind that will make possible both the exercise of professional judgement and the translation of this into professional practice. It is for this reason that we prefer to use the term 'teacher education' with its emphasis, at least in our eyes, on the notion of the development of understanding and powers of decision-making, or 'teacher preparation', a largely neutral term, to that of 'teacher training', a phrase which suggests to us the development of a much more limited range of skilled techniques, of a kind which, in themselves, will not take any teacher very far in the schools of today.

Among the professional skills that teachers need — and we would want to argue that all teachers need these whether they are committed to our view of education or not — are several which we would like to pick out as especially relevant to our case.

They will, of course, need a range of practical skills which will enable them to carry out what they decide to do, skills to produce the materials, the displays and the equipment which will forward their teaching, skills to organize their classroom and their children, skills to deal with the dozens of day-to-day problems their pupils will present them with, and many more.

All such skills, however, important as they are and necessary as it is to assist aspiring teachers to acquire them, are largely useless, and in fact positively counter-productive to education, if they are not backed by something far more profound. A doctor highly skilled at removing appendices but totally lacking in the understanding needed to make decisions about when his skill should be employed would not be merely ineffective he would be a positive menace to life and limb. Similarly, a teacher with a range of teaching skills but no basis upon which to make the judgements that are a necessary prerequisite to the exercising of such skills will be both ineffective and, indeed, harmful. The preparation of teachers, then, must include the development of this kind of professional awareness and understanding. This is what is necessary if teachers are to be educated rather than merely trained. And it is the proper function of their Education courses, both theoretical and professional, to assist them towards this kind of professional development. It is also, incidentally, vital that this assistance be maintained throughout their careers in teaching and especially during the first few years.

There are many aspects of the professional awareness and understanding we are attempting to identify. Several of these we would like to emphasize here. First, we would stress the importance of the teacher developing an awareness of the many dimensions of children's learning which our earlier chapters have drawn attention to. To see learning as a purely cognitive activity is to miss all or most of its educational point. The important things, in our view, for teachers to be asking about children's learning are not just how skilled they have become or how much knowledge they have stored away but how this has contributed to their growth and development. That is a question which introduces to the scene considerations of many other aspects of their development, social, emotional and moral as well as intellectual. It is the lack of attention given to these dimensions of education that is at the root of many of the problems faced by schools today.

An awareness of the multi-faceted nature of education must bring with it also a sensitivity to the individuality of children, as expressed both in their needs and in their reactions to the experiences they are offered. Too many teachers have a preconceived idea of the reaction they wish to see to what they offer their pupils, so that they are inclined to regard any different form of reaction as unacceptable, as 'wrong' or even as subversive. An appreciation of the individuality of each pupil and of the need to promote this — for it is difficult to justify the use of schools to try to cast everyone in the same mould — must lead to the idea of individual provision for individual needs and of the need not only for tolerance of individual reactions but even for a welcoming acceptance and encouragement of them. This is not an attitude that comes easy to a teacher faced by thirty-five such individuals, but the more stress we place on conformity the less we are likely to assist the personal growth of our charges.

This must in turn lead to the adoption of a more 'open' approach to knowledge, to a rejection of that traditional dogmatism over what shall count and what shall not count as worthwhile knowledge, and thus as the 'proper' concern of schools. For to be dogmatic over this is to restrict our offerings to that 'educational' knowledge (Keddie 1971) which some of our sociologists have for some time been suggesting is a major factor in the alienation of many pupils from their schooling, and to deny the validity of the children's existing knowledge, that 'commonsense' knowledge which has to be the starting-point for any learning that is to be truly developmental.

These are just a few of the features of the enhanced awareness on the part of teachers that we regard as essential for the development of education as we view it. They are features which suggest to us that we need to rethink many of our traditional attitudes to the preparation of teachers. In particular, they suggest the need for courses which lay more stress on the study of children and of the complex processes of education than on the study of traditional subjects. For the latter kind of emphasis must lead to that dogmatism and those entrenched positions that militate against the attainment of the former. In general, then, these are considerations which lead us to claim that teachers of the kind we wish to see can only be produced in any quantity by the longer, three- or four-year courses of teacher education. To offer an intending teacher a short course of preparation lasting one year at the end of a period of three years spent studying one or two subjects is in our view to invite that very subject-centred attitude to schooling that we find unsatisfactory.

This, then, becomes the first point to be made when we turn from trying to identify the qualities and professional 'skills' teachers need to some attempt to suggest how they can be helped to develop these qualities and skills. For our first point must be that it is very difficult to help any but the most outstanding recruits to the profession to do this in a one-year course, particularly when, as we have just suggested, the mere existence of such a route to the profession might well be interpreted as implying that knowledge of a subject forms a very large part of the teacher's armoury, a view which is often compounded by the emphasis placed in the education year on 'subject-method'. Time is needed to assist the young teacher to grow in the ways we have suggested are desirable.

Time, however, in itself is not enough. The right kind of help also is vital so that the right kind of use is made of this time. And we must now turn to a consideration of some of the forms this might take.

The major elements and emphases of this kind of course

One of the major advantages offered by the longer courses of teacher preparation is the scope they provide for the interweaving of the various elements of
the course. To say that they provide this scope is not, of course, to say that
advantage is always taken of it. But, in our view, a very important aspect of a
proper form of teacher education is this interweaving of the elements and,
before we begin to identify the elements themselves, this general point about
their important interrelationships must be made. If the course does not deliberately set out to assist the student to relate the professional skills that are
being developed, the theoretical understanding that is being fostered and the
knowledge-content that is being acquired so that they add up to a coherent
and cohesive totality, then the teachers it produces will be unbalanced in their
competences. Clearly, a course in which the study of a subject or subjects is
completed before the professional preparation is begun (or, in some cases,
even contemplated) will offer far less scope for this kind of integration than
one in which all aspects are to be developed concurrently.

Several ways in which this integretion can be achieved will emerge as we
discuss the individual elements. It is worth stressing here, however, that it
requires a collaborative effort on the part of all concerned. It requires that
tutors responsible for various aspects of the course should plan and work
together. It requires that in the long-term we achieve a proper balance
between all the stages of teacher education — initial preparation, the first
years of teaching, including the all-important probationary year, and in-
service education. To blame the inadequacies of any one of these for poor
teaching performance is to lose sight of their total interdependence. It is naive
to think that teachers can be adequately prepared merely by working in
schools, since this will lead to an undue emphasis on the purely practical
aspects of their work. It is naive to think that they can be adequately prepared
if the focus of their work is too directly centred on the College or Department
of Education, since this will lead to an undue emphasis on the theoretical. And
it is naive to believe that we will produce good teachers if we expect to see them
emerge as 'the finished product' from any course of preparation, since this will
lead to inadequate follow-up support and continued education. If we are to
achieve a balance of the several elements of the preparation of teachers we
must also achieve a balance of the various stages of that preparation and this
necessitates the collaboration of all concerned at every stage.

Having stressed the general point that the prime need in courses of teacher
preparation is for the integration of their major elements, we can now turn to

an examination of these several elements. In broad terms, there are three of these — the development of professional skills, the promotion of theoretical understanding and the acquisition of appropriate knowledge-content — and we must look briefly at each of these in turn.

At one level, the development of professional skills suggests the acquisition of techniques for the creation of materials and displays. There is much work to be done here and many such techniques to acquire if the teacher is to be fully equipped for the job. The main point to be stressed, however, is that if our concept of 'professional skills' does not extend well beyond this level, the teacher will not be fully equipped for the job. As we suggested earlier, there are many skills the teacher needs that go well beyond the creation of teaching materials. Prime examples of such skills would include the ability to make perceptive observations of the work of children, their reactions and their interactions, and, allied to this, the ability to make helpful and constructive evaluations of their own performance in the classroom and that of others.

This clearly necessitates the provision of ample opportunities to observe the work of other teachers and fellow students. It also necessitates regular contact with a tutor or tutors whose task it is to assist in the enhancing of the student's levels of observation and resultant powers of evaluation. Much has been achieved in recent years by the development in this direction of some Professional Studies courses. In fact it might be argued that a more relevant form of intellectual rigour has entered the arena of teacher education by this route than by any other. In this connection, it is interesting to record the comment of a student on learning that we were putting this book together. She asked if we had found it more difficult than the writing of The Primary Curriculum, since she had found the written work set in connection with the Professional Studies element of her course by far the most intellectually demanding of all the tasks she had been asked to perform.

It is the linking of professional preparation with theoretical issues that creates these demands and that provides the clue for the appropriate kind of approach to the theoretical elements of the course — it must address itself to issues that are real, especially in the eyes of the students. To say this does not mean that we must only tackle those issues the student already recognizes as real; it does mean, however, that we must be able to demonstrate the relevance of whatever issues we do raise and that we must realize there is little point in raising them unless we can show the student that they are relevant.

This is best done, of course, by that linking of theoretical study to the developing first-hand experience of the student to which we continually return. It also means, however, — and this we cannot stress too highly — that the issues we raise must be genuine educational issues; an arid form of pseudo-intellectualism must result from presenting them with issues which are primarily related to the study of philosophy, psychology, sociology or the history of education. All of these may have a relevance but that relevance will derive from a prior educational relevance. In short, the only useful direction of theoretical study is from a genuine educational issue *outwards* to whatever that is of value that any other discipline can contribute rather than from the researches of those other disciplines *inwards* to education. The inadequacies of the latter approach should not need to be spelled out here; in themselves they constitute perhaps the strongest case for adopting the former line. The right kind of intellectual rigour in the study of education is that which results from a properly rigorous study of educational practices; that which derives from the study of associated disciplines must always be second-hand, largely spurious and often counter-productive.

The third major element in the preparation of teachers must, of course, be the acquisition of the knowledge that is to be shared with pupils. Much that we have said in this book, and indeed in this chapter, may suggest that we believe that this is not important. We must, therefore, begin by dispelling any such misapprehension. To stress the importance of seeing education in terms of its processes is not to argue that its content is not important; it is to claim, however, that its subject-content should not be the first and central concern. That is our position, and we must reiterate that it implies that educational planning must begin not with statements of the knowledge to be acquired but with an analysis of the processes to be promoted. And we are claiming that decisions about the knowledge to be acquired are secondary to that analysis. To use the new catch-phrase, we are concerned to promote learning *through* subjects rather than the learning *of* subjects.

This has several implications for the preparation of teachers. It suggests, for example, that if there is to be a major subject component of their courses, that component cannot be properly justified in its own terms nor in terms of what used to be called the 'personal development' of the student. The development of the student can be quite adequately attended to by other elements of the course. The justification of any subject component must be found in relation to its role in the development of the children.

This implies in turn that the selection not only of appropriate subjects but also of the appropriate content for subject courses for teachers must be made by reference to that kind of consideration. Again we may note the advantages offered here by concurrent courses which do make possible the planning of syllabuses expressly designed for intending teachers and thus of greater relevance to their needs than many courses they will pursue as part of other degree programmes. In this connection it is interesting to remember those degree courses, especially in science, where attempts have been made to introduce an element of concurrence in order to be able to plan the subject content in relation to the needs of intending teachers.

A second implication of this view of the place of subject-content in the preparation of teachers is its suggestion that for all non-specialist teachers — and, in our view, this would include at least all Primary and Middle School teachers — the provision of a range of subjects may well offer more than the intensive study of one or two. Certainly, all Primary teachers need courses in language development, in literature and in mathematics, and it cannot but be an advantage to offer them opportunities to work in one or two other areas too. To lay heavy stress on one or two subjects may be to limit seriously the teacher's scope; it is certainly to assume a continuing value and importance for the subject concerned and this is becoming increasingly more questionable.

A good deal of attention, therefore, needs to be given to the problem of finding a suitable form for the knowledge-content of teacher education courses. For it is no longer possible to make the bland assumption that to study any traditional subject must *ipso facto* be of value to the intending teacher. We must look here, as much as in other areas of the course, for the relevance and significance of the study to the professional development of the teacher.

All these elements of the course can best be attended to, and certainly the integration of them with each other can best be achieved, if they are seen to come together and focus on one central experience — that gained from the close and sustained contact of the student with children in a variety of settings. Again, a strength of the concurrent course is that it enables this kind of contact to continue over a longer period and makes possible a wider range of contexts in which the student can work with children. If there can be contact with children on educational visits, for example, in play-groups or in even more informal settings, much can be learned and a vast store of experience acquired which is applicable not only to these contexts but to the classroom itself.

Such continuous contact, however, is of limited value if it is not undertaken under the supervision and with the help of a tutor. It is naive to assume that merely to send a student to work with children is to ensure that value will be gained from the experience. Students need expert help and guidance in making observations and in analysing these, so that a tutor is needed who both shares the experience and can then, as soon as possible, discuss it with the student or students concerned.

It is at this point that it becomes possible to bring the elements of the course together. For it is in this kind of situation that the tutor can help the student to relate theoretical considerations to what has been observed in practice or, conversely, to extract theoretical questions from practical problems that have arisen. Thus the development of professional skills and of theoretical understanding can proceed hand-in-hand.

To illustrate how this might be achieved, we offer the following examples of notes we have given to some of our First School students to help them both to get the best value from their observational visits to schools and to reflect productively on those visits after they have been made.

At the very outset of the course — Year One, Term One:

Reflections on school visits: term 1

1. What kinds of response did the children make to your provision? What did you learn from their responses that will help you when you make provision in the future?

2. Comment on some of the problems you encountered when organizing your materials. How would you solve these problems if the classroom was yours?

3. Which were the most difficult aspects of the afternoon and why? Similarly, which were the most successful aspects?

4. What have you learned about selecting stories for children of this age? How much have you learned about being a story teller and how have you improved in this sphere?

5. Choose one aspect of your provision and, in the light of your reading, comment on the use that these children made of the provision and discuss what the children gained from the experience.

Please make your answers as concise as possible, drawing upon observations, actual experiences in school and background reading, where appropriate, to support your comments.

Next, some forward thinking and planning — also Year One, Term One:

Discussion points

1. How may the provision extend a child's experience? What might young children learn as a result of using the materials?

2. Discuss the variety of classroom settings in which the provision might be used. Can it be used in a variety of ways by the children or by you? List a variety of purposes to which it can be put.

3. Examine the design and organization of the materials. Suggest ways in which either or both could be improved.

4. How could the provision be added to, extended and improved?

5. Discuss both the use and the storage of the materials in the classroom.

6. Discuss the professional skills that were necessary when you produced the materials. How can you improve these skills?

7. Consider the adaptations that might be necessary when children of different ages or at different stages of development make use of the provision.

8. Discuss background reading that has helped you to deepen your understanding of this provision.

And, later, in Year Two, an example of a piece of Professional Studies work focused on a particular aspect of the curriculum, mathematics:

Mathematics in the Environment: Case Study
The Cockcroft Committee argues that teachers should try:
'. . . to develop in children *an attitude* to mathematics and *an awareness of its power to communicate and explain* which will result in mathematics being used wherever it can *illuminate* or make *more precise* an argument or enable the result of an investigation to be presented in a way which will *assist clarity and understanding* '(DES 1982, para. 329, p.96).
Bear this assertion in mind as you discuss the mathematical possibilities present in the area that your group has been given. Work as a team and prepare to report on your findings to the rest of the group.
The following points should guide your exploration of the environment.
A. List the possibilities for extending mathematical understanding whilst exploring the environment.
B. Highlight the opportunities for using mathematics to explain aspects of the environment and for communicating these aspects to others. Examine both of these elements from two points of view: in relation to your understanding as an adult, and in relation to what would possibly interest and extend the understanding of a young child.

When you discuss the possibilities for work with children, pay particular attention to the following:

a. Equipment needed to support the work.

b. Problems that could be posed that would enlist the children's interest.

c. The mathematical language that is used.

d. The kinds of measure that are necessary.

e. When a level of mathematical understanding would be necessary to explain the problem.

f. The ways that findings could be recorded (both in the field and later in the classroom).

g. When mathematical understanding was related to other experiences or helped to clarify experiences.

h. How interests would differ depending on the child's age or level of understanding and skill.

It is by encouraging this kind of reflection on experience with children, and by emphasizing that as a basis for forward planning rather than the formal planning itself, that one can lead students to an appreciation of the need to understand the processes of education, and to attain clarity over the principles upon which their work will be based, at a level which 'stating the aims and objectives of your lesson' can never bring them to. Reflective evaluation of the experiences of both teacher and children is far more important in the development of a teacher's work than detailed prestating of objectives which have never carried any teacher, whose work was not rooted in a rigid dogmatism, beyond the first few minutes of any 'lesson'. This is also the best route to the development of those professional skills we referred to earlier. For they too are far more subtle than we often appreciate and can only be developed by reflection on one's own work, and indeed on one's own mistakes.

The following extract from one student's report on her school observation visits reveals all these processes under way, and indicates that already, at the start of the second year, one student at least is beginning to appreciate at first-hand some of the principles elucidated in the earlier chapters of this book.

We started each session with a discussion related to what we were going to do. The children were always eager to participate and their level of general knowledge was good, and often greater than I had anticipated. My use of home-made reference books and cards was a great help in guiding the conversation and the pictures appeared to stimulate ideas; of greatest interest were the photos I had taken in the area around the school. The children found it amazing that 'their' environment should be in a book. They were also eager to read what I had written and would often look through the book again in pairs or individually while drinking their milk.

The children worked well at the more practical work that they did and and were able to co-operate as a group and help each other. This was very apparent when we were measuring in the playground where they used a trundle-wheel and peg-board in pairs. They had to be aware of their partner's problems and both work at the same speed to gain an accurate result, and where two children measured the same length they were within ½ metre of each other.

The general response to writing was not so enthusiastic, especially initially. The children appeared to regard writing as 'work', unrelated to other things that went on in the classroom. I attempted to make the practical work of writing easier by providing clip-boards with ruled lines so that they could write on a firm surface and could see the lines through the paper as a guide. I also provided good pencils, and work-cards so that they could work without continually coming to me for words. These provisions made their writing easier, but they still often appeared unaware of how to record what they had done. I attempted to help them by discussing exactly what they wanted to say before they started writing and by making several books of their work. I did this initially to show the children that there was a reason for recording what they had done. When I produced the first book on 'The Playground' they laughed at their own work when in a group, but enjoyed looking at the book individually. With the next book we made I talked about making the book more interesting by writing about different aspects of the use of masks. The children found this difficult to start with and did not know what to write, but having got started they all enjoyed their writing and did not want to go out at playtime or stop at lunch-time. They were still critical and rude about the finished book on masks when I showed it to them as a group, but individually they obviously enjoyed it. The children have a poor concept of themselves as both writers and artists, and it would take a long time to alter this view completely.

From the children's responses I learned the value of materials made to suit their understanding, drawing where possible on material from their own environment. Also the need to make their work meaningful, for example, not just writing because they have to write each day. Children need to understand why they do things, that writing can be used to inform others, as in the case of a reference book on masks, or to record information in a clear way so that they can use it at a later date, as with measuring the playground etc.

I became aware of the need for good materials and organisation to enable the children to work to the best of their abilities. This was obvious from the improved standard of writing after I introduced my practical writing provisions. (Jane Brett)

We would also suggest that yet again this passage further reveals the need for intending teachers to be given ample time to develop their thinking as well as their professional skills. For it does not require a great deal of imagination to envisage what good tutors will be able to achieve over a further period of three years with students who show this level of understanding at the end of one year.

Finally, the longer courses can also provide opportunities in their later stages for students to pursue a special interest or adopt a special focus for their work. For once a solid foundation has been laid along the lines we have attempted to describe, this can be built upon and issues of particular interest identified in the earlier stages can be pursued in greater depth. There is an increasing need in schools of all kinds for teachers with special kinds of expertise. Sometimes these special kinds of expertise will be in curriculum areas such as language development or mathematics or science. Increasingly, however, there is a need for teachers with expert understanding of other kinds — understanding of children with special needs, for example, whether these be the result of race, of gender, of physical, intellectual or social handicap, or understanding of the general pastoral and moral aspects of schooling. It is important that teachers be encouraged to identify interests they may have in any of these areas and to begin to develop an appropriate expertise as soon as possible. The right kind of in-service opportunities must build on this but it is not satisfactory to leave the process entirely until then.

These, then, are the elements which we regard as vital to a proper course of teacher education, particularly if it is to produce teachers who can meet the demands of education as we view it. If there is one general principle that underlies it, it is that if teachers are to be helped to develop such qualities as will enable them to support the development of each of their pupils as an individual, they must be assisted towards this by teacher-educators who possess and display exactly the same qualities as they are endeavouring to develop in their students.

However, there are a number of recent events which seem to us to put the development of this kind of approach to teacher education very much at risk and it is to a consideration of some of these that we now turn.

Recent and current developments and their implications

There is no doubt that the record of teacher education in the United Kingdom is not a distinguished one. Far too high a proportion of teachers have reacted with something approaching contempt to the courses they have been provided with, suggesting, perhaps particularly in the context of one-year courses, that the only useful experience the courses have provided has been the period of teaching practice, that most of the theoretical input to their preparation has been professionally irrelevant and often academically inadequate, and that in general it might have been better to have gone straight into a school and learned how to teach by actually teaching. To this must now be added the evidence of a recent survey by HMI of young entrants to the teaching profession that many of those teachers who have been prepared for teaching by three- or four-year B.Ed. courses are critical of the amount of time that has been devoted to the study of a 'main subject' (DES 1982d).

To some extent, of course, this reflects a mistaken attitude on the part of such students themselves. For it is clear that, at least in part, these reactions are those of people whose expectations of their courses have been somewhat limited and naive. It must also be recognized that many of the more successful teachers have not reacted in this way and have gained far more value from their initial preparation than this. It would be wrong, however, to lay the blame entirely on the recipients of these offerings. There have been, and still are, some major inadequacies in the offerings themselves, for which the providers must accept responsibility. In fact, there have been more inadequacies than the students themselves have often detected, especially when the courses are viewed from the perspective of those whose notion of education is akin to that outlined in this book.

It will be helpful, therefore, if we begin this discussion of the present scene with an examination of some of the features of past and present courses of teacher education which are at odds with the view of education we are concerned to promote.

Some common inadequacies of teacher education programmes

One of the major ways in which arrangements for the preparation of teachers can go and often has gone wrong is through the provision of an unsuitable form of theoretical input. We would understandably be surprised to discover that a major element in the training of a doctor or a lawyer was a study of the works of Plato, in spite of the fact that Plato had almost as much to say about health and fitness and about the law as he did about education. We would hope and believe that too much progress had been made in the development of those professions for what Plato had to say about them to be regarded as almost the last word on the subject. Yet until recently this was a major element of many one-year courses of teacher education and what has replaced it has not always been much more convincing.

A prime reason for this, of course, is that those who have been providing the courses have been anxious to convince their colleagues that what they were engaged in was every bit as respectable academically as anything going on in any other sector of Higher Education. They have not succeeded, since the academic level of their offerings, consisting as these often have of snippets of philosophy or psychology or sociology or history or whatever, has never been high and the recipients of them, some of them already the possessors of good first degrees in these disciplines, have not found it easy to take them seriously. Nevertheless, this has been the aim.

It is clearly a totally inappropriate aim. For aspiring teachers need much more than such snippets; they need to have their attention and their energies closely directed at real current educational issues and to be introduced to theoretical considerations of a kind that they can see have a direct bearing on and relevance for these. Recent developments in some institutions have shown that this can be done, as we indicated in the first half of this chapter. However, there is still a long way to go before we achieve a general recognition that this kind of approach to the education of teachers is in fact more respectable academically as well as professionally, that it can be intellectually demanding as well as professionally significant. Once the intellectual rigour necessary for this kind of study is appreciated, the study of Education will free itself of its dependence on the so-called 'contributory disciplines'.

If we are to produce teachers who can attend properly to the needs of curriculum development, then, we must begin to overhaul our methods of preparing them and, in particular, we must change quite radically the theoretical input to their initial courses.

A second major mistake in our view of many traditional and existing courses of teacher education is the emphasis they often place on subject content. It is only recently that courses have appeared which offer the student the

opportunity to spend all or most of his or her time studying aspects of education. A few institutions have begun to offer 'all-Education' B.Ed. courses, conceived and planned on the assumption that teachers at most levels, but perhaps especially in the Primary schools, need to acquire an extensive understanding of children, of the society in which we live, of the problems and techniques of curriculum development, of the processes of education and of many
other related issues rather than to achieve a deep knowledge of one or two
particular subjects.

We believe that a strong case can be made from every angle for the view
that children's development should be in the hands of teachers who understand what that responsibility entails rather than of those who have good
honours degrees or even doctorates in history or mathematics or any other traditional curriculum subject. The emphasis on subjects has led to the production of many teachers who continue to regard subject content as the prime
consideration in educational planning and who, as a result, are not only incap-
able of viewing the process of education in a wider context but also find it difficult to envisage a curriculum in which their subject does not figure in something like its traditional form. Thus their views both of the process of education and of curriculum development are severely restricted.

If education is to keep pace with changes in society, its development must
be in the hands of people who possess the kind of understanding to attend to it.
Such understanding will come not from the study of history or mathematics or
any other area of the traditional curriculum; it can only come from the study
of education itself.

The emphasis in teacher education, then, must shift away from its subject
content towards the acquisition of a theoretical understanding of education as
a process. This, we believe, is true of the preparation of teachers for all levels
of the education service. It is, of course, particularly true for teachers who are
to take responsibility for the development of education of the kind described in
this book.

A third aspect of many courses of teacher education which militates against
the kind of development this book is intended to promote is the emphasis that
continues to be placed on the use of objectives-based models in the planning of
'lessons'. The concept of a 'lesson' itself needs closer attention than it has
often been given, but the problems associated with the view of education
which the use of that term suggests are compounded when students are led to
believe that the starting point for the planning of every 'lesson' must be a
statement of objectives to be attained. Enough has been said in the earlier

chapters of this book and in *The Primary Curriculum* to draw attention to the problematic nature of this approach. It will be sufficent to say here, then, that too many teachers continue to emerge from their training courses with no awareness of the problems this model raises or with no appreciation of the fact that the debate in the literature about the use of objectives in curriculum planning, which sometimes they are familiar with, applies with equal if not greater force to the preparation and planning of their own work with pupils.

It must be recognized, of course, that the use of objectives provides a structure, or at least the appearance of a structure, and that this is something which the young, inexperienced teacher clearly needs. However, enough has been said already to indicate that in many contexts it provides an inappropriate structure and one which may, in a fundamental sense, be at odds with what the teacher is endeavouring to do. This is why many student teachers have come to regard statements of the objectives of their 'lessons' as exercises to be performed to satisfy their tutors rather than as useful aids in their work; for one of the strongest arguments against this approach to planning has long been its ineffectiveness in a practical setting, a point which teachers quickly come to recognize when they discover how early in any 'lesson' they have to modify their objectives if they are to achieve anything worthwhile (Kelly 1977, 1982; Blenkin and Kelly 1981). Furthermore, we hope enough has been said in the earlier chapters of this book and in the earlier part of this chapter to show that teachers, and student teachers too, can be helped to develop structures for their work on other bases than the use of objectives.

The suggestion, often still made to young teachers, that statements of objectives are the only basis for the planning of their work is thus another way in which many courses of teacher preparation hinder the development of the kinds of approach to education we are advocating here.

Finally, it must be stressed that these inadequacies, although not solely confined to the short, one-year courses of teacher training, are more likely to be in evidence there than in the three- or four-year concurrent courses. Or, to put it differently, it is the concurrent courses which have offered more scope for progress towards the elimination of these inadequacies. For the one-year course, following three years spent in studying a subject area, is clearly predicated on the belief that 75 percent of what the intending teacher needs from his sojourn in Higher Education is a study of one or two subjects. This is reflected too in the dominant part often played by subject-method courses in the teacher-training programme. It is in this kind of short course also, especially perhaps those conducted within a University setting, that the wrong kind of academicism is most often to be seen. And it is the student who has least time to mature as a teacher and to develop his or her professional skills who is most likely to latch on to the spurious sense of structure that the use of objectives seems to offer.

In short, it is in one-year courses of teacher preparation that, not surprisingly, we see an emphasis on the production of teachers rather than of educators, of journeyman practitioners rather than professionals. When such teachers rise above the limitations of such courses, as many clearly do, they do so more often in spite of rather than because of them, and this is clearly unsatisfactory. As we said earlier, to educate someone is a much more complex undertaking than merely to teach them something. It is an undertaking for which only the highly talented can be adequately prepared in one year.

The importance of this cannot be overstated. Few teachers will be able to undertake the kind of work in schools we have been describing in this book after only one year of preparation. This point becomes particularly crucial when we note the current trend towards a proliferation of such courses, at Primary as well as at Secondary level. It is to a consideration of some of the reasons for this trend that we must now turn.

Recent trends and developments

The most significant factor in the planning of courses of teacher education in the United Kingdom for more than a decade has been the fluctuations in the birth-rate. A planned massive expansion in the output of teachers in the late 1960s resulted in an equally massive overproduction of teachers throughout most of the 1970s, as a dramatic fall in the number of children born led to a reduction in the number of teachers needed first of all in Primary schools and later in Secondary schools. It could be suggested, and with some cogency, that the legalization of abortion and the wider availability of relatively easy methods of contraception might have indicated to a wiser government that it would be not unreasonable to expect a fall in the birth-rate, but the truth is that the planned expansion of teacher output was contemporaneous with those measures.

Whatever the reason, however, a rapid contraction of the nation's teacher education programme was necessarily undertaken during the 1970s. This resulted in the closure of many institutions, in the merging of others and in an extensive reorganization. This process has continued into the 1980s, as the smaller cohorts of pupils have progressed through our Secondary schools and proposals have been made at this very time of writing for further closures and mergers of courses and institutions.

In the meantime, however, for reasons which are less easy to identify, there has been an upsurge in the birth-rate which will necessitate a gradual expansion of provision at Primary level in the second half of the 1980s and subsequently, of course, at Secondary level too. The increased number of teachers that this will require, however, will have to be met from those much-reduced cohorts which are now reaching the stage of Higher Education. We thus have a rather complicated equation and one which has led to certain trends and developments which we must now attempt to pick out.

Two major developments have occurred as a result of the recent contraction of the teacher education programme. The first of these has been the progress that has been made towards establishing teaching as a degreed profession. A major reduction in the scale of teacher education has made it possible to phase out all non-degree courses, except for certain short courses in shortage subject areas. This has meant that the old three-year Teachers' Certificate has been replaced by a B.Ed. course for all students seeking a concurrent course.

A prime intention of this development, of course, has been to raise standards. Admission to a degree course is limited to applicants with at least two GCE 'A' level passes, whereas admission to Teachers' Certificate courses required a minimum of only five passes at 'O' level. There has been a corresponding rise in the level of the courses themselves.

There are two ways of viewing this development, however, and indeed of implementing it. One is to stress the academic content of the courses in the kinds of way we were expressing concern about earlier. It is clear that this has happened in many cases and, when it has happened, it has taken the form of increasing the emphasis on the subject-content of the courses and/or raising the 'academic' content of the Education component. In other cases, however, the need for introducing a proper kind of academic rigour has been recognized and the opportunities offered for developing properly relevant and rigorous forms of professional preparation have been seized. The resultant trend, therefore, is an ambiguous one. We shall see shortly, however, that more recent developments are tending to promote the former rather than the latter kind of movement.

The second major result of the contractions of recent years has been the expansion of provision for the in-service education of teachers. This has not been on the scale originally envisaged (HMSO 1972), but it has been significant in its impact on the scene. Again, the issue centres on the quality rather than the quantity of such provision and we shall see shortly that other trends are currently of great significance for this. But the importance of continuing educational opportunities for teachers is, in our view, a major factor in the development of education, so that the arrival of the notion in the consciousness of most teachers represents a step in a direction that could be highly advantageous to what we are promoting here.

The factor that has complicated these trends, however, is the recent upsurge in the child population. This has presented the administrators with two problems, each of which has led to certain proposals which are of crucial significance for the development of teacher education and thus of education itself. First, it has created an immediate need for a vast increase in the force of teachers skilled to work with Primary children. Secondly, it has raised longer-term questions of how we can develop machinery or make arrangements which will be able to cope with constant fluctations in the birth-rate.

It is apparent that the first problem cannot be resolved merely by increasing the admissions to intitial courses. It is unrealistic to expect that, from those reduced cohorts we mentioned earlier as now entering Higher Education, we can find enough who are both able and willing to enter the teaching profession. Thus attention has been turned towards the establishment of courses for the retraining of people who have withdrawn from teaching and now may wish to return to it, and for redundant Secondary teachers who may wish, or may be directed, to retrain to work with Primary children. In this context, it is plain that everything will depend on the quality of these retraining courses. Early indications, however, are far from reassuring. We have already heard of one local authority which believes that such retraining can be accomplished by courses lasting a mere two weeks, and it is clear that no Secondary Head-teacher is likely to declare redundant the most outstanding members of his staff, so that those to be retrained will inevitably be teachers who have most to learn or relearn or even unlearn. The dangers of subject-bound attitudes, objectives-based planning and inadequate theoretical perspectives begin, therefore, to loom very large.

The same picture emerges from an examination of the attempts being made by the administrators to develop procedures which will meet not only this current problem but also the likelihood of continuing fluctuations in the school population. For, first, there is a clear preference for one-year courses of training, not because of any conviction that these are more satisfactory, but because they offer a quicker means of regulating and adjusting the output of teachers than do the longer, three- or four-year courses. This, of course, increases those dangers we suggested earlier are most readily associated with such courses. Secondly, there is an obvious desire to see a greater stress on the subject component of courses of training for Primary teachers (DES 1983) — not necessarily only out of a conviction that this will make better teachers at that level, but also because it will lead to a greater mobility within the teaching profession by making it easier to move such teachers into the relevant subject department of a Secondary school, if and when this becomes necessary.

Associated with this has been a move towards excluding from postgraduate teacher education courses graduates in subjects which are not regarded as cognate to the Primary school curriculum. It could be argued that a graduate in philosophy or psychology or anthropology might *ipso facto* have many quali-ties that would enable him or her to develop, with the right kind of help, into exactly the kind of teacher we are claiming our schools need. On current trends, however, such persons will be overlooked in favour of those with expertise in traditional subject areas of the curriculum, a development which must have the effect of reasserting the significance of subject-content.

Lastly, there is serious discussion at present, prompted by the DES, of proposals for relating the award of qualified teacher status directly to subject-specialism and age-range. Thus, whereas at present in the United Kingdom, although not in most other countries, qualified teacher status permits one to seek employment in any kind of school and to teach any subject, current pro-posals are for much more specific forms of qualification. It is difficult to under-stand how such proposals are likely to assist towards the achievement of a more flexible teaching profession. It is apparent, however, that this again must have the effect of stressing those aspects of teacher education which we have been suggesting are its least desirable features.

It will be clear, then, that, while there are obvious possibilities for the improvement of teacher education in recent developments, there are rather more potential dangers, so that these developments need to be watched very carefully over the next few years. For, as we said at the beginning of this chapter, unless we get the preparation of teachers right, we cannot expect to attain the kind of education for our children that we want to see.

Induction and in-service education

It has long been acknowledged that many of the problems facing those respon-sible for the initial education of teachers could be resolved by the institution of adequate and compulsory in-service provision. Most of the problems presented by the brevity of one-year courses and those of achieving the right kind of balance in all courses would disappear almost overnight if in-service opportunities were to be made available on a proper scale. For it would not matter nearly so much that a teacher cannot be properly prepared in one year, if those concerned with these courses could be confident that their task was merely to lay the foundations of his or her professional training and that others would soon be building on these. And it would not be necessary to attempt to open the young teacher's eyes to every dimension of his or her work in the initial course programme, if one could be sure that those aspects one might decide to leave for a later date would in fact be taken up later. As it is, some teachers receive little or nothing beyond their initial courses and the awareness of this places great strain on those courses.

This was a major reason why an extensive expansion of in-service provision was being advocated more than a decade ago. For example, a detailed survey of teacher education within the purview of the University of London (University of London Institute of Education 1971) began its chapter on in-service training with the following paragraph:

> We need a very considerable expansion of provision for in-service training and for three reasons. The pace of change, educational and social, is greater now than ever before, and teachers cannot possibly keep in tune with the times if they have no training throughout their professional career. Secondly, as we have seen, there is great need to lighten the syllabus while increasing the intensity of initial training and this cannot be done while it is impossible to assume that in-service training will follow. Thirdly, you cannot keep your mind fresh without such courses from time to time: the teacher who ceases to learn will soon find that he has ceased to teach as he should (op. cit., p.51).

This chapter concluded with some positive recommendations: 'that *there be a substantial increase in the provision of in-service training, though we know that this will cost money;* and that *the equivalent of a week a year be allowed to every teacher . . . for in-service training in school time'* (op. cit., p.53). The italics are those of the original report and the case has, if anything, come to merit even greater stress in the intervening years.

Several things have happened since this kind of recommendation was being made. Firstly, the case was taken up officially in the James Report (DES 1972) and in that government White Paper (HMSO 1972) to which we have already referred and which was to have provided the blueprint for the development of teacher education in the last decade. For, entitled *Education: A Framework for Expansion,* that document set out a programme for the contraction of initial training provision, because of a dramatic fall in the birth rate, and its title could only be justified by its attempts to match this contraction by planned development elsewhere. The two areas it chose for such development included the in-service education of teachers (the other was Nursery education). This was thus a major item in what it called its 'ten-year strategy for the education service' (op. cit., p.2). What this amounted to was that the first two objectives specified by the James Committee (DES 1972) had been, along with the remaining four, given 'universal acclaim' in the White Paper. These two objectives were 'a large and systematic expansion of in-service training' and 'a planned reinforcement of the process of induction in the first year in school' (op. cit., p.16).

Unfortunately, both of these objectives were to become early casualties. For the second event which we must note as of relevance here was that economic recession which followed the 'oil crisis' in 1974. The most immediate effect of the resultant cutback in expenditure on education was the disappearance of the, often quite extensive, plans which many local authorities had developed for in-service education in response to the encouragement of the White Paper. In part, of course, the choice of this area for economies can be explained in terms of its having little immediate significance for parents; it represents a diminution in the quality of education offered to pupils but of a kind that does not have the obvious impact of increased class sizes, reduced material resources or even the disappearance of free milk. And it is this factor that explains why on several occasions subsequent governments have had to take positive steps to discourage local authorities from too readily adopting this solution to their economic difficulties. Nevertheless, its effect on educational provision must not be underrated. There is ample evidence of this in the fact that one of the most significant implications of that recent survey of young teachers to which we have already referred (DES 1982d) is the continued inadequacy of induction and in-service provision.

This development (or rather lack of development) is even more disturbing when viewed against the backcloth of the massive changes which have occurred in the context of the teacher's work and the demands made on the teacher's expertise during the intervening decade, many of which have emerged very clearly in our earlier chapters. We have seen how these have been reflected in some courses of initial preparation, but we can also see that they cry out for the continued education of teachers. One message of every chapter in this book, in fact, has been that the continued development of the curriculum — in any form — requires the continued development of teachers.

And this can only be achieved if improvements in initial teacher education are matched, complemented and extended by similar improvements and a massive expansion of the arrangements for the induction of young teachers into the profession and their continued in-service education.

This brings us to a further development that needs to be noted here, one which perhaps merits rather fuller discussion. For the changes which have occurred in education in the last decade have led, amongst many other things, to the emergence of the idea not only of school-based curriculum development but also to that of school-based in-service education. How this has come about will be clear from the accounts given in Chapters 8 and 9 of curriculum development in schools and the support which can be provided for this from outside. Whether initiatives are to come from the school itself or teachers are to be expected to respond to promptings from without, it is now clear that it is the teachers who will be at the centre of the process and not only their role but also, and especially, their ability to fulfil that role will be crucial. Furthermore, we noted earlier, in our discussion of the initial preparation of teachers, how the theoretical perspectives we offer them must be linked to their developing practical experience by being directly and specifically related to that experience rather than being allowed to remain at the level of generality. The same must be true of the perspectives offered by in-service courses and this must lead us to the idea of school-based or school-focused provision.

There is no doubt that this area of the educational debate may currently be notable rather more for its rhetoric than for its practical recommendations, 'that hope, faith and optimism do not so much permeate the discussions and evaluations of SCI (school-centred innovation) as consume them' (Hargreaves 1982, p.252). We need a good deal more analysis of a critical and constructive kind of what the notion of school-centred innovation or development implies for curriculum planning than has hitherto occurred. However, what is central to our case here is that this process of constructive and critical analysis should embrace not only school-centred curriculum development but also the in-service education of teachers which we are arguing must go hand-in-hand with it. For we need to know much more about that too and about how it can best be promoted. For, if we are concerned about the theory/practice dichotomy in initial teacher education, we must be concerned about it at the in-service level too. And if we are right to claim that the solution to it in initial courses is to be found in a more school-centred approach, then we must pursue the possibilities of that approach at the in-service level also.

Thus, the school-centred developments which Elaine Ball discussed in the previous two chapters not only lead us to an awareness of the need for increased in-service provision, they also offer us clues as to the form such provision might take. The implications of this for all providers of such courses, not only local authorities but also all those institutions which have traditionally provided award-bearing courses of all kinds in Education, are far-reaching and must soon be faced.

Summary and conclusions

This chapter has endeavoured to indicate ways in which teachers can be prepared by their initial courses to undertake in schools work of the kind this book has described. It has suggested that in order to achieve this we need to engage in an extensive rethinking of some of the assumptions that can be seen to lie behind traditional and existing practices. We suggested that there is evidence that in some places this process is well under way. However, we then considered some recent trends and developments in the field of teacher education and pointed out that there is little encouragement there for us to be sanguine about the future. Administrative procedures are tending to reinforce those traditional assumptions we have argued need to be questioned and are unlikely to promote the developments we are favouring.

One area that does hold out some hope is that of in-service education. The need for this seems to have been accepted at all levels, so that it is not unreasonable to expect to see significant developments in this sphere. To a large extent, of course, if we can get this right, it may compensate for some of the inadequacies of initial courses. Clearly, however, it would be far more advantageous to all concerned if it could be directed at assisting teachers to improve skills and understanding they already possess rather than, as too often is the case at present, having to undertake the somewhat negative task of compensating for the inadequacies of their earlier courses. For we must not lose sight of the fact that, while an inadequately trained teacher is acquiring the experience upon which an in-service course to correct his or her inadequacies can be built, the children who are providing that experience are real children deserving of fully adequate provision.

PART FOUR

BEYOND THE PRIMARY SCHOOL

INTRODUCTION TO PART FOUR

It has been stressed several times, both in *The Primary Curriculum* and in this present book, that the approach to education and curriculum planning we are endeavouring to explore and promote is not, and certainly need not be, limited to the education of younger children. If we continue to discuss it mainly in the context of the Primary school, it is because it is there where it is most often to be found and it is there where it has had the official blessing of two major government reports. However, one of our constantly reiterated claims is that one important reason for attempting to elucidate its major principles is to encourage its extension into and adoption in other sectors of the school system.

It is to this issue that the present section turns. For here we attempt to go 'beyond the Primary school' to consider what advantages there might be in adopting this approach elsewhere and what peculiar difficulties or problems such a development might throw up. And again our method has been to invite accounts of first-hand experience in this area.

The two accounts we offer describe two quite different educational contexts, one being from the field of Special Education and the other an account of work in a Secondary school. These are contexts which in many respects are quite different from each other and from that of the Primary schools we have focused on hitherto. For one offers all the problems attendant on educational handicap of all kinds and the other those of an area of schooling which has long been dominated by a subject-centred philosophy and by the monolithic system of public examinations.

Again, however, what proves to be most significant is the common ground which appears, both in terms of the shared conviction of the value of certain fundamental educational principles and the recognition of certain forms of planning and certain kinds of activity as not conducive to their practice. Thus again we note a rejection of prestated objectives as a basis for planning; again we hear doubts expressed about the validity of subject barriers; again we see an emphasis on development of all kinds; and again we are encouraged to recognize the value of art work, drama and language work in promoting this kind of development. It all adds to our conviction that education is education is education . . . and that there is no valid justification for the fact that it is often offered in quite different forms in different sectors of our school system.

The field of Special Education is one in which the pseudo-scientific influence we referred to earlier has held long and wide sway. Often one finds the curriculum of Special schools being controlled by psychologists, and even members of the medical profession, rather than by teachers, as extrapolations are made — quite improperly — from medical or psychiatric prescriptions to decisions about curriculum, so that the basis of their theory, their planning and their practice is psychological rather than educational — and thus behavioural rather than developmental. Indeed the term 'behaviour modification' is often openly applied to schooling in this sector and this is, in our view, an exact description for a curriculum planned on the basis of behavioural objectives. The implications of this, however, for the attitudes thus adopted towards the human beings who are the recipients of this form of schooling are serious and wide-reaching. One might argue, therefore, that nowhere is there greater need for a questioning of this approach to curriculum planning and an exploration of the potential of a process-based curriculum and of the principles which might underpin its practice. It is exactly this that is undertaken in Chapter 11, where a discussion of the inadequacies of the objectives base is followed by an account of the kind of practical provision that can be made once one is clear about one's educational principles.

In the Secondary sector the context and the problems are different again. Here traditionally the focus has been on subject-content, on the acquisition of knowledge, and this has been matched by a concern with public examinations as devices which have not only tested the extent to which such knowledge has been acquired but also, in most cases, have controlled and decided what knowledge shall be purveyed. In short, the curriculum has been dominated by a subject-centred examination system and, even in the recent age of planned curriculum development and innovation, such development and innovation has gone on largely within subjects and little development across subject boundaries has been possible. Certainly, there has been little scope for planning a curriculum according to some notion of educational processes, since it has usually been dictated by the demands of subject-content. Again, therefore, an exploration of the possibilities of a different approach is long overdue and a rethinking of our assumptions about schooling at this level, particularly in the context of rapid technological advance and rising unemployment, is badly needed. This is what is undertaken in Chapter 12, which offers an account of how the project, Man: A Course of Study, has been used in one Secondary school and how the principles embodied in that project have been extended into further courses up to and including those leading to public examination. Suddenly we see children blossoming under the same kinds of experience we have seen others being offered in the Primary schools but at their own level and in the context of their newly emerging adolescent interests. The need for, and the way to, a major overhaul of our thinking about education at this level becomes ever clearer, as we begin to appreciate the possibilities which exist and the potential which too often remains untapped.

The Primary school, then, remains our most prolific source of examples of what teaching by processes might mean. But there is strong evidence here for its development 'beyond the Primary school'.

CHAPTER 11

PROCESSES IN SPECIAL EDUCATION
ALAN GODDARD

It seems, then, that the new findings in developmental research point in precisely the same direction as the requirements for an interventionist psychology in special education practice: the need for PROCESS MODELS. We do not yet really possess such models, but there are clues to their possible form (Sinha 1981).

I was most excited and encouraged when I read *The Practice of Special Education*, edited by Will Swann (1981). I found Chris Sinha's contribution 'The role of psychological research in Special Education' particularly relevant, for it was the first time I had come across any published work concerning Special Education that stresses the need to view education as a form of *process*. Sinha concludes that in the past psychologists' preoccupation with standardizing (tests, responses and teaching methods) has led them to neglect processes, and he thinks that now is the appropriate time to redress the balance. I am in full agreement with these sentiments. The time is surely ripe; processes have been grossly neglected, often ignored, in Special Education, and this chapter is a small attempt to rectify this serious situation.

When I started teaching at my present school, the responsibility for the education of 'severely subnormal' children had only recently been transferred from the Department of Health and Social Security to the Department of Education and Science. ESN(S) schools had formerly been called 'Junior *Training* Centres' and much of the philosophy behind that title remains.

Coming to this school, then, rekindled my interest and enthusiasm for education, and I started serious study again. I was most fortunate in that my head-teacher, Mary Eglington, was flexible in her approach and allowed and encouraged me to 'feel my way' with my new class. She has given me much-needed support over the years.

On becoming deputy head in the mid-seventies, I was also made curriculum coordinator throughout the school, which provided me with a wonderful opportunity of gaining first-hand experience of working with all the children and the teachers. It also made me think more deeply about curriculum development. I soon discovered that much of the literature on curricular matters at all levels took for granted that some form of 'objectives' approach must be used.

This situation gave me feelings of considerable unease, for the use of objectives ran counter to my experiences as a teacher in both 'mainstream' and 'special' schools. I therefore decided to examine 'objectives', for there was, and still is, great pressure on teachers to state at the start the objectives of their teaching, and these pressures are increasing, nowhere more than in the sphere of Special Education. A basic assumption held by many is that curriculum evaluation is not possible without the prespecification of objectives.

Most current leading literature on curricular matters in Special Education adopts and is dependent on 'objectives'. Even the most cursory glance at these writings, and others of the last decade, will reveal a binding bias towards 'objectives', and an approach by way of objectives (for the most part *behavioural* objectives) has often been uncritically accepted as a basis for curriculum planning and development.

This behavioural approach to teaching, which also embraces behaviour modification, thus currently dominates the field of Special Education, especially in ESN(S) and ESN(M) schools, and is also making its mark in remedial education. In fact it can now be seen at all levels of our educational system.

My examination of objectives in curriculum development revealed, and is revealing, most serious deficiencies, especially in what might be termed the 'behavioural objectives model'. Thus, this is a model which I reject, and I take as a viable and valid alternative the view of education as process — an approach that looks at the curriculum not in terms of its subject-content nor its goals, but the principles of procedure that constitute the work of teachers and pupils, and emphasizes the developmental processes that I consider to be the proper concern of education.

A further reason why I continued to study curriculum development and, in particular, to explore alternatives to the behavioural objectives approach was that I thought it of great importance to make myself accountable as a teacher. That sense of accountability was further heightened by my appointment as Headteacher.

So for some time I have consciously been attempting to develop education and to promote curriculum development in terms of processes. I use the word 'consciously' for I am of the opinion that many experienced practising teachers in Special Education, along with many in the Primary sector (Blenkin and Kelly 1981), intuitively, albeit unwittingly, already use a form of process planning in their classroom teaching. This stems from practice rather than theory, but obviously a sound theoretical rationale to back up practice is both necessary and essential.

It is my contention that this practice is currently at risk due to the ever-increasing pressures on teachers to prespecify the objectives of their teaching, pressures that are further intensified by the claim that such objectives play a central role in teacher accountability. It is only right and proper that teachers should, indeed must, be accountable for their teaching, but behavioural objectives offer merely an apparent answer to the question of accountability. All these pressures may be openly witnessed where teachers are being pressed into translating their aims into behavioural objectives, and so accepting what I consider to be an unsuitable curriculum model.

I am ever aware, I hope, of the dangers of having a theory first and then trying to make it 'fit', as tends to happen in the hypothetico-deductive method, a doctrine traditionally used by 'scientific' psychologists. John Dewey says, 'A very humble experience is capable of generating and carrying any amount of theory (or intellectual content), but a theory apart from experience cannot be grasped even as a theory' (Dewey 1916, p.169). It is of the utmost importance, therefore, that those with day-by-day, year-by-year, practical experience, namely teachers, must play a vital and central role in educational matters.

This is what I find so refreshing, and attractive in the idea of the teacher as researcher (Stenhouse 1975). In similar vein Malcolm Skilbeck (1973, 1976) suggests that teachers should be encouraged to examine their own teaching and to redesign curricula. And also Meriel Downey and Vic Kelly stress that curriculum development is teacher development, and to recognize this is to adopt a more viable approach 'than to attempt to manipulate them like puppets from somewhere above and beyond the real educational stage' (Downey and Kelly 1979, p.247).

Anyone hoping to find tips on how to teach, therefore, or who is looking for recipes or packages in this chapter will be totally thwarted. Publications abound in Special Education, usually recommending prescriptive planning and emphasizing the 'how' and the 'what' rather than the 'why'. If one accepts the statement that 'curriculum development is teacher development', as I do, then one may appreciate my deep concern at the emergence of what might be termed the 'check-list syndrome', and the current proliferation of professionally (and often commercially) produced curriculum 'packages' and 'kits' based on behavioural objectives. A typical example is the Portage Guide to Early Education (Shearer and Shearer 1972, Bluma et al. 1976) so eagerly adopted by many.

How, I ask, does the use of packages and the like develop the teacher either personally or professionally? For the role of both teacher and pupil is greatly diminished, if not demeaned, and there is a very real danger that curriculum development as such could cease.

Furthermore, another disquieting aspect of the use of such simplistic approaches is that they give the illusion that we know precisely what we are about. As Elliott Eisner so sensibly states, 'The hunt for recipes, rules, formulas, and other nostrums to solve educational problems is a hopeless one. Contexts change and the configurations of schooling within those contexts also change'; we must 'anticipate that "final" solutions will always be temporary at best' (Eisner 1979a, p.35). He continues by saying that he is not arguing for innocence on the part of the educational scholar, or professionals — 'I am arguing against unrealistic aspirations, pseudo science, and the host of other bandwagons, bad analogies, and panaceas that emerge in the field each year . . . For the curriculum planner this means a life of continual uncertainty' (ibid.). 'Uncertainty' must always be the order of the day when considering educational phenomena. I am weary of the scientific 'certainty' and pseudo-security so often displayed in the behavioural approach, where teaching practices are based on so-called 'sound psychological principles'.

Many appear to have been side-tracked by the 'scientific', 'technological' approach to education, but fortunately an increasing number are now realizing this and reacting accordingly. It is in this vein that I shall proceed, in a dual attempt at trying to improve both my own understanding, following Kelly (1955), and the understanding of children, the latter being the central theme of Michael Armstrong's so sensitively written work *Closely Observed Children* (1980).

The dominant influence of behavioural objectives on the development of Special Education

One might expect that the behavioural objectives model would have a major influence on Special Education in America, and it has. American Special Education laws insist on the use of an individual education programme (I.E.P.) (Booth 1982), which involves the use of short-term instructional objectives very much within the behaviourist tradition in education. Booth states, 'one view of what makes special education special is that it should have a rigorously defined and structured curriculum. The curriculum is analysed into skills, which are, in turn, broken down into smaller learning units. Before teaching begins, a child's level on a set curriculum is assessed, and then teaching objectives are prepared which specify the particular behaviour that a child will master in a particular time to a particular level of success, using predefined materials and methods. Extensive records are kept as a means of evaluation and accountability' (op. cit., p.34). He adds that this approach often involves 'diagnostic-prescriptive teaching'. He has found very few writers on Special Education in America who do not approve of this behavioural approach.

A similar situation exists in this country *at the moment*, and I shall now turn my attention to reviewing the influence of behavioural objectives on curriculum development in Britain.

R. Gulliford's *Special Educational Needs* (1971) reflects the curricular thinking of that period, which is still very much in evidence today. He stresses the need to be clear about educational objectives and considers that Taylor (1966, 1970) 'has provided an outline of the steps required in formulating a curriculum plan' (op. cit., p.26). The Taylor model is dependent on behavioural objectives.

This behavioural approach was also adopted in the early days of the Hester Adrian Research Centre for the Study of Learning Processes in the Mentally Handicapped (Mittler 1970), and continues to this day. The members of the Thomas Coram Research Unit in London also popularize behavioural methods, as do those of the British Institute of Mental Handicap, in common with most leading writers in the field. For example, although John McMaster (1973) admits that 'it would seem obvious that educational theory relating to the mentally handicapped has not as yet been born' (op. cit., p.20), he thinks that the potential of operant conditioning necessarily involving shaping and control of behaviour is 'so great that it deserves considerable prominence' (op. cit., p.60). Like Taylor, he too speaks approvingly of Bloom's taxonomy

(Bloom 1956), and gives reasons why objectives are so vitally important.

> Firstly, they are essential for assessment and evaluation. Secondly, they offer an articulate means of discussing in detail the content of an educational programme, and thereby allow for meaningful communication.
>
> A third major reason for the importance of clearly stated objectives is that they can help determine the most appropriate teaching methods and give guidance to the activities which will be selected for the children (op. cit., p. 123).

The very title of Wilfred Brennan's book, *Shaping the Education of Slow Learners* (1974), is indicative of his bias towards behavioural methods. He contends that behavioural objectives should be the prime concern of curriculum planning. He approves of the principles of modern curriculum design advocated by Wheeler (1967), and also recommends Taylor's (1970) proposals for compensatory education. He ends his book, 'Clarity of terminal and intermediate objectives in the curriculum is seen as essential if the teacher is to use the total learning situation in order to continuously "shape" the development of the pupil in an on-going process of interaction' (op.cit., p.97). More recently, in Schools Council Working Paper 63 (1979), Brennan again champions the Wheeler model, and more recently still talks of the importance of objectives, claims that the steps to attain these must be carefully worked out and once more stresses the need for a clear knowledge of objectives that will shape 'the choice of experiences, materials and teaching and learning methods to be utilized by the teacher in her work' (Brennan 1982, p.97).

The British Institute of Mental Handicap appears to be totally committed to behavioural methods, as the programmes for their conferences clearly show, as do Perkins et al. (1976), in a book published by the then Institute of Mental Subnormality, the title of which is *Helping the Retarded: A Systematic Behavioural Approach.* In their first chapter, 'Basic principles of the behavioural approach', it is blatantly stated that 'we all learn according to these basic principles' (op. cit., p.7). The book is full of terms such as reinforcing, prompting, fading, shaping, chaining, extinction — all part of the jargon that so commonly constitutes the behavioural psychologists' repertoire.

In the book *Teaching the Handicapped Child* (Jeffree et al. 1977), which was primarily designed as a companion volume to the 'Let Me . . .' books, emphasis is placed on an overall approach to teaching, irrespective of content, and again objectives play a central and essential role in the approach adopted. In summarizing the chapter on 'The Teaching Objective' it is stated

The teaching objective describes:
a) the activity of the child;
b) a specific observable activity;
c) an activity which the child should be able to demonstrate in the near, rather than the distant, future;
d) the conditions under which the activity should occur.

(op. cit., p.53)

This theme is continued in *Starting Off* (Kiernan et al. 1978), where it is claimed that, as the mentally handicapped child does not learn spontaneously, he does not teach himself. The basic approach used in the book is 'to discover what the child lacks, and to teach so as to fill in the gaps' (op. cit., p.19).

Another major boost to the 'objectives' cause came with the publication of the Warnock Report (DES 1978b). In the chapter 'The Nature of the Curriculum' a typical Tylerian tack is taken, where it is claimed that four interrelated elements contribute to the development of a curriculum:

> They are: (i) setting of objectives; (ii) choice of materials and experiences; (iii) choice of teaching and learning methods to attain the objectives; and (iv) appraisal of the appropriateness of the objectives and the effectiveness of the means of achieving them (op. cit., p.206).

The Report commends current work in curriculum development for children with severe learning difficulties, for 'it is now recognized that the tasks and skills to be learned by these children have to be analysed precisely and that the setting of small, clearly defined incremental objectives for individual children is a necessary part of programme planning' (op. cit., p.221).

Further heavy weight was added with the Schools Council Curriculum Bulletin 8 (1979), where a behavioural objectives model is used.

> When we refer to objectives we refer to observable and measurable behaviours . . . Objectives must be coherently related to aims . . . Objectives are observable behaviours which the child will be able to perform at the end of the learning experience that he could not perform at the beginning. . . . Objectives are clear, precise, observable and measurable behaviours, that make it possible to evaluate the effectiveness of the child's learning (Leeming et al. 1979, p. 42).

Although the illustrations and examples used are exclusively from the area of language and communication, they declare that 'the principles apply with equal force to other areas of the curriculum for mentally handicapped children' (op. cit., p.67). They continue, 'the only way we can hope to change children, and know we have succeeded, is to change their behaviour. This is the basis for the use of an objectives approach to the curriculum' (op. cit., p.68).

Language curriculum packages are also discussed, where reference is made to C.E. Osgood. The language model evolved from Osgood's work sees language as a number of separate sub-skills, which, although they come from independent bases, each affect the working of the total system. This model is used in the Illinois Test of Psycholinguistic Abilities (ITPA) which lists skills which are claimed to work together to produce language ability, and well known language development kits, for example the 'Peabody', are based on Osgood's model. It is admitted that there is very little in the way of developed curricula for teaching language and communication to ESN(S) children, but it is considered that McMaster (1973) has produced a useful basis for the development of such a curriculum.

In the same year Peter Mittler talks of the lack of books, materials and curricula for ESN(S) schools and also that 'there is little in the way of a sound theoretical rationale in this field, though the foundations have been ably laid by McMaster (1973)' (Mittler 1979, p.87). He advocates the use of a systematic approach towards teaching methods, and summarizes a number of essential components

1. Assessment
2. Selection and analysis of task.
3. Presentation of task.
4. Evaluation.

(op. cit., p.91)

Mittler states that the approach to education that he outlines is broadly behavioural, very much relying on assessment, developmental planning and prescription.

He then has a few, a very few, words to say on 'creative activities', such as drama, music, physical education, swimming, games, sports and a wide range of recreational activities, and adds that such activities 'can often provide the means for self-expression and a source of satisfaction' (op. cit., pp.95-96). It is my contention that these and other interrelated activities can provide much, much more than this, as I hope to illustrate later.

Recent projects from the Hester Adrian Research Centre (1979) continue to display a strong behavioural influence. One such project 'Teaching and the Severely Subnormal', developed by the Huddersfield Polytechnic in association with the HARC, aims to develop skills needed to run structured teaching sessions, and it is claimed 'that there is now in existence a considerable body of research evidence on learning processes in the severely mentally handicapped which could be used to inform their education and training (e.g. Clarke and Clarke 1974)', and that 'this evidence provides clear and unambiguous implications for teaching (Clarke and Clarke 1975)' (HARC 1979, p.33).

John Presland's (1980) paper further illustrates what appears to be an overwhelming commitment to the objectives approach and emphasizes the need for systematic teaching. 'Psychological research generally indicates that, at least for children with learning difficulties, their learning should be planned in a definite sequence, from the simple to the more complex, and reinforcement may often need to be given in a carefully planned way' (op. cit., p.28). See also Presland and Roberts 1980.

Further current pressures on teachers in Special Education to use behavioural methods may be seen in *Language Development Through Structured Teaching* developed by Project TASS (Teaching and the Severely Subnormal) (Robson 1980), and *Training Staff in Behavioural Methods: The Education of the Developmentally Young — The E.D.Y. Project* (Foxton and McBrien 1981; McBrien and Foxton 1981). Also, in a recent paper, Mittler (1981), in discussing the topic of teacher training in Special Education, lists the skills and knowledge needed, which include proficiency in the specification of behavioural objectives, task analysis, programme writing, prompting, shaping, chaining and reinforcement techniques and generalization training.

Ainscow and Tweddle (1979) also use the behavioural objectives approach in planning education for children with learning difficulties, as do the authors of *In Search of a Curriculum* (Rectory Paddock School 1982), who incidentally are practising teachers. They offer the most unfortunate mechanistic analogy of a car with a faulty engine as an aid to an understanding of the mentally handicapped child.

Finally, I shall give an example from the most recent edition to hand of *Special Education* (June 1982), which encapsulates aspects of present theory and practice in the behavioural mould. Raybould and Solity (1982) show enthusiasm for precision teaching and add that although this approach is relatively new in this country it has been used for a decade or more in the USA, Canada and Australia. (Much more than a decade — see Lindsley 1964.) They write that precision teaching uses many important behavioural principles, and state that this type of teaching offers a systematic approach for teaching children with learning difficulties in ordinary and Special schools.

They go on to argue that a prerequisite for precision teaching is that teaching targets, in terms of behavioural outcomes, must be formulated — it is necessary that the desired behaviour of the pupils must be observable and measurable. Mention is made of Mager (1962), Popham (1975) and Gronlund (1978), and they claim that increasing use is being made of specifying pupil performance in terms of objectives in the teaching of children with learning difficulties in this country. They give as examples Ainscow and Tweddle (1977, 1979) and argue that 'unless pupil performance can be stated in this way it will not be possible to determine whether or not the child has acquired the appropriate skill' (Raybould and Solity 1982, p.10).

What I find so depressing is that this behavioural approach to curriculum development appears to be seen by some as something of a new discovery, which of course it is not; leaving aside the fact that this type of curriculum development has so many deficiencies both in theory and in practice. I am suggesting that the use of this model *at any level* gives not only a most limited and limiting view of education, but may even be counter-productive to the enterprise of education itself.

Although powerful and most convincing objections have been eloquently directed towards the debilitating limitations of the behavioural approach towards curriculum planning by an increasing number of writers (I have listed some sixty or so serious limitations to using behavioural objectives), it is only recently that I have come across similar criticisms of this approach applied to Special Education, and I shall be discussing some of these a little later.

Before this, however, I must mention Lawrence Stenhouse's (1975) orderly alternative to the objectives model — a process model. For it is my contention that viewing education and curriculum development in terms of processes is admirably compatible with the ever-evolving practice in our own ESN(S) school. I shall tentatively try to describe some of the theory and practice involved in attempting to implement this alternative approach there, for 'it is increasingly apparent that real and effective curriculum development must go on within individual schools rather than by the creation of projects or other innovations hatched out in some central place detached from the realities of any actual school situation' (Kelly 1982, p.24).

A process approach to curriculum development in Special Education

I must reiterate my earlier suggestion that many experienced practising teachers use a form of process planning in their teaching. It is absolutely vital and essential that this practice must continue if 'education' itself is to survive. For, as Dewey said,

> The primary root of all educative activity is in the instinctive, impulsive attitudes and activities of the child, and not in the presentation and application of external material . . . and . . . accordingly, numberless spontaneous activities of children . . . are capable of educational use, nay, are the foundation-stones of educational method (Dewey 1900, p.27).

When my present school first opened in 1970 many of the staff had been teaching in the Junior Training Centre and there was comparatively little literature in this area of education. However, the teachers, under the leadership of the former Headteacher, who has never been inhibited by dogma, were influenced by the work of Mildred Stevens and earlier educationalists such as Froebel and Dewey.

Mildred Stevens managed most effectively to merge practice with theory. She anticipated a major recommendation of the Warnock Report by a decade; 'As a teacher I cannot think of the group of children ascertained as severely subnormal in any way other than that they are children with special learning difficulties, who go to school like all other children' (Stevens 1968, p.x). She advocates a dynamic approach to the education of such children, framed in terms of their 'happiness, interest, response and development', in which teachers must be able to *withstand the sway of educational fashion'* (Stevens 1971, p.viii). She reminds the reader of the impact of educational philosophy (some of it centuries old), and supports Dewey's assertion that it is the child's own instincts and powers that both furnish the material and provide the starting point for all education.

In her chapter 'General Educational Needs', she stresses the need for first-hand experiences, lists essentials for educational development, and talks of opportunities and reasons for spontaneous movement, adding 'It is truly a joy to see handicapped children busily employed in individual, representative and dramatic play and in creative pursuits. How interesting and exciting to be with them on their journeys' (op. cit., p.17). Later she offers some suggestions for activities with individual children, and makes the most salient point, which I shall be discussing later, on the topic of 'sequence' in activities, when suggesting that 'the handicapped do not seem to proceed from (a) to (b) in the steps we want them to pass through' so that 'the teacher should always be ready to abandon her own preconceived plan and follow the response of the child' (op. cit., p.37). She gives much practical advice on classroom arrangement, and also the need for children to move out of the school on various outings and visits.

Finally, in 'Understood Play', she lists important reasons for including play in the curriculum, one of which is that 'the skilful teacher can use play as a vehicle for introducing relevant language at the moment when it is most understood' (op. cit., p.54). And she talks of child psychologists such as Piaget, who see play as an important aspect of intellectual development, concluding that 'in play even severely subnormal children are given the chance to reconstruct and reorganize their experiences. As Dewey says, "it is this (reconstructing and reorganizing) which adds to the meaning of experience and increases the ability to direct the course of subsequent experience"' (op. cit., p.55).

These influences (along with other progressive ideas on primary education), coupled with an abundance of sound, and ever increasing practical experiences of working with the children in this 'special' school, were very much in evidence when I was fortunate enough to join the staff and become the senior boys' class-teacher. The school was alive with activities, based on a child-centred approach, where the child was seen as an active learner, an approach which now could be termed 'process-orientated'. Furthermore I was very attracted by the happy atmosphere that permeated the school. It would be difficult to describe what a wonderful effect this school has had on me, and how much I have learned from the children.

Every Thursday morning we had 'drama' in the school hall. It was chaotic to begin with — neither the children nor I could handle the situation — but ideas slowly evolved and these were shared and developed. After a couple of terms or so drama gradually became the highlight of our week. The boys began to be much more co-operative with each other. Our activities in the hall sparked off many ideas for work back in the classroom. When I became deputy head I continued taking drama/music/movement and started introducing children from other classes into the group. The older, more experienced children helped the younger ones.

As I mentioned earlier, I also became curriculum coordinator, and at that time was asked to write a one-page article to be included in the Year Book for the local Society of Mentally Handicapped Children, the title being 'The

Curriculum'. The following passages are taken from that brief article.

At Mayfair School, we try to create a stimulating, purposeful and happy environment, and this is reflected in the curriculum. The curriculum must be continually developing and based on individual and group needs. These needs are never constant. No one scheme, kit or programme is going to provide the answer. Although it is important to be aware of educational developments in our field, it is also most important to be selective, to never get imprisoned in a method.

Our children are encouraged to be active, for they can learn through their own actions, and also to experience what they are being taught. Furthermore, education should be enjoyable for all concerned.

We generally work in group situations, but time is also provided for work of a more individual nature.

Lack of space prohibits me from listing all our activities, but they include P.E., football, cricket, battington, swimming, inter-school sports, play in its various forms, the many moods of music, music and movement, rhythm, singing, stories, the experience of drama, of colour and form in painting, in craftwork, cookery, hygiene, shopping, self-help, project work, the use of television, records, cassette recordings, films (including our own), links with the community at large, with other schools, with Beck House [the Adult Training Centre], with the Gateway Club, educational visits, and our week at Earl's Orchard Field Studies Centre.

It must be stressed that all areas of the curriculum are inter-related and nothing must be seen in isolation. (Also communication, both verbal and non-verbal, enters into every aspect of the curriculum).

However, the curriculum means much more than this — it involves the delicate task of helping the individual child to unfold his or her unique personality. This further involves the building up of personal relationships, for the quality of interpersonal relationships is of the utmost importance throughout the whole of life.

In all we attempt to provide an environment in which a child can keep on growing and learning.

I include these extracts because:

(a) it was my first public statement on curriculum;

(b) there was nothing new or spectacular about the approach and activities mentioned, which could no doubt be seen in many other similar types of school;

(c) in retrospect it is in line with the philosophy of education expressed in the Hadow Report — 'Applying these considerations to the problem before us, we see that the curriculum is to be thought of in terms of activity and experience . . .' (Board of Education 1931, p.93) — and the Plowden Report — 'It lays special stress on individual discovery, on first hand experience and on opportunities for creative work. It insists that knowledge does not fall into neatly separate compartments and that work and play are not opposite but complementary' (CACE 1967, p.188);

(d) a similar approach was, and is, used to great effect by the local Gateway Club, run by parents and others with much personal and practical experience and involvement with mentally handicapped children, involving activities and providing experiences which I consider to be truly educative in the widest sense; and

(e) it came at a time when I was comparatively naive about curriculum development, but had decided to remedy this situation, and had begun my own studies, especially on the role of objectives in curriculum development at all levels of our educational system.

My examination of objectives led me to the conclusion that just as the 'scientific' approach had earlier superseded the ideas of Dewey in America, so the lead suggested by the likes of Mildred Stevens in Special Education is being stifled by the 'scientific' behaviourist approach, with its reliance on behavioural objectives — at least by most of the theorists, if not by the practitioners.

As Headteacher, I am now forever attempting to develop curriculum within the school, supporting teachers by trying to provide a theoretical framework necessary to make more explicit the experiential knowledge that each possesses. In part of a staff hand-out 'Curriculum Development and Special Educational Needs: An Introduction', I sketched in some of the general principles embodied in education as process.

I started by mentioning Stenhouse (1970, 1975) and his orderly alternative to the objectives model — a process model. He writes a critique of the objectives model, and thinks that there is a good case for claiming that the objectives approach, designed to improve practice by increasing clarity about ends, is not in fact the way to improve practice. He attempts to explore the possibilities offered by arriving 'at a useful specification of curriculum and the educational process without starting by pre-specifying the anticipated outcomes of that process in the form of objectives' (Stenhouse 1975, p.84).He points out that the weakness of the process model is that it rests upon the quality of the teacher, but claims that this is also its greatest strength. The adoption of the model is more demanding and also far more difficult to put into practice, but 'it offers a higher degree of personal and professional development' (op. cit, p.97). On the question of evaluation he considers the complete problem of criteria, and does not think that the criteria employed in the classical model of evaluation, where success or failure are judged by measured student behaviour, are appropriate. He concludes his chapter on evaluation by saying that curriculum research must be 'illuminative' rather than recommendatory. Finally, he agrees with Skilbeck (1971) — in fact he goes further — 'in doubting the effectiveness of pre-planned change as opposed to change evolving from process' (op. cit., p. 223).

My staff hand-out went on to point out that the notion of education as process is further developed by Geva Blenkin and Vic Kelly in *The Primary Curriculum* (1981) and I briefly summarized their chapter 'Education as Process':

1. An ever-present concern should be that the activities that we encourage children to be engaged in should have intrinsic value for them — not merely as a means to achieve certain ends.

2. The influence of developmental psychology adds a second dimension to the continuation of the educational process.

3. The combination of 1 and 2 leads to a view of education in the light of the developing experience of the child.

In order to provide these kinds of experience, several important principles must guide our practice:

1. the context of education — the child must be given freedom to explore and experience — also there must be appropriate and skilful intervention from the teacher;

2. the importance of both the warmth and the intensity of the relationship between pupil and teacher;

3. the areas of interest must also be genuine areas of experience;

4. they must not be selected or pursued merely to satisfy the teacher's demands;

5. the teacher must assist the child to develop ways of dealing with elements of the child's own enquiries, thus promoting the child's intellectual growth;

6. the concern is with the process of education rather than the products;

7. the teaching of basic skills must not be separated from the wider aspects of children's development.

I end the hand-out by looking briefly at some implications of viewing education as process in developing a curriculum for children with special educational needs, suggesting that the Warnock Report (DES 1978b) can be seen to provide a basis of some *activities* that may help to constitute a curriculum, with its stress on wider aspects of English and mathematics, for example, and also on the vital importance of language (both verbal and non-verbal). The value of music, art, drama and physical education are emphasized as being particularly important for children with special needs, as well as education in the forming of relationships with others.

A process curriculum in practice

All these interrelated activities should be experienced in a 'playful' and an intrinsically meaningful way (Piaget and Bruner both stress the enormous importance of play). In *The Dramatic Curriculum* (1980), Richard Courtney, in claiming that the entire curriculum can be viewed in dramatic terms, quotes both Caldwell Cook and Dewey and their assertion that *doing, play* and *spontaneity* are the keys to learning. Seeing education as concerned with processes puts many of our school activities into proper perspective, placing emphasis on the whole development of the child, encouraging emotional, intellectual, physical, perceptual, social, aesthetic and creative growth, and what better vehicle for fostering this 'interrelatedness' than play, which can actively involve all learning.

Herbert Read helps me here. He sees schooling as an activity which grows insensibly into living and argues that the process is one of initiation. And, although 'play' may be objected to as being not good enough for 'such a solemn rite', and therefore the word 'art' is substituted, nevertheless Caldwell Cook's (1914) description is, according to Read, the best that could be quoted:

> 'Play, as I mean it,' he says — ART as I mean it, 'goes far deeper than study; it passes beyond reasoning, and lighting up the chambers of the imagination, quickens the body of thought, and proves all things in action . . . but even today learning is often KNOWING without much care for FEELING, and mostly none at all for DOING. Learning may remain detached, as a garment, unidentified with self. But by Play (Art) I mean DOING anything ONE KNOWS with one's heart in it. The final appreciation in life and in study is to put oneself into the thing studied and to live there ACTIVE.'

Read adds 'Caldwell Cook was a schoolmaster, and his theory arose out of his practice' (Read 1943, pp.231-232).

Earlier I mentioned how our drama lessons became the highlight of our week. The Bullock Report makes the observation that 'in most schools drama has yet to realise its potential in helping the child to communicate with others, to express his own feelings and thoughts, and to gain confidence in a variety of contexts' (DES 1975, p.157). I find Ian Petrie's *Drama and Handicapped Children* (1974) also of interest. In the Foreword Peter Slade states that 'any person handling "special" children may have to structure more to start with then try to offer more responsibility to those taking part in drama — little tasks to see how they get on by themselves'. Petrie says that in Special Education teachers are 'basically attempting to provide experiences which meet the needs of handicapped children and creative drama may contribute towards meeting these needs' (op. cit., p.3).

I find most relevant his point that the methods which have been devised to *change behaviour* at surface level, based on techniques of behaviour modification (involving the use of behavioural objectives), 'are unacceptable to many psychologists and teachers who believe that social and emotional development is fostered more through personal relationships than principles of conditioning' (op. cit., p.8).

He also discusses the relationship between creative drama and play, although he differentiates between them, and he argues that play is an *active* process and in its relationship to creative drama emphasis is given to *active* learning, a view of education related to children's natural interests and modes of responding.

Another publication I find useful is Gordon Pidgeon's *Towards Creative Play* (1980) — a guide to using Child Drama with those of special educational need. Pidgeon believes that in drama activities there is no right 'method'. He restates the relationship between Child Drama and play. He thinks that there is too much concentration upon the *cognitive* aspects of failure whilst the *emotional* aspects of learning are neglected. In 'Practical Work' he makes the pertinent point, which I agree with entirely, that 'at all times teachers should look for what the children can do rather than what they cannot do' (op. cit., p.9). He concludes:

> There is support for the belief that we learn by doing. If we learn to draw by drawing it follows that we learn to talk by talking and the growth of language must develop through opportunities to use language. Whether this is non-verbal, or verbal language, children will develop a richer vocabulary by involvement in

situations which require expression. I have found that children and adults who have opportunities for regular relationship play become more physically confident, more sociable and consequently more communicative. I also believe that the activities which I use, although they may not be accepted by some teachers as 'drama', also contribute to the development of children's language, thought and socialization. Consequently, they require consideration as important aspects of the curriculum (op. cit., pp.46-47).

This theme is reflected in *Drama in Primary Schools* (Stabler 1978), where as part of the educational value of drama it is stated that 'it fosters fundamental learning involving many curricular areas', (op. cit., p.2). Emphasized too is children's natural approach to drama and the intrinsic strength of interest and motivation that 'can make it such a powerful educational force . . . encouraging language, expression and communication, organizing information, solving problems, formulating and testing hypotheses' (ibid.). These authors also stress the development of social understanding and an ability to work constructively in groups. The importance of dramatic play is stated, bringing together both the individual experiences and the resources of those involved, and also the sharing of dramatic play, which encourages children to move from egocentric tendencies towards co-operating within the group, thus making group activity possible. Through play children can learn 'tolerance, mutual help, trust and that give and take which enables group planning and decisions to be undertaken' (op. cit., p.3). It is also added that the functions of dramatic play encourage the child in its own creative power, and also, very importantly, I think, develops the individual child as an active agent in his or her own world.

Dorothy Heathcote (1981), who has done much excellent and pioneering work involving children with learning difficulties, views drama in a wide educational setting which incorporates many educational principles. Drama is a social activity which uses the human body as an agent of expression. In that sense she thinks it is the closest art to the process of living and thus integral to education. 'Finally, having spent a long time wondering why I have for years been irritated by the cry of "Let's have more drama in our schools", I now realize why I always wanted to say, "Don't lobby for dramatics, lobby for better learning"' (op. cit., p.15).

I have chosen to examine 'drama' first for it shows:

(a) what a potent learning medium it can be;

(b) how it supports curriculum unity, and the idea of education as process; and

(c) how it relates both to the overall development of the *curriculum* and to *assessment* (which includes record-keeping), aspects of which I shall now consider.

Assessment in my school is carried out by the teachers in two ways. The teaching staff have always been expected and encouraged to keep 'notes' on individual children, these being of a personal and informal nature — in similar fashion to Derek Rowntree's description of a more basic idea of assessment in education, 'to some extent or other it is an attempt to KNOW that person. In this light, assessment can be seen as human encounter' (Rowntree 1977, p.4). Rowntree also recommends circumspection and a decent humility with all methods of assessment. He makes the most important point that we must go 'beyond behaviour', as behaviour has meaning, and quotes an old Roman saying, 'If two people do the same thing, it is not the same thing' (op. cit., p.175). He also mentions that the assessor would need to report on important unanticipated qualities — the use of a more open assessment, such as the 'Free Response' report, 'in which we describe everything significant we happen to have noticed about the student in a particular piece of work or during a particular period of time' (op. cit., p.220).

Over the years these reports have given us a fascinating and fruitful insight into the child as a person — a unique individual.

The second more formal system of assessment is more problematic, for it is here that we run the risk of 'segmenting' the child into various areas. 'The standard chapter headings of memory, cognition, motivation, perception, emotion, the senses and so forth are the ultimate denial of the person as the subject matter of psychology. They substitute for the person functions to be studied separately in spite of the fact that they cannot be LIVED separately' (Bannister and Fransella 1971, p.52). Tony Booth also stresses the de-humanizing effects of much psychological writing and suggests that the difficulty of it is that 'its subject matter seems to bear little resemblance to anything remotely human. It is often about bits of people' (Booth 1975, p.8).

Although for convenience sake, then, I have asked the staff to write about each child in various 'traditional' areas, it must be stressed that all areas are interrelated, as I hope to illustrate further. The areas are: Gross Movement (including sporting interests and swimming progress); Body Image (including awareness of body parts); Fine Movement; Books, Paper and Pencil Work, Drawing, Writing, Reading; Time; Early Mathematics (pre-number/ number); Language, (verbal and non-verbal, including comprehension and expressive); Self-help (eating and drinking, home activities, shopping, domestic tasks, dressing, toileting, washing and general hygiene); and Play (different kinds of play overlap and classification is difficult — play is a total activity which involves the child's whole thought and action — however, we may tentatively look at social, domestic, construction, make-believe, natural materials, outdoor and dramatic play).

How these areas are interrelated to promote the development of the whole child, by emphasizing processes rather than products, and how that inter-relationship can be reflected in the assessment procedures adopted, I shall now try to demonstrate, as I did in discussing 'drama', by the following examples.

In *Art Activities for the Handicapped*, Sally Atack (1980) bases her work on observations of young children participating in undirected art activities, which have convinced her of the value of these activities in developing the skills and personalities of maturing people. She explains 'How Art is Helpful' —

1. Control and Awareness of Self.
Learning how to make something happen — physical control. Getting it better — physical dexterity. Stretching out — the physical possibility.

2. Awareness and Discrimination of Things.
Exploring the difference. Learning the difference. Making a choice. Choosing the right thing — personal organization. Making the right choices, and getting the desired result on one's own — self-reliance.

3. Communication.
Having something to share. Art as language — a contact without words. Having something to talk about. This is how I see 'it' — making a picture about how it looks to me. Placing a value — respecting one's own and others' contribution, however small.

4. Contact with Others.
Joining in. Something to give. Letting experience be the beginning of art.

5. Pleasure and Success.
Pleasure gained from handling a variety of materials. Pleasure and success felt when the result is as it was intended. Pleasure gained through giving (Atack 1980).

In cookery the children are not only learning about self-help and indepen-dence, but are also using fine and gross movements; hand-eye coordination; mathematical experiences in concrete situations — weighing, dividing, counting, returning working utensils to their respective places; listening, co-operating, developing language in a meaningful context, etc. — plus the joy of taking 'their' cooking home.

Similar areas merge, say in the playing of battington or table tennis — most of our children have poor body image, and are encouraged to participate wherever possible in many activities including naming, touching and moving different body parts in different ways. Without an awareness of his or her own body and its movements, the child will be unable to learn from observing other people's bodies and their movements. Our children are encouraged to have as wide a range of movement experiences as possible, to build up their physical and emotional sense of security. 'Movement has a great deal to contribute to children's development . . . the effect of movement on children's concentration, effort and co-ordination may in the long term be a far more efficient method of dealing with learning difficulties than the repetition of methods that have previously led to failure' (Rosen and Rosen 1973, p.196). Much emphasis is put on PE, swimming, team games, music/movement/drama and dance, encompassing both functional and expressive movement.

Certainly music and movement have made a great difference to my own personal development and I can now join in sessions with willingness and without embarrassment, as if it is the most natural thing in the world, which of course it is. I hope the children under my care feel this too.

Music plays a most important role in our school life. We have our own band which plays at events within the school and also at 'outside' functions. Most of our children readily respond to the many moods that music can provide. We do much rhythmic work, action games and action songs. These activities not only provide opportunities for rhythm work, but also for movement linked with language, and for early mathematical experiences.

I find *Mathematics for Young Children — a comparison of three Schools Council Projects* (Cooper and Whitfield 1981) most helpful, where the view of mathematics taken can be summed up:

> Children begin to absorb mathematical ideas from a very early age and as their use and understanding of language progresses, so they are able to convey ideas to other children and people around them . . . The same learning process goes on as they explore the whole gamut of toys, books, music and physical activity, gaining experience in the way material may be manipulated . . . This gradual collecting and storing up of information leads children towards acquiring concepts (Schools Council 1978, p. 3).

Cooper and Whitfield continue 'Thus, mathematics is active; it can be acquired through a wide variety of apparently non-mathematical activity; and it involves the children in acquiring concepts' (op. cit., p.35).

All three projects discussed in that article see learning as an active process. 'Structuring Play' suggests children learn 'by active and direct participation in concrete situations where the basis of problem solving and creative thinking is laid' (Manning and Sharp 1977, p.12). In 'Early Mathematical Experiences' it is argued 'In the past, because children have been able to chant numbers in order (1, 2, 3 . . .), it has sometimes been assumed that they understood them and so were ready for sums . . . Young children need to experience the ideas through play. It is practical activity that is important; the handling of a whole range of materials.' And it continues, 'The help of a skilled adult, who can stand back and observe and who is ready also to join with a child as he plays, to focus his attention and talk with him, is also important' (Schools Council 1978b, p.3). Examples are given concerning the individual child's total development, as mathematics naturally involves many other activities; but there are 'also examples of records for more specifically mathematical notions such as concepts of size and position, and the ability to make comparisons' (Cooper and Whitfield 1981, p.37).

Language development, verbal and non-verbal, touches on every aspect of the curriculum. Some children are unable to communicate verbally, yet many are able to communicate by non-verbal means and some of them accompany their gestures with sound. In the case of children who are either late in speech development or who do not develop expressive language at all, an alternative method of communication should be explored and preferably this should not preclude the possibility of later speech development.

In the General Introduction to *Language Development* (Lee 1979) an important distinction is made between language acquisition and language variation. 'There is a danger that language development might be identified with language acquisition. The inclusion of a substantial section on language variation emphasises the importance of CONTEXT to the acquisition of language' (op. cit., p.11). I find Dennis Fry's *How did we learn to do it?* (Fry 1977) a most excellent introduction to an overview of language acquisition. He makes this most important observation: 'To speak of the stage a child has reached is only to give a hint as to the general character of the activity he will be most engaged in. Stages in speech development, like those in every other type of learning, merge into each other and cannot be marked off by dates and times' (op. cit., p.19). This is a point which reinforces much of what Marian Whitehead said of language development in Chapter 3.

Also of much help and interest is *Learning through Interaction: the Study of Language Development*, by Gordon Wells (1981). The first part of the book contains chapters on an overview of linguistic communication and its development. It is argued that conversation provides the natural context of language development and that the child learns through exploring his world in interaction with other people. The second part looks at similarities and differences between the talk that occurs at home and at school and stresses the need for continuity.

Also Wells (1978) describes and illustrates characteristics of much parent-child talk — it is child initiated; arises from meaningful activity; involves negotiation of meaning. He argues that talk in classrooms is too often restricted to teacher-dominated *uncontextualized* question-answer routines, and calls for a varied style of interaction in the classroom, building upon children's strengths and also incorporating characteristics of home talk. Time and time again Wells stresses the importance of finding out what the child is currently interested in. It is important to sustain and extend the initiations the child makes — the adult sensitively following, rather than imposing his or her view on where the child is going.

In support of another point Marian Whitehead made in Chapter 3, the importance of listening to stories for children's language development is also highlighted — both as a highly desirable experience in its own right, and also because of the power written language has to create a context, thus preparing the child for highly symbolic situations. On the topic of stories Pat D'Arcy (1973) mentions the function of fantasy in stories for young children, how it helps in the emotional and mental development of the child, and also the strong fantasy element in nursery rhymes. She adds that, as well as books, many television programmes 'offer the opportunity for children to project their inner fantasies' (D'Arcy 1973, p.8). She also mentions the importance of nursery rhymes, where the strong rhythmic pattern encourages the child to join in.

Self-help comes naturally into many of our activities, for example undressing and dressing for swimming and PE, which of course involves movement and coordination. So too does eating and drinking. The staff take lunch with the children and this provides many excellent teaching and learning situations, carried out in a meaningful context, and including social education as well as a fruitful ground for language development. At the same time it provides opportunities for building up both the confidence and independence of the individual child.

We also take the children on as many educational visits as possible. This is an integral and essential aspect of our curriculum, which can, and often does, provide ideas on various forms of project work. Most terms we take a group of children to Weardale for the week, where we do all our own cooking etc., and the term 'learning through living' really takes on a true meaning. I have often been on such visits and the educational value of such ventures would merit a chapter to itself; they also provide us with much additional information through observations of the children in a different environment.

Other related professions are actively involved in the life of our school too. Very frequent medical inspections are held, which invariably involve parents. The school nurses visit on many occasions during the week. Medical reports add yet more useful and essential information on children — as do reports and advice from our physiotherapist, speech therapist, educational psychologist, community nurses, school-based social worker, and other social workers and school welfare officer.

Parental support is most necessary — it is so important that we all work together — and parents must be kept informed of their child's progress. If a parent requires a progress report it is written in the form of a personal letter, utilizing all available information, which includes my own involvement. For I teach every day and run a football/social club each day during the lunch-break, so I am in constant contact with the children and the teachers. Parents are also welcome to come to the school at all times. We have a school swimming club every Thursday evening and parents and friends are most welcome. We hold informal parents' meetings on Friday mornings, which involve staff and often our physiotherapist, speech therapist, educational psy-chologist and school nurses. Many of our older children are members of the Gateway Club and benefit greatly from the facilities and friendship provided there. A junior section has recently been established and all parents and children are most welcome to join.

At the end of each term we send out a Newsletter of School Events. The curriculum is evaluated in its own terms, on the principles of process rather than products or intended learning outcomes; curriculum development is a dynamic, living, continuous process, which is emergent, not established, and thus may be evaluated in a 'formative' as opposed to a 'summative' manner, using 'illuminative' evaluation.

I have tried to condense my account of how one can meet the needs of assessment and record-keeping while at the same time offering a unified curriculum into a few pages, and have taken the risk of over-simplifying a complex process, in the hope that it supports and illustrates my claims that there is a valuable and workable alternative to the 'objectives model' of curriculum development in Special Education and that to adopt it need not put the assessment of pupils at risk.

It appears then that it is not only *possible* to develop, assess and evaluate a curriculum in Special Education, and to allow for accountability, without the prespecification of behavioural objectives; it is also, I think, *preferable*.

Some recent developments in Special Education and other related issues

It was only very recently that I discovered other literature concerning Special Education that is not in agreement with basing a curriculum on the behavioural approach. Will Swann, in attempting to understand some of the current movements in this field, explains that one feature 'that is currently booming in many areas is the use of behavioural approaches to teaching. It appears as behaviour modification when applied to maladjustment, and "teaching by objectives" when applied to learning difficulties' (Swann 1981, p.5). He continues that the central problem of teaching by objectives 'is that it is sold as a curriculum, but it is nothing of the kind. The important questions of what should be taught, why and how are avoided or glossed over quickly' (op. cit., p.7). He illustrates this by reference to some of the example programmes provided by Ainscow and Tweddle (1979). He also states that what we often want to teach is not behaviour, neither can it be reduced to behaviour, and he illustrates this point by citing Presland and Roberts (1980). Acts take place within social contexts and this must be taken into account.

These, and other arguments (Pring 1981), have persuaded him that 'a behavioural approach is wrong in principle as a basis for a curriculum' (op. cit., p.10). His argument is 'that behavioural approaches cannot form part of an integrated system because they amount to a form of curricular segregation, whether they involve teaching academic skills through behavioural objectives, or classroom management techniques' (op. cit., pp. 14-15).

I was also delighted to come across *Minds of Their Own: One Teacher's Philosophy*, (Serpell-Morris 1982). Gerry Serpell-Morris was formerly a Senior Lecturer in Special Education, and is now Headteacher of a school for children with severe learning difficulties. When he was lecturing he felt he should include practical books in his courses — 'books advocating careful prescriptive planning, largely based around what is called the behavioural objectives approach. However, now I am personally facing these problems (of what teaching action to take with a particular child) I find little assistance from such material.' He continues that he has been struggling 'with the philosophy of the curriculum because once I have established clear principles on which to proceed I feel that I shall have a basis for a more consistent course of action — a more consistent curriculum' (op. cit., p.176). In discussing the teachers' role, he thinks they should 'arrange things so as to capitalize on what they (the children) can do — not emphasize their disabilities' (op. cit., p.177). This last point is so important, and is applicable at all levels of education.

In a recent personal correspondence he writes of 'the naive logic of the terminal and intermediate objectives approach so popular at the present time, largely one suspects because of the apparent ease of assessing teaching and learning it is supposed to offer'. He adds that 'a curriculum strategy for mentally handicapped children which subscribes to the present received wisdom of the objectives approach has no educational significance'. 'Education' is reduced to training. He contends that 'education must be perceived not as a period of rigidly planned and prescribed preparation for some eventual "end state" but as an incremental strategy of amelioration which will continue throughout the mentally handicapped person's life of which schooling is but a part.'

This raises the question, why should behavioural approaches be any more valid in Special Education than in 'ordinary' education? The Warnock Report states 'we believe that the general aims of education are the same for all children' (DES 1978b, p.205). Mildred Stevens quotes Mary Lindsay (1963) 'Nothing in my experience as a teacher of the mentally handicapped children, nor what I have seen so widely of other people's work leads me to believe that the fundamental needs of mentally handicapped children are different from those of normal children' (Stevens 1968, p.4.) And 'In one sense every child's educational needs are "special"' (DES 1980, p.10), which basic fact is restated in Povey (1980). I suggest that there are two possible reasons why the behavioural approach is still considered by so many as being so suitable for Special Education. I believe it is based on two myths. One concerns 'structured teaching' and the other 'basic skills'.

The myth of structured teaching

There is an assumption, which has rarely been challenged, that children with severe learning difficulties do not learn vicariously from experience. Hence there must be a 'special' curriculum, where all is carefully 'structured' — based on behavioural objectives, of course. But the experimental evidence on which this assumption is based is not strong, and does not provide, as it has been claimed, 'clear and unambiguous implications for teaching' (Clarke and

Clarke 1975). In fact, one hardly needs to carry out scientific experiments to realize that the assumption is clearly false. I am constantly amazed how the children, with whom I have had the pleasure of being associated over the past decade, come to know and understand so much, both in and out of school, without the aid of highly structured 'intended learning outcomes', and also how a child can influence his or her own learning and that of other children. I am sure I am not alone in my observations.

Will Swann hits the nail squarely on the head on this issue, writing again in personal correspondence:

> The vicarious learning myth supports the structured teaching myth, which is where behavioural objectives find their niche. As I argued in Unit 12 of E241 this idea is also deeply flawed because the distinction between structured and unstructured teaching is a semantic trick. All teaching, all environments have a structure, and the question of the kinds of structure that are conducive to mental, bodily and spiritual growth is sidestepped by the orthodoxy, and artificially buttressed by the mirage, of achievement measured by behaviour.

In the Open University course 'Special Needs in Education', to which he refers, he states:

> In virtually all attempts to apply the psychology of child development to teaching mentally handicapped children has been the idea that the best kind of teaching is highly structured individual sessions, generally involving the specification of objectives to be achieved within that session. This is often coupled with the idea, expressed earlier in this section by Chris Kiernan and his colleagues, that if we can identify in more detail the components of development then these can become the objectives of individual teaching sessions. In effect we would be teaching development.

He continues, 'teaching the products of development does not amount to development itself. Development for normal children is a process of constant and varied interaction with the environment, and this can be no more circumvented for normal children than it can for mentally handicapped children.' He thinks that one should be 'led back to the everyday tasks that children perform in their day-to-day lives, and to selecting those tasks which are most relevant to the child's interests and capabilities. This requires understanding children not as collections of developmental products . . . but as doing certain things in certain ways in certain contexts . . . The task of teaching then becomes one of supporting children in their natural environment, and extending their power to deal with that environment' (Swann 1982, pp.34-35).

The myth of 'basic skills'

'Back to basics' is a rallying cry which is being heard more and more both in this country and in the USA. Children in Special Education find skills learning difficult. In America much Federal money has been spent on programmed instructional materials, aided and abetted by workbooks, packages and an assortment of other skill-drill materials, and this approach fitted in admirably with the behavioural objectives model of curriculum development. Indeed the behavioural objectives and back-to-basics movements developed hand-in-hand. In discussing 'A Unified Curriculum', Geva Blenkin and Vic Kelly (1981) consider the teaching and learning of skills in some detail, and some of the points made there have been developed more fully by Geva Blenkin in Chapter 2 of this book. Aspects of this discussion I shall briefly summarize, with a few added observations.

It is often suggested that skills are learned through training rather than education, and that the teaching of skills should be viewed in isolation from other types of teaching — that they are learned in a sequential and linear manner, and therefore ideally suited for the behavioural objectives approach. But skills in themselves are not necessarily educative and the use of the model can be both inappropriate and counter-productive. In the teaching and learning of skills in an educational context it is necessary to realize that both are part and parcel of the process of education, and it can no longer be assumed that skills can be either taught or learned in isolated units, nor that skills are learned independently of the context in which they are used. They must not be learned for their own sake but must be developed in living contexts. If skills are taught in isolation, out of context of the child's real-life experiences and understanding, as often happens in the use of packages and kits (many instrumental language programmes offer clear examples), then the learning of splinter skills could well ensue. Merely teaching a skilled performance at a behavioural level in itself has no educational significance — such practices could in fact be seen as being anti-educational.

> If a skill such as reading is to be viewed as supportive of an educational activity, if not an educational activity in itself, an approach to the teaching of it by way of pre-specified behavioural objectives and a concentration on skills of a simple kind is not only inappropriate, it is also counter-productive. Parallels can be drawn in the skills of numeracy, for not only may children be encouraged to 'bark at print' or become non-readers that can decipher print, but also — and perhaps more commonly — they can learn to recite computations without being aware of either the rules or the concepts that govern the activity (Blenkin and Kelly 1981, p.122).

In conclusion they state, 'This led us to the realization that the only proper way to view the teaching and learning of skills in an educational context is to see that both are an integral and inseparable part of the process of education and to recognize that their prime function and purpose is to promote the kinds of intellectual development of which education itself consists' (op. cit., p.135).

It was felt by many, and still is, that the so called 'frills' (such as art, drama, music etc.) were responsible for neglecting the development of skills, and were merely 'fringe' activities of secondary significance, or even superfluous, to cognitive development. I have argued earlier that this is not the case. As Fred Hechinger writes in *The New York Times*, in an article entitled 'Frills in Schools Are Often Basic', 'If the "basic school" — one without such frills as art, music, after-school activities, books and personal instruction — becomes the standard pattern, particularly in financially pressed cities, then city schools will soon again become "poor schools", as they were called before the advent of universal access to public education' (Hechinger 1979).

And in a most illuminating paper 'The Contribution of Painting to Children's Cognitive Development', Eisner asks 'what students learn when they paint, or sculpt, or draw. In short, what do children learn when they make visual images?' (Eisner 1979b, p.109). He goes on to discuss in some detail nine forms of learning that add to children's cognitive development.

Finally, Gavin Bolton in *Towards a Theory of Drama in Education* (1979), on the topic of language says:

> Expressive skills, however, must be seen within the larger context to which they clearly belong: language ... Many recent educational publications claim an important relationship between drama and the acquisition of language skills, including communication skills, but I would go further than this by suggesting that in many ways drama is language ... It is as if drama is a cobweb and language its strands: you cannot conceive of one without the other.
>
> I am talking about language in its very broadest sense of course, as a nonverbal/verbal code for encapsulating and sharing experience. It is a currency for handling meaning (op. cit., p.119).

In discussing 'Reading and writing', he thinks that 'it is ironical that at the time of writing this book there is an educational trend "back to basics". Infant teachers tell me that they have no time for drama as they must raise the standard of reading and writing, so they drop the very tool that would help them' (op. cit., p.123). In a more recent publication he states that 'the rest of education may at this moment in time be rushing lemming-like "back to basics". Conceptually, for drama teachers this is no problem ... for drama *is* basic' (Bolton 1982, p.31). He thinks drama may be seen 'as a vehicle for cognitive development giving significance to the learning of those kinds of concepts which, while cutting across the traditional subject barriers, are nevertheless of central importance to living' (op. cit., p.42).

Summary and Conclusions

Many 'standard' practices in Special Education have now been challenged. For example, the King IQ appears to have abdicated. The Frostig Development Tests of Visual Perception, along with the Frostig-Horne teaching materials, had 'a tremendous bandwagon effect in the 1960s and are still quite widely used' (Harris 1976, p.442). The results of the wealth of research on the Frostig programme and authoritative views of such research are most disappointing, to say the least, as is the effectiveness of the Illinois Test of Psycholinguistic Abilities (ITPA). Harris declares 'It would seem that a programme of training specific abilities based on the ITPA rests on fairly shaky ground. Furthermore, there is very little evidence as to the degree to which deficient abilities in children can be improved by special training' (op. cit., p.443). In *Diagnostic Teaching* (1982) Swann and Briggs sum up the situation thus, 'This identification and training of fundamental psychological processes looks very appealing, as if we are getting to the heart of the problem. Unfortunately it doesn't work' (op. cit., p.4.11).

The sociological approach too has often been neglected. 'It takes as its subject matter the recurring relationships between human beings . . . Hence, rather than, as is the case with educational psychology, focusing on the needs and dispositions of the individual child, the sociologist insists that they must be seen in conjunction with the social structures (family, peer group, classroom, school, and educational, industrial and class system) in which the child is enmeshed' (Lane 1981, p.8).

I have argued that the current practice of basing a curriculum on the behavioural objectives model in Special Education is totally inadequate, as it is at any level of education. I have offered an alternative approach, using an 'open system' (Downey 1980), searching for and encouraging the strengths of individuals in an attempt to build up the confidence, self-esteem and self-motivation of all concerned, everyone being active participants in the process of their own unique and ever-evolving education, where teachers play a central role in curriculum development which is genuinely school-based.

I started by quoting from Sinha's paper and shall conclude in similar fashion. He talks about the nature of learning processes in mentally handicapped (and normal) children. He states that few active researchers in developmental psychology would consider behaviourism to be an adequate theory, and continues that in the field of Special Education the developmental theory of Piaget is only just starting to displace the previously 'unchallenged hegemony of behaviourism' (Sinha 1981, p.403). Behaviourism, according to Sinha, is *not* a developmental theory and, he argues, it is a developmental theory which is needed. He mentions Wells' (1981) work where the importance of the processes of social interaction and negotiation in both linguistic and cognitive development is discussed; and, following Donaldson (1978), it seems that children's thinking is embedded in context. He also quotes Vygotsky that 'learning awakens a variety of internal developmental processes that are able to operate only when the child is interacting with people in his environment and in co-operation with his peers. Once these processes are internalized, they become part of the child's independent developmental achievement' (op. cit., p.410).

To develop an educational curriculum in Special Education priority must, I believe, be given to processes.

CHAPTER 12

PROCESSES IN THE SECONDARY SCHOOL: MACOS AND BEYOND

GWYN EDWARDS

In this chapter I hope to demonstrate that the model of education elucidated so cogently in *The Primary Curriculum* (Blenkin and Kelly 1981) and given practical expression in some of the earlier chapters of this book is both desirable and possible in Secondary schools, despite formidable constraints such as external examinations and internal administrative structures. In one important respect the title of the book is a misnomer in that its basic message is as relevant to teachers in the Secondary and Tertiary sectors as it is to their Primary colleagues. Unfortunately, 'progressive' education has been much maligned in Secondary schools, due partly perhaps to excesses perpetrated in its name by practitioners with a limited understanding of its basic features. The authors of *The Primary Curriculum*, in undertaking a thorough re-examination of the nature and purpose of education, have provided all interested teachers with a detailed blueprint for action. The message they offer is both loud and clear and it is now up to schools and teachers who accept its importance to respond to their challenge by developing curricula that give practical realization to the conceptual framework they have explicated.

This chapter will focus on the way in which the Humanities Department at Meopham School, Kent, has faced up to such a challenge. From the outset the difficulties inherent in the task must be emphasized. It is not an enterprise that a school or department undertakes without considerable commitment and thought. A non-hierarchical structure which facilitates and encourages openness and dialogue is an essential prerequisite. It assumes the professional and intellectual development of staff to be of paramount importance. Moreover, in Secondary schools in particular, there is a need for a fundamental reappraisal of many long-standing pedagogical and epistemological assumptions. To bring about the kind of education envisaged in *The Primary Curriculum* requires not only a radical reordering of the way in which knowledge is defined but also a shift from a pedagogy that emphasizes the transmission of knowledge and skills to one that focuses on the processes of education.

The school setting

Meopham School opened in September 1976 as an 11—17 high school operating within the scheme for Secondary education in the Gravesham Division of North Kent. Secondary schools in this area are organized in a two-tier system. At eleven all children transfer to high schools without any form of selection. At thirteen there is a process whereby some pupils transfer, by guided parental choice, to 13—18 upper schools to follow courses designed to lead to 'A' level examinations. It is an integral part of the scheme that pupils who remain in high schools have the opportunity to follow courses leading to public examinations at 16+. Meopham School currently receives a seven-form intake with approximately 25 percent of these pupils transferring to upper schools at the end of their second year.

Internally the school is organized on rather traditional lines, reflecting the usual pastoral/curriculum dichotomy, although there has always been an emphasis on the integration of these functions, and increasingly so in recent years. A more detailed description of the internal structure of the school is not considered relevant to the purpose of this chapter.

The Humanities Department

The Humanities Department occupies a number of rooms built around a central resources area which it shares with the English Department. It makes extensive use of a purpose-built lecture theatre, with banked seating for approximately 80—90 pupils, which adjoins the area. In years one to three pupils pursue an integrated Humanities course, of which the American curriculum project Man: A Course of Study forms a major component, taking up a term and a half in both the first and second years. The importance of this project in the development of the Department's thinking will be examined in due course.

In years four and five the Department offers as options four subject-based courses, Geography, History, Social Science, Religion and Modern Living, leading to CSE and 'O'-level examinations. The Upper School option system is designed in a way that ensures all pupils pursue at least one Humanities course. Pupils are taught in mixed ability groups in all years, although it should be pointed out that because of transfer at 13+ the ability range in the remaining years is somewhat compressed. It is the Department's view that examinations should not be allowed to dominate or distort the curriculum and the courses it offers in years four and five have been developed to reflect and facilitate its fundamental philosophy of education as process. This is particularly true of the CSE Mode 3 Social Science course which will be reviewed later in the chapter as an exemplar of the Department's practice.

Man: A Course of Study

Man: A Course of Study (MACOS) was developed in the USA during the 1960s by Education Development Center Inc., under the direction of Peter Dow, with grants from the National Science Foundation. In Britain the project is disseminated by the Centre for Advanced Research in Education (CARE) at the University of East Anglia which also provides training facilities for teachers using or intending to use it. Indeed, such is the desire to protect the integrity of the course that officially it is only sold to those schools employing a member of staff trained in its use. The course was initially aimed at 10—12 year olds but it has subsequently been used with pupils ranging from 9 to 16 years of age.

The most significant feature of the course is that it attempts to give practical expression to the learning and instructional theories of the American psychologist, Jerome S. Bruner, who was the chief consultant in the early stages of its development. Detailed expositions of his key ideas are to be found in *The Process of Education* (1960), *Towards a Theory of Instruction* (1966) and *The Relevance of Education* (1971), the last a collection of papers spanning a number of years. Although the implications of his writings are far-reaching and complex, and to some extent have shifted in focus over the years, they are held together by a number of powerful concepts.

Central to his thesis is the view that education is a process by which cognitive growth is facilitated rather than propositional knowledge acquired. Cognitive growth can be conceived as the development of capacities by which human beings explicate and gain mastery over a complex world. The learner is an active participant in the process, constantly restructuring knowledge and generating new thinking strategies in order to resolve problems presented by the environment. Bruner recognizes three 'modes of representation' which enable the individual to make sense of his world: the enactive mode in which knowing is linked to a set of appropriate actions, the iconic mode whereby knowledge is assimilated through a set of images or graphics that 'stand for a concept without fully defining it' (Bruner 1966, p.44) and the symbolic mode in which complex symbolism, mainly language, is increasingly employed. This is the basis of Bruner's 'spiral curriculum' where 'the basic principles, under-lying axioms and pervasive themes' (Bruner 1977, p.ix) of a subject are re-examined constantly at an increasingly sophisticated level. As Bruner himself puts it, 'In time one visits and revisits the same general principles, rendering them increasingly more abstract and formal, more precise, more powerful, more generative' (1971, p.138). He maintains that provided that it is pre-sented in a mode that is accessible to the learner, 'any subject can be taught effectively in some intellectually honest form to any child at any stage of development' (1960, p.33).

Closely related to this claim is Bruner's view that the structure of a body of knowledge is as integral to the process of learning as the mode of representa-tion. The structure of a discipline consists of a set of basic principles and inter-related concepts that give it definition and allow a multitude of items to be related to it in a meaningful way, its merit depending on its power to simplify information, generate new propositions and increase the manipulability of a body of knowledge. Structure, he argues, is not absolute but relative and should always be related to the needs of the learner. In this sense it becomes clear that Bruner's concern with structure is psychological not philosophical; he is not subscribing to the rationalist perspective that sees knowledge as hier-archical, inert, revealed or God-given. Rather he envisages the mastery of structure as an enabling device that gives the learner's endeavours a sense of purpose and direction. It provides a processing apparatus that allows individ-uals to 'go beyond the information given' (1966, p.95) and generate modes of thought, knowledge and opinions of their own. He writes 'We are extra-polative. We easily go beyond the information given by processes of inference that come as naturally as breathing' (1971, p.142).

Bruner makes four claims for the importance of a mastery of structure in the learning process:

1. A subject is made more comprehensible

2. It aids memory

3. It is the basis of the transference of learning

4. It reduces the gap between elementary and advanced knowledge in a given field.

In Chapter 6 of *Towards a Theory of Instruction* (1966), entitled 'The Will to Learn', Bruner expounds what he considers to be the basic features of human motivation. To him the 'single most characteristic thing about human beings is that they learn' (op. cit., p.113). This will to learn he sees as being a product of intrinsic motivation where reward resides in the successful completion of an activity or 'even the activity itself' (op. cit., p.114). He identifies three distinct, though related, aspects of intrinsic motivation: curiosity, competence and reciprocity.

Curiosity, Bruner claims, is a function of man's biological need for novelty, a response to ambiguity and uncertainty. 'Our attention is attracted to something that is unclear, unfinished or uncertain. We sustain our attention until the matter in hand becomes clear, finished or certain. The achievement of clarity or merely the search for it is what satisfies' (ibid.).

Competence is a motive that goes beyond the satisfaction of mere curiosity. It is the drive an individual has to master a complex world, and behaviour which helps achieve this mastery is inherently satisfying. It finds expression in the pleasure derived from developing and practising a new skill. In Bruner's words 'we get interested in what we are good at' (op. cit., p.118). The learner acquires this motive through interaction with others who have mastered a desired skill, whether manipulatory, intellectual or social, and thus serve as competence models.

Bruner describes reciprocity as 'a deep human need to respond to others and operate jointly with them towards an objective' (op. cit., p.125). As with curiosity and competence 'its exercise seems to be its sole reward' (ibid.). In an educational setting pupils have a basic social motive to comply with the goals of the social group in which they find themselves, in order to become accepted members of the learning community. This does not imply conformity for it is a feature of reciprocally operative groups that specialized roles develop, for example the leader, the helper, the critic etc.

The idea that human learning is largely a product of intrinsic motivation, that is, engaged in for its own sake, may be viewed with some scepticism by those teachers familiar with the problems of psychological truancy and disaffection, where pupils respond, if at all, only to extrinsic stimuli such as examination requirements. In response to such scepticism I would wish to argue that often situations perceived as pupil problems are in fact curricular problems. As Bruner points out, 'The will to learn becomes a "problem" only under specialized circumstances like those of a school where a curriculum is set, students confined and a path fixed. The problem exists not so much in learning itself, but in the fact that what the school imposes often fails to enlist the natural energies that sustain spontaneous learning — curiosity, a desire for competence, aspirations to emulate a model, and a deep-seated commitment to the web of social reciprocity' (op. cit., p.127).

Bruner describes the content of MACOS as 'man: his nature as a species, the forces that shaped and continue to shape his humanity' (1966, p.74). Three fundamental questions reverberate throughout the course: What is human about human beings? How did they get that way? How can they be made more so? These questions are pursued through an exploration of five interrelated 'great humanizing forces', namely tool making, language, social organization, the management of man's prolonged childhood and man's urge to explain his world, which, Bruner contends, define man's distinctiveness and continue to shape his humanity.

The materials provide pupils with an opportunity to explore fundamental issues associated with modern man through a series of comparisons with animals — the Pacific salmon, the herring gull, the baboon troop, the chimpanzee — and a preliterate human group — the Netsilik Eskimo. Throughout the course there is an emphasis on structure with concepts, such as life cycle, aggression, adaption, structure and function, social organization, communication and technology, being analysed at increasingly sophisticated levels in relation to the five humanizing forces.

The aim of the course is not a mastery of structure *per se* but a mastery of structure 'so that it assists in the thinking process and becomes a tool for raising and exploring important questions' (Dow 1970a, p.13). The intention is to provide a framework within which pupils research, speculate, analyse and discuss rather than passively assimilate a body of facts or concepts.

The course materials are designed to utilize to the full Bruner's three modes of representing reality. They include games, simulations, constructional activities and problem-solving exercises where the emphasis is on making or doing. For example, given the raw materials (illustrated on cards) that are available to the Netsilik Eskimo, pupils are asked to design their own version of a sled. Records, filmstrips, photographs and high-quality film provide valuable sources of primary evidence, from which hypotheses can be formulated and tested. This is supplemented by other sources of original data including a selection from the field notes of the eminent anthropologist Irven DeVore who studied the baboon troop, and extracts from the journal of the Danish ethnographer Knud Rasmussen, giving an account of his travels among the Netsilik. Concept booklets, such as 'Innate and Learned Behaviour', use illustrative graphics to reduce complex ideas into relatively simple propositions, thus rendering them more accessible to the learner. Other booklets include collections of Netsilik myths, songs and poetry and supplementary information of a more descriptive kind on the animals studied.

The take-up of MACOS in Britain has been relatively small: currently it is used in approximately one hundred Primary, Middle and Secondary schools. This is understandable considering the immense cost involved which presently amounts to approximately £2000 for the complete package. In a period of financial stringency this is beyond the means of most schools. However, the response of those adopting the project is generally one of enthusiasm, despite a degree of criticism levelled against it.

Apart from the emotive, though influential, outcry of certain sections of American society, who see MACOS as 'Marxist' and anti-Christian, a number of influential educational critiques have been articulated. Adams (1976) expresses concern about the moral and philosophical implications of the project and both he and Jones (1972) perceive an excessive concentration upon rationality at the expense of the affective domain. Even Ruddock, in charge of its dissemination at CARE, advises caution: 'It is important to ask whether, in practice, the studies become instrumental to the acquisition of concepts, or whether the concepts can be kept in place and regarded as a means towards an understanding of studies which are interesting in their own right' (1972, p.120). Jenkins, on a similar tack, draws our attention to 'the much expressed view that there is a persistent antinomy ... between the cognitive map embedded in the materials and its commitment to enquiry-based learning' (1980, p.128).

In the context of this chapter, however, there is little to be gained from pursuing these particular criticisms and ambiguities in greater depth. This does not imply a refutation of their validity but rather a recognition that such an examination could detract from a wider appreciation of the positive contributions of MACOS to the development of education as process.

For, despite the criticism it has aroused, there is no denying the importance of MACOS in furthering educational thinking and understanding in recent years. It is the most coherent and articulate expression of process curriculum in the humanities sphere and even Adams (1976, p.88), a vehement critic, 'is impressed by the imagination, ingenuity and enthusiasm behind the actual teaching techniques'. Another endearing feature is its potential as a vehicle for the intellectual and professional growth of teachers. This is of paramount importance in the 1980s with the recognition that curriculum innovation and teacher development are interdependent and should proceed simultaneously.

In this respect Bruner (1980) is right when he claims,

> ... the course was ultimately designed with change in mind. I always had the feeling that the main thing that was worthy about the course was that it could be used as well for teacher training and that used in that way it would produce quite unpredictable results in what teachers would do with the course afterwards. (Bruner 1980, p.225).

It is my contention that an appreciation of the weaknesses as well as the strengths of the project is fundamental in promoting the interest, dialogue and sense of challenge that leads the innovatory teacher beyond MACOS.

Beyond MACOS — theoretical considerations

In the final unit of MACOS the course developers state, 'This course has no ending. An understanding of what makes man human is a continuing process' (Dow 1970b, p.89). In this sense MACOS is an unfinished curriculum: the 'great questions, themes and substantive issues' (Jenkins 1980, p.217) around which it is organized remain unresolved and the means by which those issues can be pursued are far from exhausted. The Humanities Department at Meopham School has undertaken the challenging task of finding the means whereby the kinds of processes and issues embodied in MACOS can be developed, thus extending the impact of the project beyond the limitations imposed by its own conceptual structure, resources and time allocation.

So far in this chapter, for reasons that I hope will now become clear, little reference has been made to the pedagogical assumptions on whch MACOS is based. The course developers have translated the pedagogy implicit in 'the Brunerian learning framework' into an explicit statement of goals which is uncompromising in its emphasis on education as process. These goals are as follows:

1. To initiate and develop in youngsters a process of question-posing (the inquiry method);

2. To teach a research methodology where children can:
   (a) Look for information to answer questions they have raised;
   (b) Use the framework developed in the course (e.g. the concept of the life cycle) and apply it to new areas;

3. To help youngsters develop the ability to use a variety of first-hand sources as evidence from which to develop hypotheses and draw conclusions;

4. To conduct classroom discussion in which youngsters learn to listen to

others as well as express their own views;

5. To legitimate the search; that is, to give sanction and support to open-ended discussions where definite answers to many questions are not found;

6. To encourage children to reflect on their own experiences;

7. To create a new role for the teacher, in which the teacher becomes a resource to children, rather than an authority.

As Dow (1970a) points out, 'It is clear that these goals centre around the process of learning rather than around the product . . . these goals put highest importance on the community of education, on exploration and on question-posing, rather than on teaching factual specifics or information *per se*' (p.13).

It is to Stenhouse that we turn for a clearer exposition of the significance of these goals. He argues that they are in fact not goals but 'a specifiction of what the teacher is to do expressed in terms of principles of procedure' (Stenhouse 1975, p.92). It is important to realize that the distinction between goals or aims and principles is conceptual rather than semantic. Aims are terminal points to which education is directed whereas principles underpin the educational process from the start. Principles and processes cannot be separated; the principles are reflected in the processes and the processes are embodied in the principles.

It is from this stance that the thinking and practice of the Humanities Department have developed over the years. For reasons outlined in earlier chapters of this book, the department eschews the use of objectives in curriculum planning, although ironically this is the model it is encouraged to use through the local authority's initiative 'Aims and Objectives in the Secondary School'. The department states,

> The Humanities curriculum is seen in terms of 'principles of procedure'. These principles are not pre-specified targets at which teaching is aimed, but criteria of judgment which help teachers get the 'process' of learning right. Working in this way, certain questions have to be borne in mind, for example; In what form are themes best raised for enquiry? How are the materials best presented? In which way can teaching stimulate questioning? Is there a correct answer or can we only explore a variety of possibilities? (from the Humanities Department contribution to the school's 'Aims and Objectives' document).

The principles of procedure viewed by the department as being essential are a slightly modified version of those proposed by Raths (1971). Thus, the department claims, all things being equal, one activity is more worthwhile than another if —

1. it permits children to make informal choices in carrying out the activity and to reflect on the consequences of their choices,

2. it assigns to students active roles in the learning situation rather than passive ones,

3. it asks students to engage in inquiry into ideas, the application of intellectual processes or current problems,

4. it involves children with real objects, materials, artefacts, data,

5. completion of the activity may be accomplished successfully by children at differing levels of ability,

6. it asks students to examine in a new setting an idea, an application of an intellectual process, or a problem which has been previously studied,

7. it requires students to examine topics or issues that citizens in our society do not normally examine,

8. it involves students and department members in 'risk' taking, not risk of life or limb but risk of success or failure,

9. it requires students to rewrite, rehearse and polish their initial efforts,

10. it involves students in the application and mastery of meaningful values, standards and discipline,

11. it gives students a chance to share the planning, the carrying out of a plan or the result of an activity with others.

It is necessary to point out that the department does not see the pedagogical aims of MACOS or Raths' principles of procedure in any sense as definitive or prescriptive; rather they are expressions of the kind of pedagogy that facilitates and promotes education as process.

It is possible, however, to make a number of generalizations regarding the model of education implicit in these principles. Firstly, this model clearly rejects the rationalist view that knowledge is 'out there' in logically discrete forms. Rather it embraces a pragmatist epistemology which portrays knowledge as hypothetical, provisional and evolutionary. Knowledge is derived from a process in which 'thought provides hypothetical ideas in response to a problem' which are then 'tested in action' (Scheffler 1965, p.4). The process is on-going in that new discoveries lead to new problems which in turn have to be hypothesized and resolved.

Secondly, this leads to a concept of education which is active rather than passive, with its central focus being problem-solving, experimentation and experience. Learners are seen as active and autonomous, imbued with the capacity for generating ideas, solving problems, developing and structuring their own knowledge and attuning their perspective in the light of new experience. Learning is seen not as an accumulation of knowledge but as a form of intellectual and emotional growth.

Thirdly, the model emphasizes the intrinsic rather than the instrumental value of education. It is something to be engaged in for its own sake. This is not to deny that society has a legitimate right to expect schools to transmit certain values and skills but to argue that the essence of education is a concern with the intellectual and emotional needs of individuals.

Lastly, in terms of a school or department faced with the task of articulating the idea of education as process, one further point needs to be stressed. The process model must be expressed in a form that is logically consistent with itself. Processes are not ends in themselves and consequently they cannot be measured or expressed as objectives. To take on board the process model of curriculum planning necessitates a total and emphatic rejection of the objectives model in any form. There is no compromise. Neither should attempts be made to isolate and lay bare individual processes in the hope of achieving greater clarity.

Processes are embodied in the phenomenon of intellectual growth and in the concept of what it means to be educated. What, for example, are the processes inherent in the notions of autonomy, rationality and understanding or in acquiring language? Processes may be ordered or random, but together they comprise a mediating system which enables individuals to make sense of their world. There are processes for generating and utilizing knowledge and for communicating it. Processes are involved in decision-making, reflecting, analysing, hypothesizing, evaluating and articulating ideas. Processes are organic in the sense that they are internal mechanisms and as such are inclined to atrophy if not provided with a wide variety of challenging and stimulating experiences.

The process curriculum in action

To elucidate the theoretical framework within which the department works is a relatively straightforward task, but to provide a portrayal of the curriculum in action, capturing its excitement, sense of purpose and vitality, is another matter. Providing the reader with a reasonably coherent picture of the practical implications of process curriculum in the Secondary school suggests a descriptive rather than analytical approach. Yet without analysis there is a danger that such a description could become anecdotal or appear prescriptive. Within the confines of this chapter it is only possible to consider a random selection of practice within the department. This may give the account a somewhat disjointed appearance but then it is not my intention to provide a rigid model to be emulated, but rather to raise awareness of what 'education as process' in practice means.

The areas examined in the remainder of this chapter are illustrated with examples of pupils' comments on the courses they follow. These have been collected over a period of years by a variety of methods, including interviews with personnel external to the school, as part of an on-going curriculum investigation. To some extent this investigation has been haphazard and spasmodic, lacking the precision and objectivity demanded by those researchers reared on the positivist tradition. I feel justified in using the material in this account, however, for two reasons. Firstly, education is such a complex and value-laden enterprise that it would be presumptuous to assume that insights gained by other means are any less problematic. There are many examples in educational research to suggest that it is often those who seek objectivity who are in fact deluded. Secondly, the comments themselves are an integral part of the educational process — a manifestation of process curriculum in action. They have been collected in an atmosphere of openness and trust, where pupils are actively encouraged to assess and articulate their educational experiences.

A specific example serves to illustrate these points. A first-year class, after four weeks at the school, was given an opportunity to discuss their initial experiences in humanities. The lesson was taped, not only to analyse the discussion at a later date, but also to familiarize the pupils with the idea of a tape recorder being used in this way. The following extracts are typical of the kind of dialogue that ensued.

'I think what we've done this morning's been good because we've been able to criticize and hear what other people think about the sheets' (worksheets)

'I like to have discussions about things because it makes me feel better and I can understand more than when I do a sheet'

'I like talking about it because you find out that you're not the only one to be worried about certain things'

'I like this discussion because it's very interesting to know how other people feel about this work . . . (Pause) . . . and I can tell people how I feel about this work'

'You can find out that other people feel the same way you feel. It helps you understand that the teacher can feel the same way that you feel'.

Individually these extracts appear unremarkable but together they point to the kind of pedagogy that gives practical realization to the notion of education as process. From the extracts it is possible to perceive education as a social process; a co-operative and interactive enterprise. There is evidence of negotiation between the pupils and the teacher, negotiation in the sense that they articulate and share ideas with each other. The teacher has endeavoured to cast off the authoritarian mantle and assume the role of a learning colleague, albeit a senior one. Of paramount significance, however, they are illustrative of a fundamental need for individuals to enter into dialogue, to communicate and to discuss — in short, to use language.

The importance of language in promoting intellectual, moral and emotional growth has long been recognized, although there is still some debate as to the exact nature of the process. Barnes (1976, p.101) states that 'through language we both *receive* a meaningful world from others, and at the same time *make meanings* by re-interpreting that world to our own ends.'

Thus stated, language is perceived as both a medium of exchange and an instrument through which the learner can bring order into the environment (Bruner 1966). Language facilitates a continuous assimilation of new experiences and in addition enables the learner actively to reinterpret or recode old experiences and represent them in new forms. Learning is not some kind of passive and accumulative block-building activity but a dynamic and creative process in which language plays a mediating role. Rosen (1971, p.126) points out that 'it is through the enormous variety of dialogue with others that we gather together the linguistic resources to dialogue in our heads; there is nowhere else to get it from. Restrict the nature and quality of dialogue and ultimately you restrict thinking capacity.'

How then does the practising teacher set about structuring the educational experience of pupils so that a 'variety of dialogue' can flourish? It requires an atmosphere where pupils can 'play with words' and 'think things out aloud'; where they 'can explore and experiment with language without fear of censure' (Downey and Kelly 1979, p.128). Dialogue must be kept on the move and not terminated prematurely or inhibited by question and answer situations. The successful practitioner is the one who 'holds our opinions highly' (second-year pupil) and who places emphasis on the community of learning, on problem-solving, question-posing and discovery rather than the transmission of inert bodies of knowledge.

The HMI survey of Secondary education (DES 1979b) is highly critical of language development in most schools. It comments:

> Although considerable research over the last 20 years into the ways in which language is acquired and extended has emphasized the part talking can play in learning, the evidence of the survey indicated that this is still not widely known among teachers. Pupils usually spent more time in reading and writing than they did in talking and listening; and in the oral exchanges between class and teacher very much more time listening than talking. Most of the talking by pupils was in response to questions (op. cit., p.94).

It highlights a typical lesson pattern consisting of exposition, recapitulation and record and concludes that very few pupils are encouraged to initiate discussion, to speculate or to offer differing views. It is clear from the survey that most Secondary schools lay emphasis on the written word, often in the form of copied or dictated notes, particularly in the fourth and fifth years. 'A fifth year group in English had written 23,000 words of dictated plot of "Far From the Madding Crowd" and would have written more when they had finished "Great Expectations", already well under way' (op. cit., p.82).

Where teachers adopt such strategies there is little hope of intellectual development taking place. It might ensure examination success but, as Stenhouse (1975) reminds us, it is possible to pass examinations without developing the kind of understanding the process-based curriculum pursues. To deny pupils access to meaningful language is to deny them intellectual growth. Consider the following extracts:

> 'I think it is good to talk about things because it makes you realize your own thoughts not other people's'. (first-year pupil)

> 'Also when you talk you can explain things better, some things you can say but not put into writing'. (second-year pupil)

> 'I think that talking instead of writing is better because you get to understand it better'. (first-year pupil)

> 'In Humanities we are aloud to exprest our fellings without getting tolled of for the kind of things we say (within reson)'. (first-year pupil)

> 'I like Humanities becaus you can speak freely'. (first-year pupil)

Here the pupils themselves have identified, evaluated and articulated the importance of dialogue in the process of learning. As the first extract succinctly puts it, talking 'makes you realize your own thoughts'; it is a vehicle for introspection as well as communication.

The Bullock Report (DES 1975), the most authoritative statement on the use of language in schools to date, also recognizes the importance of 'exploratory talk' (Barnes 1976) in the learning process. It advocates that talk should take place in large and small groups with an emphasis on the latter. Small, mutually supportive groups generate talk that is tentative and discursive, characterized by constant repetition, rephrasing and restructuring of thought. This extract of a taped discussion, in which a group of second-year pupils grapple with a certain aspect of the MACOS question 'What makes man human?' is illustrative:

P.1 I think its because we've got . . . um . . . a . . . well . . . don't know how to say it . . .

P.2 (helpfully) a real world and an imaginary . . .

P.1 (interrupts) Yeh . . . whereas animals they have to . . . they're . . . they're hunters . . . and . . . and they're hunted . . . all the time.

T   Do you think animals lack imagination then?

P.3 Well they're . . . I don't think they keep inventing new things to help their life by. They just learn it from their parents and stick to that.

Notice here how the teacher adopts a role of intervention rather than direction, reflecting a question back to the pupils, not to test understanding or to elicit propositional knowledge but in order to develop, clarify or extend points in their thinking.

Such a tolerant, collaborative enterprise provides the security for pupils to take risks and try things out. This contrasts sharply within the kind of whole class 'discussion' found in many Secondary schools where the more articulate and confident pupils compete with each other, either for the teacher's approval or to guess what is in his mind, whilst the introverted and less articulate, often forming a majority, remain silent for fear of being corrected, censured or even ridiculed.

It is important to realize that without structure and guidance group discussions can be unproductive and aimless in educational terms. Exploratory talk ensues when pupils are presented with problems which engage their natural curiosity and harness their drive for competence by 'legitimizing the search', that is opening up areas for investigation and enquiry. The curriculum offered by the Humanities Department is replete with challenging and stimulating open-ended activities which, having no final answers, prompt pupils to 'bounce ideas and raise hypotheses with each other' (Arnold and Watson 1979), thus keeping conversation, discussion and dialogue on the move.

The 'Mystery of Mark Pullen', an exercise taken from the Schools Council 13—16 History Project pre-examination kit entitled 'What is History', is indicative of the department's commitment to this enquiry-based approach. Pupils are presented with a folder containing the police accident report on a young male student found dead at the side of a main road, together with the contents of his wallet. Using the evidence presented, pupils are asked to reconstruct the movements of the young man on the day he died, to speculate on the kind of person he was and to form hypotheses to account for his death. On completing this task, the members of a first-year class were asked to describe briefly what they perceived to be the main benefits of the exercise. Again their responses are clearly framed in terms of processes:

'I think this exercise has taught us how to build up ideas on just a little base. I also think we have learned that not all questions have answers.'

'I think we have done this exercise because it has taught us how to work out things but not to jump to conclusions. Also we have learned to work in groups . . .'

'How to use facts to discover, to use our imagination, to think, to ask questions.'

'I think we did this work so we could research and fit things together. I have also learnt how to ask questions and not always get answers.'

At this stage it should be pointed out that the attention the department gives to promoting exploratory talk, generally through small group work, should not be conceived as a rejection of the more formal, polished and precise 'final draft language' (Barnes 1976, p.108), which, in most secondary schools forms the bulk of the linguistic experiences planned for pupils. Rather it implies a recognition that the former is a natural and crucial prerequisite to the latter. Exploratory talk helps develop the cognitive structures which facilitate understanding. Without these structures final draft langauge can only be an expression of rote learning.

A major advantage of seeing education in terms of processes is the greater freedom and flexibility it allows in terms of curriculum planning. With no pre-specified body of knowledge to get across or objectives to pursue the teacher is able to utilize to the full any unexpected learning opportunity that may arise. Thus a particular class, having completed the 'Mystery of Mark Pullen', suggested that, working in small groups, they produce their own mystery folders. The inventiveness and originality of many of the 'mysteries' that materialized was equal to that of the commercial product, although the presentation was obviously of an inferior standard. Of interest here is the way in which problem-solvers had become problem-posers, a point which will be examined in greater depth in due course.

The 'Mystery of Mark Pullen' exercise provides a prelude to a school-produced curriculum unit designed to introduce pupils to the idea of handling evidence. Using a variety of primary and secondary sources pupils carry out an enquiry-based investigation of local issues, mainly from an historical perspective. During a unit on 'Crime and Punishment' there arose for one class an opportunity to pursue the topic in an interesting and contemporary setting. The class sought permission to hold a trial to ascertain the guilt of three of its members who had arrived late for their Humanities lesson with an unconvincing excuse.

It is difficult in words fully to convey the sense of drama, excitement and solemnity which the trial generated. Neither is it possible to portray in essence the dedication of the 'C.I.D.' as they searched for clues and set about obtaining taped interviews from key witnesses, the perceptive and penetrating questioning of the 'defence' and 'prosecution', the articulate and sensitive summing up of the 'judge' or the long and searching deliberations of the 'jury'. The pupils' comments tell their own story.

'I found today's work very interesting. I thought of it as a sort of follow up to our detective work. The jury (which I was in) had to decide whether they were guilty and we found this difficult and time-consuming. I enjoyed this work immensely.'

'I thought it was very helpful having witnesses so that we could have more evidence against the accused and so we could ask more questions. I also thought it was a good idea for the three accused and the witnesses to swear on the Bible. I was very glad we could interview the witnesses who could not come to the court.'

'I thought the lesson was enjoyable and interesting. I had the part of spokesman for the jury and I feel this gave me some experience of talking for a group and listening to their views.'

'I thought it was very clever how something like this had timed itself so well to come in when we are doing work on Crime and Punishment, anybody would think that it was planned!'

'I found it, in places, funny and amusing, yet in others very serious. I never had done anything like this before . . .'

A central feature of the department's educational philosophy is its claim that one of the main concerns of the educative process is the fostering and development of personal autonomy, particularly in a democratic and pluralist society. Autonomy, however, like understanding, is a developmental process. It is a relative state of mind rather than an end in itself and as such can be inhibited or enhanced but never fully realized. To talk of autonomy is to recognize that man is active and dynamic and capable of shaping his own destiny. The mental faculties which define autonomy cannot be isolated from other activities of the mind, for the concept implies that autonomous individuals have developed critical awareness and discriminatory powers and are able to think independently on intellectual, social and moral issues. Also included in the concept is the notion of individuals coming to terms with the constraints imposed on their freedom, including those arising out of their own limitations (Downey and Kelly 1979).

From an educational perspective the important point to bear in mind is that individuals cannot become more autonomous unless they are allowed to exercise the autonomy they already possess. Thus situations in which knowledge is imposed on individuals from a higher authority, or where learning is uncritical, unreflective or assumes consensus, do not facilitate the growth of personal autonomy.

In pursuit of personal autonomy the department endeavours to give pupils greater control over their learning experiences. Meaning is negotiated rather than imposed, divergent views are protected and materials and tasks are presented in a way that enable pupils to develop their own thinking strategies. By encouraging pupils to seek solutions to queries and problems they themselves have identified the emphasis shifts from problem-solving to problem-posing. It is a matter of recognizing pertinent questions as well as providing possible answers.

Assuming that the effective curriculum is what each pupil takes away, then the following extracts are indicative of what the department actually achieves.

'In Humanities we raise some very interesting questions like how did man come about? Why are we here? Main questions that get the mind boggling'. (first-year pupil)

'The part of Humanities which I have enjoyed so far is the part when we split up into groups and we had to work out our own hypothesis. It interested me because we had found an answer in a way that I had never thought of before.' (first-year pupil)

'Mr . . . doesn't tell us the answers like other teachers but he makes us find answers for ourselves. He lets us go away and think about things.' (second-year pupil)

'The piece of work on animals . . . realy caused us to use our brains. It also made us talk about it intelligently, about whether animals and humans having bones is realy worth writing down, whether it was a realy important factor.' (first-year pupil)

'During Humanities we raise some very good questions but they are sometimes difficult to answer or answers are sometimes difficult to explain.' (first-year pupil)

'I like it better than subjects like . . . because in those subjects you sometimes do not like to answer questions because you are scared of being wrong. In Humanities you can never be wrong.' (first-year pupil)

'In . . . you know how to do it because you've been told but in Humanities you have to find things out for yourself. I think Humanities is a subject that teaches you to ask sensible questions that are relevant to the work we're doing.' (second-year pupil)

'This work I found interesting because it was left to us to organize our hypothesis and to prove it.' (first-year pupil)

'Our second subject was the class profile . . . we had to think ahead on how to set it out and also it is interesting to delve further into the hypothesis results and put it as a percentage or split girls and boys up . . . there's loads of things you can do with a simple hypothesis.' (first-year pupil)

'I sometimes have difficulties sorting out the evidence to make it point one way or the other but I became better at thing (this) as I was faced with more.' (third-year pupil)

It was pointed out earlier in the chapter that MACOS has been criticized for placing excessive emphasis on rationality and intellectual development to the detriment of the affective dimension. This is a claim that the course developers are at pains to refute:

> The emphasis on organizing ideas should not obscure our equal interest in what educators call the affective domain — the emotional, artistic and spiritual life of the child (Dow 1970, p.14).

Jones (1972) maintains that MACOS materials encourage teachers to examine in the classroom highly emotive issues in an emotionally neutral context. He adopts a contrary view and argues that controlled emotional unmasking is an essential part of the learning process. He states (p.174) 'The value of emotional involvement in the learning process thus lies in its potential for aiding assimilation of new or remote experiences in idiomatically, illuminating ways.' Bruner (1977, p.x), in response to Jones's accusation that he advocates a rationalist perspective, contends that 'there need be no conflict between fostering intellectual power and cultivating emotional maturity'. Dow (1970a, p.14), in a similar vein, takes the view that in MACOS 'the manipulative, expressive, creative activities are critical accompaniments to the verbal interplay'.

What seems to emerge from these arguments is the view that to talk of the cognitive and affective domains or intellectual and emotional skills as if they were distinct entities is to create false and misleading dichotomies. This is not to deny that there are recognizable dimensions to the human condition but to argue that human growth is a far more complex and integrative process than some would have us believe. Such a stance provides the platform from which it is possible to maintain confidently, if not to posit as a fundamental educational truth, the notion that all learning, and by implication all knowledge, is a unity.

Such a perspective is far removed from the practices of most Secondary schools where knowledge and skills are 'disintegrated' from the processes of human development and parcelled into discrete subject areas. Attempts at reintegration have been carried out from a philosophical rather than a psychological point of view, resulting in no more than the uncritical throwing together of bodies of knowledge into an incoherent amalgam (Blenkin and Kelly 1981).

It would be foolish to deny the existence of 'public traditions of awareness' or 'socially developed modes of thinking' (Pring 1976, p.10) or to argue that they have no place in the education of young people. What must be remembered, however, is that learning is a process of assimilation from within rather than imposition from without. Bodies of knowledge, skills and modes of thought are redundant unless they are closely related to the personal needs of the learner or until they assist in the organization of his own knowledge and experiences.

This kind of thinking is evident in much of the work carried out in the department in all years. To adopt the main conceptual configuration of Roy Richards' chapter, pupils learn *through* Humanities rather than *of* Humanities. The department is aware of the need to develop *in* pupils a range of 'capacities and competencies' (Blenkin and Kelly 1981) rather than transmit *to* them certain bodies of knowledge or modes of thought.

The Humanities curriculum is unified in the sense that it views the intellectual, moral, social, aesthetic and emotional growth of individuals as an integrated and integrative whole which knows no boundaries. Traditional subject boundaries are frequently 'violated' as pupils endeavour to master and communicate the conceptual framework in which they operate. The concepts embodied in the materials and activities of the courses they follow are seen as enabling devices, which once assimilated through action and experience, permit the learner to go beyond the information given and speculate, hypothesize and experience anew; to develop what the department calls 'extension skills'. This contrasts sharply with the approach adopted by many Secondary school departments where concepts are learned and frequently regurgitated but never become fully part of the learner's cognitive strategies. Indeed, it is my contention that the move from facts to concepts in the Secondary sector represents only a marginal shift in its educational thinking, for the concepts pupils now learn are as remote and redundant as the facts that constituted their previous diet, in many cases, perhaps, even more so.

To facilitate the kind of education advocated in this chapter the department places considerable emphasis on actively doing, making or experiencing rather than passively receiving. Ideas are made more meaningful through role play, simulation exercises, visits and audio-visual stimulus. Concepts are acquired, developed and articulated through a variety of activities which could be broadly defined as the expressive arts — designing, drawing, painting, model-making, drama etc. In this area there is considerable potential for creating meaningful links with other departments and possible avenues are now being explored. The subject-based approach to Secondary education, however, makes this exceedingly difficult and the 'timetable' must be seen as a major constraint to developing process curriculum in the Secondary school. As a first-year pupil points out:

'I would like Humanities lessons to have more time because once you get interested the pips go' (signalling the end of a lesson).

It should also be pointed out that interdepartmental co-operation is unlikely to flourish unless the departments, to some extent, embrace the same educational philosophy.

The various creative and expressive activities outlined above are viewed by the department not as soft options or light relief but as an integral part of the learning process. Eisner (1979b) identifies nine aspects of learning that can be enhanced by participation in artistic activities. The general trend of his argument is that such activities are devices for the clarification and inner articulation of thought as well as means of communicating ideas, in that 'the public manifestation of the image is a second-order symbol, the first being the conceptualization itself' (p.111).

Some of Eisner's ideas can be illustrated by a specific example. Figure 12.1 shows a piece of work produced in response to a MACOS exercise which requires pupils to design an animal which would survive in the Arctic environment. In addition to arousing the pupils' imagination the exercise enables them to grapple with concepts such as structure, function and adaptation which are introduced in earlier materials. It is not an easy task to extrapolate what is educationally significant from such a piece of work, but in spite of this a number of insights can be gained.

The exercise itself held some intrinsic value in that from personal observation I feel justified in claiming that the intellectual challenge engaged the pupils' curiosity and aroused a drive for competence.

The example helps substantiate Eisner's view that two processes are involved in the transformation of an idea into a visual public image. Firstly, to conceptualize the 'slidegal' involved a rearticulation or reordering of a plethora of previous experiences, for example, knowledge of the Arctic environment, and concepts such as structure, function and adaptation, and,

My Arctic Animal

NANCY CASTLE 2·G.

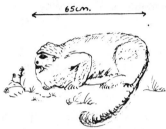

This is a slidegal, it is about the size of a dog. It has fairly long legs but it is usually seen with them tucked under.

It is a fairly fat animal covered by a light grey hair which is very slightly darker underneath it. The slidegal is a mammal. It is a solitary animal. It's mainly carnivorous.

Picture A shows the face of the slidegal. Its features are positioned high on its head. In snow blizzards this animal can lower a flap of skin over its face.

It wraps its large furry tail around it to keep warm. It can also with-draw its dangerous claws like a cat.

The slidegal has a unique feature in its slippery skin on its under side.

This means the mammal can reach high speeds. Its long sharp claws which are also on its rear elbows act as brakes. It eats birds and animals which it chases, or catches injured animals.

Figure 12.1

secondly, to communicate the visual concept required the invention of a suitable graphic image to give it form. To illustrate further, this view is implicit in the following comments:

'If you draw instead of write you can see what your doing and you understand it.' (second-year pupil) (This is also a manifestation of the power of Bruner's iconic mode of representation in the learning process.)

'I quite enjoyed setting out and making booklets. It made you think about how to explain clearly what you had learnt and I like explaining things with drawings.' (second-year pupil)

It would be folly to think that work of this nature could be assessed by some kind of objective means for there are no standards. This, Eisner maintains, shifts the locus of evaluation from the external to the internal for, in activities where the criteria for judgement are more subjective, individuals must learn to rely on their 'own sensibilities and perceptions'. Thus, through the process of self-evaluation, pupils develop the kind of intellectual independence and personal autonomy outlined earlier in the chapter.

This leads naturally into the whole question of assessment in Secondary schools, an issue which has received increasing attention in recent years. At the time of writing, in terms of external certification, thinking appears to have polarized. On the one hand there is a tangible movement towards greater central control and standardization of the public examination system and on the other a gathering chorus for more meaningful and educationally justifiable forms of assessment, particularly in the latter part of the pupil's school career. A number of 'profile' schemes have been piloted and found wanting, the most insidious of these consisting of detailed check-lists of educational objectives against which pupils are measured.

Public examinations, of course, form only a small part of the total assessment carried out in Secondary schools but their techniques and emphases have a backwash effect. Therefore the majority of assessment procedures currently employed are incompatible with the notion of education as process, for their main focus is to ascertain what propositional knowledge pupils have acquired, be it factual or conceptual, thus promoting an instrumental view of education.

With no radical reform of public examinations in sight any advances in this field will have to be made within the system. It is from this standpoint that the department has developed a CSE Mode 3 Social Science Course, committed to education as process and to the principle that, to use the well-worn phrase, the examination tail should not wag the curriculum dog.

The course itself is organized around the same procedural principles that underpin the lower school curriculum and in many respects is an extension of it. The emphasis is on the development of conceptual structures through action and experience which take the learners beyond the information given and enable them to travel their own journey in thought. Two pedagogical dimensions are discernible, the quantitative, based on first-hand research, and the qualitative, concerned with an exploration of human, social and political issues through discussion and role play, set against a common backcloth of empathy, curiosity, openness, flexibility, compassion and a willingness to share with others. Little would be gained from giving a detailed account of the course but a few selected examples of it in action should serve to capture its essence.

For six weeks during the summer term, pupils spend one afternoon per week in institutions, such as hospitals, old people's homes, mental hospitals and Primary schools, carrying out a piece of original research. Pupils are asked to formulate and test a hypothesis of their own choice, selecting, with teacher collaboration, whatever techniques they consider appropriate. It is obvious that the critical awareness developed by such an activity cannot, and should not, be divorced from the social awareness and empathy it generates, or the key concepts such as restriction, freedom, autonomy, power and interdependence etc., which give it meaning. By way of illustration, one fourth-year pupil chose to examine the changing reaction of his peers to the patients of a mental hospital over the six-week period, with questionnaires, interviews, surreptitious tape recordings and systematic observation of behaviour, such as physical contact between patients and pupils, constituting his investigatory repertoire. This resulted in a highly sophisticated piece of research but of equal significance educationally was the sense of 'awkwardness and insecurity' he experienced on his first visit and the 'very nice feeling' which contact with the patients generated.

Original research forms an integral and important part of the course. Whilst undertaking such work pupils keep a diary which helps them explore ideas and at the same time keeps the teachers in touch with their progress. The following extract is taken from the diary of a fourth-year pupil's 'Youth Culture' research project, which constituted an investigation of the relationship between social class and musical taste:

> 'During this week and the next I shall be collecting my thoughts and making rough notes. Mr ... gave me a useful book with a chapter regarding class. From this I was able to devise my own way of dividing people into classes by using some of my own ideas and some of his ideas from the book.
>
> The book showed me that sociologists' views on class differ greatly and they do not have very precise boundaries to work by.'

In choosing to reject the Registrar General's classification the pupil claimed 'it is fairly old (1911) and out of touch with the ways and the situations of today's society'.

This is a classic example of the kind of intellectual autonomy the department wishes to foster. Book knowledge is only seen as useful in that it enables the pupil to develop and articulate his own ideas. It has no authority or sanctity as of right. Not only does he reject a particular view of class but he is prepared to offer a reasoned critique for doing so.

The research projects form one-third of the continuously assessed coursework which contributes 50 percent to the final CSE grade, the other half being a terminal examination. To design a formal examination which meets the Examination Board's requirements but at the same time is compatible with the notion of education as process, as illustrated in this book, is a formidable challenge but one which the department has readily accepted.

Questions are designed in such a way that the examination itself is part of the learning process. The intention is to provide the pupils with an intellectual challenge in which they are expected to generate new knowledge and articulate original ideas rather than recall learned and rehearsed information, whether it be of a factual or more analytic kind. Many of the questions are based on stimulus materials which the department itself has designed and produced. Its most successful endeavours include two short video programmes which pupils watch immediately prior to attempting the respective questions. The following example is taken from Paper 2 of the 1981 examination.

Question 1

You should spend about 40 minutes on this question.

Following a controversial TV documentary, which suggested that teachers' views of pupils did as much to hinder their educational achievement as their social background, this letter appeared in a well-known national newspaper.

Dear Editor,

As a practising teacher of 15 years, I must register my disgust at the recent TV documentary 'Pygmalion in the Classroom Revisited'. Since J.W.B. Douglas published his book 'The Home and the School' in 1964 it has been an accepted fact that family background is the most important factor in determining the educational achievement of school children. To suggest that teachers are in any way responsible for hindering the progress of their pupils is not only nonsense but also damaging to the teaching profession. In my own experience I have always found teachers to be competent, caring and totally unbiased in their dealings with pupils. However, unlike the media, I am in a position to support my arguments with concrete facts as a result of a piece of research I recently undertook in my own school.

I am a Geography teacher in a large boys' comprehensive school near the centre of Manchester. Although we have many of the problems associated with the inner city areas, by applying firm discipline we have achieved very good examination results over the years. Each year in the school is divided into three bands, Upper, Middle and Lower, and within each band there are three classes. Allocation to bands is based on the pupils' ability when they enter the school and so accurate are the primary schools in their assessments that we have never found it necessary to move pupils between bands. The three classes in each band are again streamed according to ability but within each band there is some movement between classes. Promotion and relegation occurs and this is based on the pupils' performance in the end of year examinations. Thus it can be seen that the structure of the school allows the pupils to achieve their potential without bias or favour and the only factor that could affect their progress, apart of course from innate intelligence, is family background.

So much for the school; what about my research? Before I started I considered a number of hypotheses but since I was not sure what my results were going to be I decided to think up my hypothesis afterwards. For my sample I took the 24 boys in my own form group, the middle class in the Middle band. I allocated the boys to social class groups using my personal knowledge of their accents, clothes, behaviour and attitude to school. On this basis I found that there were 8 middle class boys and 15 working class boys in my form. One boy I found difficult to place so I put him in the working class group to make it easier to compute my results. At the end of the school year when the examination results were published I made a graph of each boy's performance and made a comparison between the performance of the middle class and working class groups. I discovered the middle class boys had achieved an average of 3 'O' levels and 4 C.S.E.'s grade 1-3, while the working class boys had achieved 1 'O' level and 5 C.S.E.'s grade 1-5. This did not surprise me as I had not expected the working class boys to perform particularly well and the middle class boys clearly fulfilled the expectations I had of them.

As a result of my research I am convinced that the hypothesis I finally decided on, 'middle class children are more intelligent than working class children', has been clearly proved.

Yours faithfully,

J. BRIGHT

You are a lecturer in Sociology with a special interest in education. Having read the letter you are far from impressed with Mr Bright's research. Write a reply, pointing out the flaws, mistakes and errors you can find in his research methods and arguments.

Set in a particular context the question has an immediacy and focus which gives it the power to extend the pupils' thinking beyond the information given. It is a problem to be contemplated rather than a question to be answered. This is far removed from the more traditional examination questions with their emphasis on factual recall or literal comprehension and those that are considered to be more searching requiring little more than the regurgitation of remote context-free abstractions; the knowledge of the textbook or the teacher rather than that of the learner. The question quoted requires a sound *functional* understanding of research methodology and sociological concepts. When pupils claim that in answering the question it is 'only common sense really' we can assume that the gap between their everyday experiences and academic knowledge has been bridged.

Some constraints

Throughout this chapter material has been used which emphasizes the positive aspects of the approach adopted by the department. However, it would be misleading to allow the reader to infer that all pupils view the experiences offered in a similar light. On the contrary many individuals are highly critical of the Humanities curriculum. Whilst it is commendable that pupils are encouraged to articulate their feelings towards their learning experiences, this itself being a part of the process curriculum, the criticisms they make give considerable cause for concern and highlight many of the tensions of Secondary education.

In the first instance pupils generally perceive school work as written exercises and therefore activities which do not conform to this pattern are considered to be of little value, even if they are inherently interesting and enjoyable.

Secondly, from an early age many pupils adopt an overtly instrumental view of education in which examinations and vocational aspirations become the main motivating force, as the following extracts clearly demonstrate.

'I like the films and the drawing and writing about the animals but I cannot see how looking at sea gulls is going to help us when we grow up or get a job.' (first-year pupil)

'I think Humanities can be rather stupid sometimes because in older life we may want to become a teacher you will not know much about History and Geography.' (second-year pupil)

Lastly, many pupils expect Secondary education to be highly structured and to some extent authoritarian. They accept a passive role and assume knowledge to be a commodity which is handed down. Lessons and knowledge are the preserve of the teacher and consequently they view their own experiences and ideas as having little currency in educational terms.

'Mr . . . he joined in. He thought of it but mostly he let us do it in *his double lesson* of Humanities.' (first-year pupil's reaction to the 'Crime and Punishment' lesson referred to earlier in the chapter)

Such a comment is significant for it highlights a formidable barrier to the full realization of process curriculum in the Secondary school. When operating within an alternative pedagogy pupils continue to evaluate their experiences in terms of the transmission paradigm in which teachers are seen as having an authoritative, dominant and custodial role. In the sense that it runs counter to the mainstream of Secondary education the process-based approach is severely inhibited if not jeopardized.

Summary and conclusions

In this chapter I hope to have demonstated that the 'canons of excellence and criteria of success' (Board of Education 1931, p. xxii), so often associated with the best tradition of British Primary education, should also constitute the essence of that which follows. The arguments put forward are based on the experiences of a group of teachers working in the Humanities, but it would be unfortunate if this was taken to imply that they are only applicable to this area of the curriculum. On the contrary, it is my contention that the paradigm outlined in this book should be taken as the blueprint for all Secondary education. Roy Richards' chapter, for example, which is a clear exposition of its practical realization in Primary school science, is a useful guide for the teaching of science in the Secondary sector, and Harriet Proudfoot's views on the educational potential of the creative arts are likewise of value at all ages and stages.

It is not a matter of alternatives for, as this book and its companion volume *The Primary Curriculum* have argued, a process-based curriculum is the only approach that is justifiable on educational grounds, and its use is imperative if society is to come to terms with the explosion of knowledge and the rapidly evolving social order. All involved in education should now direct their attention to exploring the potential of the technological revolution rather than perpetuating its industrial precursor. For, as Rogers points out,

> We are . . . faced with an entirely new situation where the goal of education, if we are to survive, is the facilitation of change and learning. The only man who is educated is the man who has learned how to learn; the man who has learned to adapt and change; the man who has realized that no knowledge is secure, that only the process of seeking knowledge gives a base for security. Changingness, a reliance on process rather than upon static knowledge, is the only thing that makes sense as a goal for education in the modern world (Rogers 1969, p.104).

Accepting this premise, how then do we set about educating people in the modern world? Perhaps the simple but potent message of a second-year pupil may show the way and appropriately conclude the chapter:

> 'When you get interested you are willing to find things out about it . . .'

POSTSCRIPT

POSTSCRIPT
GEVA BLENKIN AND VIC KELLY

Some attempt must now be made to draw together into a coherent pattern many of the strands which have run through all the different contributions of the earlier chapters. For there have been many common elements there; there is a major and significant LCM or HCF; but to a large extent these elements have been implicit in what has been said and we must now attempt to render them explicit. To do this we will need to reiterate some of the points which were made in Part One, but we hope that the chapters which have intervened will now enable us to make these points with more force and with greater effectiveness. For we believe that they constitute a case for, and indeed form the basis of, a major overhaul of our thinking about education.

There are several perspectives from which one can view the upbringing of the young. One can endeavour to see it from the point of view of social needs. One can emphasize the vocational needs or aspirations of the individual. One can from both of these perspectives stress the acquisition of skills. Or one can see it as a process of individual growth, of the development of whatever talents or capacities the individual possesses or shows aptitude for — a raising of the levels of functioning of the individual human being.

Only the latter perspective has traditionally been designated by the term 'education'. However widely the debate has raged over what this concept entails or encapsulates, no-one, from Plato through to the present day, has ever engaged in theorizing at a serious level about *education* without making the, often tacit, assumption that the concern was with the intellectual and moral development of the individual. Indeed, even those people — parents, employers or politicians — who are most vociferous in their demands for the teaching of 'basic skills', the maintenance of 'standards' and the meeting of the demands of developing technology are equally urgent in their demands that the young should be 'brought up proper'. The concern is with the development of 'character' as well as of basic competence. It is often assumed by such people that the two go hand in hand. It is time we recognized that they do not and that too great an emphasis on the latter can even be counter-productive to the former. We must recognize, therefore, that the implication of a view of education as necessarily concerned with the development of the individual must be squarely faced. It cannot be left to happen by chance as a by-product of a largely vocational form of training.

There is now another compelling reason why this issue must be faced. The sheer rate of technological advance makes it impossible to base our educational planning on the needs of society, the vocational interests of the individual or the development of 'basic skills'. For who possesses the crystal ball that will tell us what any of these are? There are few young persons today who are not in a position to obtain from a pocket-calculator at the touch of a button the computations they spent many — often unhappy — hours learning to do themselves at school. Furthermore, a society which must learn to live with unemployment as a permanent result of its technological advance, which, indeed, must learn to embrace it as a major break-through in human existence rather than complain at the disappearance of the need for vast armies of workers to spend much of their lives in mind-numbing activity, must acknowledge that it needs from its schools a very different kind of service from that which it has received and, indeed, demanded in the past. Recent events in Brixton, Toxteth and elsewhere must be recognized as being as much a result of the lack of a proper education as of the lack of employment.

Before it is too late, then, the process of rethinking must begin and it must begin from a recognition that many of the notions with which educational discussion is littered — among professionals as much as among lay persons — are outmoded categories which trail with them assumptions which it is no longer reasonable to make and which no longer enjoy whatever validity they might once have had. The sheer rapidity of present-day technological advance makes a nonsense of notions like those of 'vocational education' and 'education in the basic skills', just as that technological advance itself, and the social changes which inevitably accompany it, makes a similar nonsense of traditional ideas such as those of 'subject-disciplines', 'intrinsically worthwhile activities' and 'forms of knowledge'. We can no longer be dogmatic about the content of pupils' learning without running the risk of offering them experiences which will be of little value to them in the context of the society and the culture they will inherit. The lesson of our age is that of the age of Heracleitus that everything is in a state of flux and it is to be hoped that we have in the meantime learned enough to discourage any latter-day Plato from attempting to impose upon this state of affairs any spurious illusion of permanence.

This is an important educational truth which has for too long remained unappreciated. In this country, however, it has been given voice in several of this century's major reports. The Crowther Report (CACE 1959) had some interesting things to say about the form which vocational education must take in a rapidly developing society (its brief was the education of the 15—18 age-group) as well as stressing the necessity of avoiding an undue emphasis on this aspect of schooling. The major statement of this view of education, however, has been that of the Hadow (Board of Education 1931) and Plowden (CACE 1967) Reports, the twin gods of Primary education, which have emphasized the need to view education from a totally different perspective and have endeavoured to establish a mode of thinking that would ensure that, at least in our Primary schools, this perspective would be adopted and the development of the individual placed at the forefront of educational planning. It should be pointed out that no-one who has avocated this view has wished to argue that social needs or the career needs of individuals are to be ignored or forgotten: they have merely wished to claim that such needs should not be allowed to continue to dominate educational planning and that they should in any case be viewed in a rather more sophisticated manner than is often to be seen. For to assume a polarity between the needs of the society and those of the individual is to adopt a simplistic view of what education is and can be. Thus the thinking that is reflected in the reports of the Hadow and Plowden committees repre-sents an attempt to assist us to begin that process of rethinking that is now needed and it is in this direction that we must look if we want to know what has already occurred in this rethinking process.

The major characteristics of the view advocated by these reports must be summarized here, since they form the underpinning philosophy of the accounts this book has offered, and it is necessary to make this clear if the per-spective from which these contributions are made is to be understood fully and the main features of the common ground upon which these teachers stand is to be appreciated.

The first principle of this view is its rejection of any kind of instrumental, means-end approach to educational theory or practice. This was the main feature of and reason for Rousseau's revolt from traditional ways of thinking and it remains the prime tenet of the philosophy his work generated. This is not the place to become involved in deep theoretical discussion of such a philosophy nor in detailed analyses of abstruse notions such as John Dewey's assertion that 'the educational process has no end beyond itself; it is its own end' (1916, p.49). But the significance of this view must not be ignored nor its implications remain unappreciated, especially in an age that seems to be increasingly concerned with utilitarian considerations not only in education but in all aspects of life.

The force of this position is brought out most effectively in Bertrand Russell's claim that 'the essence of what is useful is that it ministers to some result which is not merely useful' (1926, p.15). For, as he goes on to argue, we cannot sensibly view existence as a series of utilities. 'Somewhere we must get beyond the chain of successive utilities, and find a peg from which the chain is to hang; if not there is no real usefulness in any link of the chain' (ibid.). 'Life must be capable of some intrinsic value: if life were merely useful as a means to other life, it would not be useful at all' (ibid.).

In simpler terms, if we plan all our educational provision on the assumption that it must be justified in utilitarian or instrumental terms, we will be denying pupils access to something of vital importance — an appreciation and understanding of the concept that some things can be valuable for their own sakes. The problem with much current educational theory and practice is that it fails to recognize this truth. It is the first principle of the view of education we have explored here that this truth is crucial to any truly educational process. It is for this reason that it represents a major act of rethinking.

Several things follow from this basic principle. One of these is that, as several contributors have stressed, there is a fundamental incompatibility between this kind of educational philosophy and the adoption of a 'product' or 'objectives' model of curriculum planning, however the products or objectives are conceived. To plan education by reference to its end-products is necessarily to view it instrumentally. To reject an instrumental approach, therefore, entails the adoption of a different planning model. Such a model must inevitably be concerned with the processes of education rather than its products and must proceed by translating these processes into educational principles rather than by translating long-term aims into short-term objectives. Much work remains to be done at the levels of both theory and practice on this approach to educational planning. Suffice it to say here that it is to such an approach that we are committed once we reject all forms of utilitarianism. Every chapter has contributed towards an elucidation of the practicalities of this form of teaching.

A further principle follows from this and that is that education must be seen in terms of experience rather than as the acquisition of knowledge or skills, as that well-known and oft-repeated sentence of the Hadow Report asserted. It is a matter of personal growth and development and, for that to occur, far more than the passive assimilation of inert ideas is required. Choice of content, material and activity must be made by reference to the individual child rather than out of deference to the claims of bodies of currently approved knowledge.

There are at least two aspects of this which need to be recognized fully and clearly. First, there is the implication that the child must be active in the learning process. This claim has too often been interpreted as implying a need for gross physical activity, so that the provision of opportunities for physical movement and work of a practical kind has sometimes been regarded as adequate for the development of this kind of curriculum. Opportunities for physical movement are, in many contexts and on many occasions, important but they do not constitute a sufficient condition for active learning. For the concept of active learning is concerned much more to stress the need for the learner to be actively engaged mentally and intellectually in the learning process in order to ensure that that process does promote his development. This is why the work of developmental psychology has been so influential in the growth of this view of education. A child can be highly active physically and learn nothing; he can be almost totally passive and learn much; in neither case will he necessarily have experienced any kind of intellectual development. It is the active engagement of his intellect, and indeed of his emotions too, that is crucial. Again much current educational practice fails to recognize the importance of this. Again, therefore, we can see the kind of rethinking that this view is urging us to undertake. We believe that the accounts in this book, particularly those in Parts Two and Four, have taken us some way towards the re-thinking of our practice in these terms.

A second aspect of this view of education as experience is that it raises important questions about the organization of knowledge. For a child to be actively engaged in the learning process, the content of that process must have meaning for him. We can only ensure that it has by planning that content in terms of his choices, his enquiries, his interests. This is a notion that has of course been debated by the theorists almost *ad nauseam* in recent years. It is, however, a corollary of the principles we have already listed. It is entirely consonant with the philosophical position on which these are based. And it does lead to the erosion of many traditional assumptions about subject boundaries and subject hierarchies. We cannot plan this form of curriculum adequately if we begin from too many preconceived notions about what is worthwhile knowledge and how this knowledge must be structured. This is why to adopt this kind of approach to educational planning is to engage in a head-on clash with the traditional subject-based curriculum. For, as Kilpatrick (1951, p.314) pointed out, 'The old (curriculum) consists of a systematically arranged *content of formulated knowledge* which the learner is to acquire. The new consists of the *total living of the child* so far as the school can affect it'. Many of the implications of this for teachers and for the education of teachers will also be apparent from our earlier chapters.

In general, then, we are dealing here with an approach to curriculum and to curriculum planning which rejects the instrumental, subject-based ethos of the traditional curriculum and lays stress on the processes rather than the content of education, on the idea of education as experience rather than as the acquisition of knowledge, on education as individual development, as a process designed to enrich the life of the individual by enhancing his intellectual, moral and aesthetic awareness rather than to provide him with a limited range of socially useful skills or knowledge.

To say that the Hadow and Plowden Reports have attempted to point Primary education in this direction is not, of course, to claim that they have succeeded in doing so on any kind of wide scale. Indeed, there is now clear evidence, in particular from the Inspectorate's survey of Primary education (DES 1978a) and the recent work of the ORACLE team (Galton, Simon and Croll 1980: Galton and Simon 1980) that what the Plowden Report itself described as a 'quickening trend' in this direction has gathered little if any further momentum since that report itself was published; and this has formed the basis of some of the criticism offered of First schools by the recent report by the Inspectorate (DES 1982a). However, the point at issue is not how widespread the practice of this form of education is; it is how far rethinking of traditional notions of education has already progressed. In fact, it may well be the external demands for the adoption of other kinds of approach which have held back the development of this kind of education in many schools. If we are right in claiming, therefore, that these demands are losing their force, even if they are, if anything, growing in volume, this merely reinforces the need to look again at what Hadow and Plowden were trying to say.

A further factor which may explain the reluctance of teachers to plan their work on this basis is the lack of opportunities for them to acquire the skills and abilities to plan and organize their work according to the principles enunciated here. Our experience leads us to believe that there are many teachers who share our view of education but who lack the skills and the understanding to translate it into practice. Thus they often lapse into or settle for less demanding and less complex forms of teaching without always recognizing that these forms not only represent a lowering of the ambitions their own views of education might give them, but also often result in styles of teaching which are incompatible with, and even sometimes counter-productive to, those views. To resolve this, we believe that all teachers need continued opportunities to reflect on and to evaluate their theory and their practice, they need to acquire the ability to articulate their views to themselves and to others, and they need to be encouraged to share experiences and ideas with colleagues of all kinds. We believe it may be more productive to help teachers to translate ideas they may have into practice by giving them access to the work of like-minded colleagues than to confirm them in their reduced aspirations by drawing their attention to the large numbers of their colleagues who are experiencing the same difficulties and seeking the same easy solutions.

One aspect of the exercise we have just completed has struck us as highly significant. It is that no-one whom we have asked to contribute to this book an account of their own practice has been able to do so without at the same time enunciating very clearly the principles upon which that practice is based. Several of the contributors have also commented on the insights they themselves have gained from being asked to analyse and articulate their own practice. We would suggest that this is further evidence both of what the continued development of the teacher requires and of the kind of link between theory and practice we should be seeking.

It is because we believe that all teachers need help in articulating their principles as well as, and contemporaneously with, developing their practice, in short, that they need to be assisted to a more sophisticated view of the relation between theory and practice in education, that we have adopted the stance which this book displays and have offered the accounts which it contains. If it helps some teachers to achieve a better match between their theory and their practice we will be well pleased.

BIBLIOGRAPHY

Adams, A. (1976) *The Humanities Jungle*. London: Ward Lock.

Adelman, C. (editor) (1981) *Uttering, Muttering: Collecting, Using and Reporting Talk for Social and Educational Research*. London: Grant McIntyre.

Ainscow, M. and Tweddle, D. (1977) Behavioural Objectives and Children with Learning Difficulties. *AEP Journal*, **4**, No. 5.

Ainscow, M. and Tweddle, D. (1979) *Preventing Classroom Failure: an objectives approach*. London: Wiley.

Archambault, R.D. (editor) (1965) *Philosophical Analysis and Education*. London: Routledge and Kegan Paul.

Argyris, C. (1970) *Intervention Theory and Method; A Behavioural Science View*. Reading, Massachusetts: Addison Wesley.

Armstrong, M. (1980) *Closely Observed Children*. Writers and Readers Publishing Co-operative Society Ltd. in association with Chameleon Books.

Arnold, C.J. and Watson, J. (1979) *What does MACOS do for pupils?* Meopham School, Kent (unpublished).

Ashton, P., Kneen, P. and Davies, F. (1975) *Aims into Practice in the Primary School*. London: University of London Press.

A.S.E. (1981) *Primary Science No. 4*. London: Association for Science Education.

Atack, S. (1980) *Art Activities for the Handicapped*. Human Horizons Series. London: Souvenir.

Bannister, D. and Fransella, F. (1971) *Inquiring Man*. Harmondsworth: Penguin Books.

Barnes, D. (1976) *From Communication to Curriculum*. Harmondsworth: Penguin Books.

Barnes, D. Britton, J. and Rosen, H. (editors) (1971) *Language, the Learner and the School*. (Revised edition) Harmondsworth: Penguin Books.

Barton, L. and Tomlinson, S. (editors) (1981) *Special Education: Policy, Practices and Social Issues*. London: Harper and Row.

Bate, M. and Smith, M. (1978) *Manual for Assessment in Nursery Education*. Windsor: National Foundation for Educational Research.

Belasco, J.A. and Alutto, J.S. (1975) Decisional Participation and Teacher Satisfaction. In Houghton et al. (1975).

Bennett, N. (1976) *Teaching Styles and Pupil Progress*. London: Open Books.

Bissex, G.L. (1980) *Gnys at Wrk. A Child Learns to Write and Read*. Cambridge, Massachusetts: Harvard University Press.

Blenkin, G. (1980) The influence of initial styles of curriculum development. 45-64 in Kelly (editor) (1980).

Blenkin, G. and Kelly, A.V. (1981) *The Primary Curriculum.* London: Harper and Row.

Bloom, B.S. (editor) (1956) *The Taxonomy of Educational Objectives. Handbook 1.* London: Longmans.

Bluma, S. et al. (1976) *Portage Guide to Early Education.* C.E.S.A. 12, Box 564, Portage, Wisconsin.

Blyth, W.A.L. (1965) *English Primary Education: a Sociological Description, Vol. 2: Background.* London: Routledge and Kegan Paul.

Bolam, R. (1978) School Focused INSET and Consultancy. *Educational Change and Development,* No. 1 April.

Bolam, R, (1980) In-Service Education and Training, in Hoyle, E. and Megarry, J. (editors) (1980).

Bolton, G. (1979) *Towards a Theory of Drama in Education.* London: Longmans.

Bolton, G. (1982) Philosophical perspectives on drama and the curriculum. 27-42 in Nixon (editor) (1982).

Booth, T. (1975) *Growing Up in Society.* Essential Psychology. London: Methuen.

Booth, T. (1982) *National Perspectives.* Special Needs in Education E241 10. Milton Keynes: The Open University Press.

Booth, T. and Statham, J. (editors) (1982) *The Nature of Special Education.* London: Croom Helm for the Open University.

Bradley, H.W. (1978) *Cost and Efficient Utilization of INSET Resources in England and Wales.* Paris: OECD.

Brennan, W.K. (1979) *Shaping the Education of Slow Learners.* London: Routledge and Kegan Paul.

Brennan, W.K. (1979) *Curricular Needs of Slow Learners.* Schools Council Working Paper 63. London: Evans/Methuen for the Schools Council.

Brennan, W.K. (1982) *Changing Special Education.* Milton Keynes: The Open University Press.

Britton, J.N. (1981) English teaching: retrospect and prospect. *English in Education* **15**, No. 2 Summer.

Brown, R. (1973) *A First Language: the early stages.* London: Allen and Unwin.

Bruner, J.S. (1960) *The Process of Education.* Cambridge, Massachusetts: Harvard University Press.

Bruner, J.S. (1964) The course of cognitive growth. *American Psychologist* **19**, reprinted in Cashdan, A. and Grugen, E. (editors) (1972).

Bruner, J.S. (1966) *Towards a Theory of Instruction.* New York: W.W. Norton (first published in this edition 1968 by arrangement with the Harvard University Press).

Bruner, J.S. (1971) *The Relevance of Education.* Harmondsworth: Penguin Books.

Bruner, J.S. (1975) The autogenesis of speech acts. *Journal of Child Language* **19**.

Bruner, J.S. (1977) *The Process of Education.* Preface to Fifteenth Printing Cambridge, Massachusetts: Harvard University Press.

Bruner, J.S. (1980) Man: A Course of Study: Response 1. 225-226 in Stenhouse, L. (editor) (1980).

Bruner, J.S., Oliver, R. and Greenfield, P.M. (1966) *Studies in Cognitive Growth.* New York: Wiley.

Butler, D. (1979) *Cushla and her books.* London: Hodder and Stoughton.

Butler, D. (1980) *Babies need books.* London: The Bodley Head.

Buxton, L. (1981) *Do You Panic About Maths?* London: Heinemann.

Calouste Gulbenkian Foundation (1982) *The Arts in Schools: Principles, Practice and Provision.* London: Calouste Gulbenkian Foundation.

Cashden, A. and Grugen, E. (editors) (1972) *Language in Education: A Source Book.* London: Routledge and Kegan Paul in association with the Open University Press.

Chapman, L.J. and P. Czerniewska (editors) (1978) *Reading from Process to Practice.* London: Routledge and Kegan Paul in association with The Open University Press.

Child, D. (editor) (1977) *Readings in Psychology for the Teacher.* New York: Holt, Rinehart and Winston.

Chomsky, N. (1957) *Syntactic Structures.* The Hague: Mouton.

Chomsky, N. (1965) *Aspects of the Theory of Syntax.* Cambridge, Massachusetts: MIT Press.

Chukovsky, K. (1963) *From Two to Five.* Los Angeles: University of California Press. Translated by Miriam Morton.

Clark, M.M. (1976) *Young Fluent Readers.* London: Heinemann Educational.

Clark, R. (1979) Assessing language in the home, in Davies (editor) (1982).

Clarke, A.M. and Clarke, A.D.B. (1974) *Mental Deficiency. The Changing Outlook.* 3rd edition. London: Methuen.

Clarke, A.D.B. and Clarke, A.M. (1975) *Recent Advances in the Study of Subnormality.* National Association for Mental Health.

Clift, P., Weiner, G. and Wilson, E. (1981) *Record Keeping in Primary Schools.* Schools Council Research Studies. London: Macmillan Education.

Cook, C. (1971) *The Play Way.* London: Heinemann.

Cooper, K. and Whitefield, K. (1981) Mathematics for Young Children - a comparison of three Schools Council Projects. *The Journal of the Association for the Study of the Curriculum,* **2**, No. 1.

Courtney, R. (1980) *The Dramatic Curriculum.* London: Heinemann.

Davies, A. (editor) (1982) *Language and Learning in Home and School.* London: Heinemann Educational.

D'Arcy, P. (1973) *Reading For Meaning 1. Learning to Read.* London: Hutchinson for the Schools Council.

Dearden, R.F. (1968) *The Philosophy of Primary Education.* London: Routledge and Kegan Paul.

Dearden, R.F. (1976) *Problems in Primary Education.* London: Routledge and Kegan Paul.

Delamont, S. and Stubbs, M. (1976) *Explorations in the Classroom.* London: Wiley.

Dewey, J. (1900) *Educational Principles.* The Elementary School Journal.

Dewey, J. (1916) *Democracy and Education.* New York: Collier-Macmillan (1966 edition).

Donaldson, M. (1978) *Children's Minds.* Glasgow: Fontana, William Collins.

Dow, P. (1970a) *Man: A Course of Study. Evaluation Strategies.* Cambridge, Massachusetts: Education Development Center.

Dow, P. (1970b) *Man: A Course of Study. The Netsilik on the Sea Ice.* Cambridge, Massachusetts: Education Development Center.

Dow, P. (1970c) *Man: A Course of Study. Talks to Teachers.* Cambridge, Massachusetts: Education Development Center.

Downey, M. (1980) The Psychological Background to Curriculum Planning. 65-82 in Kelly (editor) (1980).

Downey, M. and Kelly, A.V. (1979) *Theory and Practice of Education.* 2nd edition. London: Harper and Row.

Ede, J. and Williamson, J. (1980) *Talking, Listening and Learning. The development of children's language.* London: Longmans.

Eisner, E. (1979a) *The Educational Imagination, on the Design and Evaluation of School Programs.* New York: Macmillan.

Eisner, E. (1979b) The Contribution of Painting to Children's Cognitive Development. *Journal of Curriculum Studies* **11**.

Elliott, J. and Adelman, C. (1973) Reflecting where the action is: the Design of the Ford Teaching Project. *Education for Teaching* 92.

Elliott, J. (1976) *Developing Hypotheses about Classrooms from Teachers' Practical Constructs.* Grand Forks, University of North Dakota.

Elliott, J. (1977) *Evaluating In-Service Activities — Above or from Below?* Cambridge: Institute of Education Mimeo.

Ennever, L. and Harlen, W. (1972) *With Objectives in Mind* Schools Council Science 5/13 Project. London: Macdonald Educational for the Schools Council.

Eraut, M. (1977) Some perspectives on Consultancy. *In-Service Education* **4**, No. 182 Winter.

Foxton, T. and McBrien, J.A. (1981) *Trainee Workbook.* Manchester: Manchester University Press.

Francis, H. (1978) Language teaching research and its effect on teachers in early education, in Davies (editor) (1982).

Fry, D. (1970) *Homo Loquens.* Cambridge: Cambridge University Press. Also 17-35 in Lee (editor) (1979).

Furumark, A.M. (1973) *A Swedish Approach to Decentralized Curriculum Innovation.* Paris: OECD/CERI Mimeo.

Galton, M., Simon, B. and Croll, P. (1980) *Inside the Primary Classroom.* London: Routledge and Kegan Paul.

Galton, M. and Simon, B. (1980) *Progress and Performance in the Primary Classroom.* London: Routledge and Kegan Paul.

Geortsina, R.H. and Mackie, J.B. (1969) *Studies in Self Cognition.* Baltimore: Wilkins and Wilkie.

Giglioli, P.P. (editor) (1972) *Language and Social Context. Selected Readings.* Harmondsworth: Penguin Books.

Golby, M., Crane, G. and Tann, N. (1981) A Strategy for Professional Development. *British Journal of In-Service Education* **7**, No. 3 Summer.

Golby, M. and Fish, M.A. (1980) School Focused Inset; Clients and Consultants. *British Journal of In-Service Education* **6**, No. 2 Spring.

Goodson, I. (1976) Towards an alternative pedagogy. In Whitty and Young (editors) (1976).

Goody, J. and Watt, I. (1963) The consequences of literacy. In Giglioli (editor) (1972).

Graves, D.H. (1976) Let's get rid of the welfare mess in the teaching of writing. *Language Arts* September.

Gray, H.L. (1979) *Implementing Innovation.* London: North East London Polytechnic Mimeo.

Gronlund, N.E. (1978) *Stating Objectives for Classroom Instruction.* 2nd edition. New York: Macmillan.

Gulliford, R. (1971) *Special Educational Needs.* London: Routledge and Kegan Paul.

Gurney, P. (editor) (1981) *Behaviour Modification in Education.* Perspectives, 5. Exeter School of Education.

Hargreaves, A. (1982) The Rhetoric of School-Centred Innovation. *Journal of Curriculum Studies* **14**, No. 3.

Harlen, W., Darwin, A. and Murphy, M. (1977) *Match and Mismatch: Raising Questions: Leader's Guide.* Edinburgh: Oliver and Boyd for the Schools Council.

Harris, A., Lawn, M. and Prescott, W. (editors) (1975) *Curriculum Innovation*, London: Croom Helm.

Harris, A.J. (1976) Practical Applications of Reading Research. *Reading Teacher* 29. Also 438-446 in Chapman et al. (editors) (1978).

Havelock, R.G. (1971) The Utilization of Educational Research and Development. 312-328 in Harris et al. (editors) (1975).

Heathcote, D. (1981) *Sign (and Portents).* Unpublished paper.

Hechinger, M.H. (1979) Frills in Schools are often Basic. *The New York Times*, 28 January 1979.

Heeks, P. (1981) *Choosing and Using Books in the First School.* London: Macmillan.

Henderson, E. (1978) The Evaluation of an Open University course, in McCabe, C.M. (editor) (1980).

Hester Adrian Research Centre (1979) *Current Research.* Manchester: Manchester University Press.

Hirst, P.H. (1969) The Logic of the Curriculum *Journal of Curriculum Studies* **1**. Also 232-250 in Hooper (editor) (1971).

Hooper, R. (editor) (1971) *The Curriculum: Context, Design and Development.* Edinburgh: Oliver and Boyd in association with the Open University Press.

Hooton, P. (1977) The Role of the Serving Teacher in Curriculum Change. *British Journal of In-Service Education* **4**, Nos. 1 and 2.

Houghton, V., McHugh, R. and Morgan, C. (1975) *Management in Education: Reader One* London: Ward Lock Educational for the Open University.

Hoyle, E. (1980) Professionalization and Deprofessionalization in Education. In Hoyle, E. and Megarry, J. (editors) (1980).

Hoyle, E. and Megarry, J. (editors) (1980) *Professional Development of Teachers.* London: Kogan Page.

I.L.E.A. (1976) *Mathematical Content.* London: Inner London Education Authority.

I.L.E.A. (1978a) *Checkpoints.* London: Inner London Education Authority.

I.L.E.A. (1978b) *Report No. 8693 Item 7. Minutes of Committee Meeting held on 16.12.78.* London: Inner London Education Authority.

I.L.E.A. (1978c) *Keeping the School Under Review.* London: Inner London Education Authority.

I.L.E.A. (1979) *Contact: Issue 22.* London: Inner London Education Authority.

I.L.E.A. (1980) *Review of In-Service Education and Training for Teachers.* London: Inner London Education Authority.

I.L.E.A. (1981) *Report No. 1106, Item 3. Priorities in In-Service Education and training for teachers.* (Schools Educational Sub-Committee). London: Inner London Education Authority.

I.L.E.A. (1981) *Priorities in In-Service Education and Training for Teachers: Report No. 1106 Item 8, 5.3.81. by Education Officer.* London: Inner London Education Authority.

Iser, W. (1978) *The Act of Reading.* London: Routledge and Kegan Paul.

Jackson, A. and Hannon, P. (1981) *The Belfield Reading Project.* Rochdale: Belfield Community Council.

Jackson, P. (1968) *Life in Classrooms.* New York: Holt, Rinehart and Winston.

James, C.M. (1968) *Young Lives at Stake.* London: Collins.

Jayne, E. (1979) *Primary Curriculum Support Teams: A Report of One Term's Work in One School, Summer term 1979* (Research and Statistics Report RS 734/79). London: Inner London Education Authority.

Jayne, E. (1981a) *Primary Curriculum Support Teams Project, Study No. 2.* (Research and Statistics Report RS 772/81). London: Inner London Education Authority.

Jayne, E. (1981b) *Primary Curriculum Support Teams Project. Report No. 3: A Survey of Heads' and Teachers' Views of the Work with the Teams.* (Research and Statistics Report RS 778/81). London: Inner London Education Authority.

Jeffree, D.M., McConkey, R. and Hewson, S. (1977) *Teaching the Handicapped Child.* Human Horizons Series. London: Souvenir.

Jenkins, D. (1975) Integrated Studies Project. In Schools Council (1975).

Jenkins, D. (1980) Man:A Course of Study. 215-224 in Stenhouse, L. (editor) (1980).

Jones, R. (1972) *Fantasy and Feeling in Education.* Harmondsworth: Penguin Books.

Keast, D.J. and Carr, V. (1979) School-Based INSET; Interim Evaluation. *British Journal of In-Service Education* **5**, No. 3.

Keddie, N. (1971) Classroom Knowledge. 133-160 in Young (editor) (1971).

Kelly, A.V. (1977) *The Curriculum: Theory and Practice.* London: Harper and Row.

Kelly, A.V. (1980) *The Curriculum: Theory and Practice.* Second edition. London: Harper and Row.

Kelly, A.V. (1978) *Mixed Ability Grouping.* London: Harper and Row.

Kelly, A.V. (editor) (1980) *Curriculum Context.* London: Harper and Row.

Kelly, A.V. (1981) Research and the Primary Curriculum. *Journal of Curriculum Studies* **13**, No. 3.

Kelly, G.A. (1955) *The Psychology of Personal Constructs.* New York: Norton.

Kiernan, C., Jordan, R. and Saunders, C. (1978) *Starting Off.* Human Horizons Series. London: Souvenir.

Kilpatrick, W.H. (1951) *Philosophy of Education.* New York: Macmillan (1963 edition).

King, R. (1978) *All Things Bright and Beautiful, A Sociological Study of Infants' Classrooms.* Chichester: John Wiley.

Klein, G. (1982) *Resources for Multi-cultural Education: An Introduction.* Schools Council Programme 4. York: Longmans for the Schools Council.

Lane, D. (1981) Foreword. 7-11 in Barton and Tomlinson (editors) (1981).

Lawrence, D.H. (1964) *Complete Poetical Works.* Harmondsworth: Penguin Books.

Lee, V. (editor) (1979) *Language Development.* London: Croom Helm for the Open University.

Leeming, K., Swann, W., Coupe, J. and Mittler, P. (1979) *Teaching Language and Communication to the Mentally Handicapped.* London: Evans/Methuen Educational for the Schools Council.

Lindsay, M. (1963) *The Training of Teachers of Mentally Handicapped Children.* International League of Societies for the Mentally Handicapped, Brussels, Belgium. In Stevens (editor) (1968).

Lindsley, O.R. (1964) Direct Measurement and Prosthesis of Retarded Behaviour. *Journal of Education* **CXLVII**.

MacDonald, B. and Walker, R. (1976) *Changing the Curriculum.* London: Open Books.

MacDonald, B. (1978) *Accountability, Standards and the Process of Schooling.* Norwich: University of East Anglia Mimeo.

Maclure, M. and French, P. (1981) A comparison of talk at home and at school. In Wells (1981).

Mager, R.F. (1962) *Preparing Instructional Objectives*. Belmon, California: Fearon.

Manning, K. and Sharp, A. (1977) *Structuring Play in the Early Years at School*. London: Ward Lock Educational in association with Drake Educational Associates for the Schools Council.

Matthews, G. (editor) (1967) *The Nuffield Mathematics Project*. London: Chambers, Murray.

McCabe, C.M. (editor) (1980) *Evaluating INSET*. Slough: National Foundation for Educational Research.

McBrien, J.A. and Foxton, T. (1981) *Instructor's Handbook*. Manchester: Manchester University Press.

McMaster, J. (1973) *Towards an Educational Theory for the Mentally Handicapped*. London: Arnold.

Meek, M. (1982) *Learning to Read*. London: The Bodley Head.

Minns, H. (1981) Separate human beings? *English in Education* **15**, No. 1 Spring.

Miles, M. (1965) Planned Change and Organisational Health; Figure and Ground. 192-203 in Harris et al. (editors) (1975).

Mittler, P. (editor) (1970) The Work of the Hester Adrian Research Centre. Published as a special monograph supplement to *Teaching and Training* **8**, Summer.

Mittler, P. (1979) *People Not Patients, Problems and Policies in Mental Handicap*. London: Methuen.

Mittler, P. (1981) Training for the 21st Century. *Special Education: Forward Trends* **8**, No. 2.

Moffett, J. (1968) *Teaching the Universe of Discourse*. Boston: Houghton Mifflin.

Nixon, J. (1982) *Drama and the Whole Curriculum*. London: Hutchinson.

Open University (1979) *Course P.333: The Reading Curriculum and the Advisory Role — action research projects*. Milton Keynes: Open University Press.

Otty, N. (1975) Getting it together. *Times Educational Supplement* **7**, November.

Paquette, J. (1982) The daily record. *The English Magazine* **9**, Spring.

Pearce, J. (1975) Schools Council Linguistics and English Teaching Project. In Schools Council (1975).

Perkins, E.A. Taylor, P.D. and Cadie, A.C. (1976) *Helping the Retarded*. Institute of Mental Subnormality.

Peters, R.S. (1965) Education as Initiation. 87-111 in Archambault (editor) (1965).

Peters, R.S. (1966) *Ethics and Education*. London: Allen and Unwin.

Petrie, I. (1974) *Drama and Handicapped Children*. Educational Drama Association.

Piaget, J. and Inhelder, B. (1971) *Mental Imagery in the Child*. London: Routledge and Kegan Paul.

Pidgeon, G. (1980) *Towards Creative Play*. Educational Drama Association.

Popham, W.J. (1975) *Educational Evaluation*. New York: Prentice Hall.

Presland, J. and Roberts, G. (1980) Aims, objectives and E.S.N.(S) Children. *Special Education: Forward Trends* **7**.

Presland, J. (1980) Educating 'Special Care' Children: A Review of the Literature. *Educational Research* **23**, November.

Pring, R. (1976) *Knowledge and Schooling*. London: Open Books.

Pring, R. (1981) Behaviour Modification: Some Reservations. In Gurney (editor) (1981).

Raths, J.D. (1971) Teaching without specific objectives. *Educational Leadership* April.

Raybould, T. and Solity, J. (1982) Teaching with Precision. *Special Education: Forward Trends* **9**.

324   The Primary Curriculum in Action

Read, H. (1943) *Education Through Art.* London: Faber and Faber.

Rectory Paddock School (1982) *In Search of a Curriculum.* Sidcup: Robin Wren Publications.

Richards, R., Collis, M. and Kincaid, D. (1980) *Learning Through Science: Formulating a School Policy.* London: Macdonald Educational for the Schools Council.

Richards, R., Collis, M., Kincaid, D. and Bailey, H. (1982) *Science Resources for Primary and Middle Schools.* Schools Council Learning Through Science Project. London: Macdonald Educational for the Schools Council.

Robson, C. (1980) *Project TASS — Phase One, Final Report.* Huddersfield Polytechnic.

Rogers, C.R. (1969) *Freedom to Learn.* Columbus, Ohio: Charles E. Merrill.

Rosen, C. and Rosen, H. (1973) *The Language of Primary School Children.* Schools Council Project on Language Development in the Primary School. Harmondsworth: Penguin Books.

Rosen, H. (1971) Towards a Language Policy Across the Curriculum. In Barnes D. et al. (1971).

Rowe, M. (1973) The Cyclical Structure of Evaluatory Schemes. *The New Era.* 1973.

Rowntree, D. (1977) *Assessing Students — How Shall We Know Them?* London: Harper and Row.

Rudduck, J. (1972) 'Man: A Course of Study'. *Cambridge Journal of Education* **2**, No. 2.

Russell, B. (1926) *On Education.* London: Unwin (1964 edition).

Ryle, A. (1975) *Frames and Cages.* Brighton: Sussex University Press.

Salmon, P. (editor) (1980) *Coming to Know.* London: Routledge and Kegan Paul.

Scheffler, I. (1965) *Conditions of Knowledge.* Chicago and London: University of Chicago Press.

Schools Council (1969) *Education Through the Use of Materials.* Working Paper 26. London: Evans/Methuen Educational for the Schools Council.

Schools Council (1975) *Evaluation in Curriculum Development: Twelve Case Studies.* London: Macmillan Education for the Schools Council.

Schools Council (1976) *Listening to Children Talking.* Schools Council Communication Skills in Early Childhood Project. London: Ward Lock Educational for the Schools Council.

Schools Council (1978) *Early Mathematical Experiences.* London: Addison-Wesley for the Schools Council.

Schools Council (1980) *Learning Through Science: Formulating a School Policy.* London: Macdonald Educational for the Schools Council.

Serpell-Morris, G. (1982) Minds of Their Own - One Teacher's Philosophy. 176-179 in Booth and Statham (editors) (1982).

Shearer, M.S. and Shearer, D. (1972) The Portage Project: A Model for Early Childhood Education. *Exceptional Children.*

Sinha, C. (1981) The Role of Psychological Research in Special Education. 400-435 in Swann (editor) (1981).

Skemp, R. (1971) *The Psychology of Learning Mathematics.* Harmondsworth: Penguin Books.

Skilbeck, M. (1971) Strategies of Curriculum Change. 27-37 in Walton (editor) (1971).

Skilbeck, M. (1973) The School and Cultural Development. *The Northern Teacher* Winter.

Slkilbeck, M. (1976) School-based Curriculum Development. 90-102 in Open University Course 203, Unit 26. Milton Keynes: The Open University Press.

Smith, F. (1973) *Psycholinguistics and Reading.* New York: Holt, Rinehart and Winston.

Smith, F. (1978) *Understanding Reading. A psycholinguistic analysis of reading and learning to read.* 2nd edition. New York: Holt, Rinehart and Winston.

Southgate, V., Arnold, H. and Johnson, S. (1981) *Extending Beginning Reading.* London: Heinemann Educational Books for the Schools Council.

Spencer, M. (1980) Handing Down the Magic. 46-62 in Salmon, P. (editor) (1980).

Stabler, T. (1978) *Drama in Primary Schools*. Schools Council Drama 5-11 Project. London: MacMillan Education for the Schools Council.

Stenhouse, L. (1970) Some Limitations of the Use of Objectives in Curriculum Research and Planning. *Paedagogica Europaea* **6**.

Stenhouse, L. (1975) *An Introduction to Curriculum Research and Development.* London: Heinemann.

Stenhousse, L. (editor) (1980) *Curriculum Research and Development in Action.* London: Heinemann.

Stevens, M. (1968) *Observing Children Who Are Severely Subnormal.* London: Edward Arnold.

Stevens, M. (1971) *The Educational Needs of Severely Subnormal Children.* London: Edward Arnold.

Swann, W. (1981) *The Practice of Special Education.* London: Blackwell in association with the Open University Press.

Swann, W. (1982) *Psychology and Special Education.* Special Needs in Education E241 12. Milton Keynes: The Open University Press.

Swann, W. and Briggs, D. (1982) *A Special Curriculum?* Special Needs in Education E241 5/6. Milton Keynes: The Open University Press.

Taylor, P. (1966) Purpose and structure in the Curriculum. 398-408 in Child (editor) (1977).

Taylor, P. (1970) *Curriculum Planning for Compensatory Education: A Suggested Procedure.* London: Schools Council.

Taylor, P.H., Reid, W.A. and Holley, B.J. (1964) *The English Sixth Form; a Case Study in Curriculum Research.* London: Routledge and Kegan Paul.

Tizard, B., Mortimore, J. and Burchell, B. (1981) *Involving Parents in Nursery and Infant Schools: a source book for teachers.* London: Grant McIntyre.

Torrey, J.W. (1969) Learning to read without a teacher: a case study. In Smith (editor) (1973).

Trudgill, P. (1975) *Accent, Dialect and the School.* London: Edward Arnold.

Tucker, N. (1981) *The Child and the Book: a psychological and literary exploration.* Cambridge: Cambridge University Press.

Tyler, R.W. (1949) *Basic Principles of Curriculum and Instruction.* Chicago: University of Chicago Press.

University of London Institute of Education (1971) *The Education and Training of Teachers.* London: University of London Institute of Education.

Vygotsky, L.S. (1962) *Thought and Language.* Cambridge, Massachusetts: MIT Press.

Vygotsky, L.S. (1978) *Mind in Society. The development of higher psychological processes.* Cambridge, Massachusetts: Harvard University Press.

Walton, J. (editor) (1971) *Curriculum Organization and Design.* London: Ward Lock Educational.

Wastnedge, E.R. (editor) (1967) *Nuffield Junior Sciences: Teachers' Guide I.* London: Collins.

Weir, R. (1962) *Language in the Crib.* The Hague: Mouton.

Wells, G. (1978) Talking with children: the complementary roles of parents and teachers. *English in Education* **12**, No. 3.

Wells, G. (1979) Influences of the home on language development. In Davies (editor) (1982).

Wells, G. (1981) *Learning through Interaction. The study of language development.* Cambridge: Cambridge University Press.

Wheeler, D.K. (1967) *Curriculum Process.* London: University of London Press.

Whitehead, A.N. (1932) *The Aims of Education.* London: Williams and Norgate.

Whitty, G. and Young, M.F.D. (editors) (1976) *Explorations in the Politics of School Knowledge.* Driffield: Nafferton Books.

Wilkinson, A., Barnsley, G., Hanna, P. and Swan, M. (1980) *Assessing Language Development.* Oxford: Oxford University Press.

Williams, E.M. and Shuard, H. (1976) *Primary Mathematics Today.* London: Longmans.

Williams, R. (1961) *The Long Revolution.* London: Chatto and Windus, also Harmondsworth: Penguin Books (1965).

Willes, M. (1981) Children Becoming Pupils: a Study of Discourse in Nursery and Reception Classes. 51-68 in Adelman, C. (editor) (1981).

Young, M.F.D. (editor) (1971) *Knowledge and Control.* New York: Collier MacMillan.

Government Reports and other official publications referred to in the text

Board of Education (1926) *The Education of the Adolescent* (The Hadow Report on Secondary Education). London: HMSO.

Board of Education (1931) *Primary Education* (The Hadow Report on Primary Education). London: HMSO.

Central Advisory Council for Education (1959) *15 to 18* (The Crowther Report). London: HMSO.

Central Advisory Council for Education (1967) *Children and Their Primary Schools* (The Plowden Report). London: HMSO.

Department of Education and Science (1972) *Teacher Education and Training* (The James report). London: HMSO.

HMSO (1972) *Education: A Framework for Expansion.* Cmnd 5174. London: HMSO.

Department of Education and Science (1975) *A Language for Life* (The Bullock Report). London: HMSO.

Department of Education and Science (1978a) *Primary Education in England and Wales. A Survey of H.M. Inspectors of Schools.* London: HMSO.

Department of Education and Science (1978b) *Special Educational Needs* (The Warnock Report). London: HMSO.

Department of Education and Science (1979a) *Mathematical Development: Primary Survey Report No. 1.* London: HMSO.

Department of Education and Science (1979b) *Aspects of Secondary Education in England. A Survey by HM Inspectors of Schools.* London: HMSO.

Department of Education and Science (1980) *Special Needs in Education.* London: HMSO.

Department of Education and Science (1981) *The School Curriculum.* London: HMSO.

Department of Education and Science (1982a) *Education 5 to 9: an illustrative survey of 80 first schools in England.* London: HMSO.

Department of Education and Science (1982b) *Mathematics Counts* (The Cockroft Report). London: HMSO.

Department of Education and Science (1982c) *Bullock Revisited, a discussion document by H.M.I.* London: HMSO.

Department of Education and Science (1982d) *The New Teacher in School.* London: HMSO.

Department of Education and Science (1983) Teaching in Schools: The Intent of Initial Training. London: HMSO.

Children's books and materials referred to in the text

Anno, M. (1975) *Anno's Alphabet.* London: Bodley Head.

Bailey, B. (1979) *The Enormous Turnip.* London: Macdonald Educational.

Bailey, B. (1979) *The Little Red Hen.* London: Macdonald Educational.

Berenstein, S. and Berenstein, J. (1971) *Bears in the Night.* London: Beginner Book.

Berenstein, S. and Berenstein, J. (1971) *Inside, Outside, Upside-down.* London: Beginner Book.

Briggs, R. (1982) *When the Wind Blows.* London: Hamish Hamilton.

Brychta, J. (1971) *Jack and the Beanstalk.* New York. Franklin Watts.

Collis, M. and Kincaid, D. (1982) *All Around.* London: Macdonald Educational.

Collis, M. and Kincaid, D. (1982) *Out of Doors.* London: Macdonald Educational.

Garner, A. (1967) *The Owl Service.* London: William Collins/Fontana: Lions.

Hargreaves, R. (1977) *Grandfather Clock.* London: Hodder and Stoughton.

Hughes, T. (1968) *The Iron Man.* London: Faber.

Hutchins, P. (1970) *Rosie's Walk.* London: The Bodley Head/Picture Puffin.

Kincaid, D. and Richards, R. (1983) *Moving Around.* London: Macdonald Educational.

Kincaid, D. and Richards, R. (1983) *On the Move.* London: Macdonld Educational.

Pienkowski, H. and Pienkoswki, J. (1976) *Mog's Mumps.* London: Puffin Books.

Richards, R. and Kincaid, D. (1981) *Colour.* London: Macdonald Educational.

Richards, R. and Kincaid, D. (1982) *Materials.* London: Macdonald Educational.

Richards, R. and Kincaid, D. (1981) *Ourselves.* London: Macdonald Educational.

Richards, R. and Kincaid, D. (1982) *Sky and Space.* London: Macdonald Educational.

Reid, J. and Low, J. (1972) *Link up 3.* London: Holmes McDougall.

Sandberg, I. and Sandberg, L. (1973) *Daniel's Mysterious Monster.* London: A. & C. Black.

Sendak, M. (1967) *Where the Wild Things Are.* London: The Bodley Head/Picture Puffin.

Southgate, V. (1968) *Jill's Toy's.* London: MacMillan Educational.

Southgate, V. (1968) *School.* London: MacMillan Educational.

AUTHOR INDEX

Adams, A., 285
Adelman, C., 31
Ainscow, M. and Tweddle, D., 256, 257, 272
Argyris, C., 203, 205
Armstrong, Henry, 96
Armstrong, Michael, 251
Arnold, C.J. and Watson, J., 294
Ashton, P., Kneen, P. and Davies, F., 20
Atack, Sally, 267-8

Bannister, D. and Fransella, F., 187, 266
Barnes, D., 31, 291, 293, 294
Bate, M. and Smith, M., 21
Belasco, J.A. and Alutto, J.S., 206
Bennett, Neville, 19
Bissex, G.L., 74, 75
Blenkin, G., 18
Blenkin, G. and Kelly, A.V., 11, 12, 18, 21,
    38, 61, 234, 250, 262, 275-6, 279, 299
Bloom, B., 253
Bluma, S. *et al*, 251
Blyth, W.A.L., 10, 15
Bolam, R., 190, 193, 200, 203, 208
Bolam, R. and Baker, 200
Bolton, Gavin, 276-7
Booth, T., 252, 266
Bradley, H.W., 193
Brennan, Wilfred, 253
Briggs, Raymond, 70
Britton, James, 57, 73
Brown, Roger, 58
Bruner, Jerome, 59, 66, 263, 281-4, 286,
    291, 298
Butler, D., 66
Buxton, Laurie, 81

Chomsky, N., 58
Chukovsky, K., 58
Clarke, A.M., 59, 62, 74, 273-4
Clarke, A.M. and Clarke, A.D.B., 256
Clift, P., Weiner, G. and Wilson, E., 21
Collis, M. and Kincaid, D., 112
Cook, Caldwell, 263
Cooper, K. and Whitfield, K., 268, 269
Courtney, Richard, 263

D'Arcy, Pat, 270
Dearden, R.F., 18, 21
Delamont, S. and Stubbs, M., 186
Dewey, John, 10, 27, 250, 258, 313
Donaldson, Margaret, 33, 35-6, 156, 278
Dow, Peter, 281, 284, 286-7, 198
Downey, Meriel, 277
Downey, Meriel and Kelly, A.V., 250, 291,
    296

Ede, Janet and Williamson, Jack, 63
Eisner, E., 251, 276, 300
Eklund, 195
Elliott, J., 186-7, 191, 204
Elliott, J. and Adelman, C., 183
Ennever, L. and Harlen, W., 97
Eraut, M., 203

Faraday, Michael, 114
Foxton, T. and McBrien, J.A., 256
Francis, H., 62
Froebel, Friedrich, 10, 27
Fry, Dennis, 269

Galton, M. and Simon, B., 315

Galton, M., Simon, B. and Croll, P., 29, 31, 34, 315
Geortsina, R.H. and Mackie, J.B., 188
Golby, M., Crane, G. and Tann, N., 204
Golby, M. and Fish, M.A., 213, 214
Goodson, I., 11
Goody, J. and Watt, I., 78
Graves, D.H., 74
Gray, H.L., 191
Gronlund, N.E., 257
Gulbenkian Foundation, 115, 120, 155
Gulliford, R., 252

Hargreaves, A., 160, 241
Harlen, W., Darwin, A. and Murphy, M., 22, 98, 99, 110
Harris, A., 277
Havelock, R.G., 189, 200, 208
Heathcote, Dorothy, 265
Hechinger, M.H., 276
Heeks, P., 66
Henderson, E., 193
Hirst, Paul, 14
Hooton, P., 203
Hoyle, E., 184
Huxley, Elspeth, 110

Iser, W., 66, 75

Jackson, A., and Hannon, P., 77
Jackson, Philip, 186
James, C.M., 10
Jayne, E., 204, 214, 217
Jeffree, D.M., McConkey, R. and Hewson, S., 253-4
Jenkins, David, 184, 285, 286
Jones, R., 285, 298

Keast, D.J. and Carr, V., 206, 208
Keddie, N., 221
Kelly, A.V., 11, 234, 251, 257
Kelly, George, 187
Kiernan, C., Jordan, R. and Saunders, C., 254
Kilpatrick, W.H., 315
King, R., 31
Klein, G., 44

Lane, D., 277
Lawrence, D.H., 153
Lee, V., 269

Leeming, K., Swann, W., Coupe, J. and Mittler, P., 254-5
Lindsay, Mary, 273
Lindsley, O.R., 256

MacDonald, B., 207
MacDonald, B. and Walker, R., 189
Maclure, M. and French, P., 79
McMaster, John, 252, 255
Mager, R., 257
Manning, K. and Sharp, A., 269
Meek, Margaret, 65, 66
Miles, Matthew, 190
Minns, H., 76
Mittler, P., 252, 255, 256
Moffatt, J., 64
Montessori, Maria, 10, 27
Moyle, 184

Osgood, C.E., 255
Otty, N., 71

Paquette, J., 73
Pearce, John, 184
Perkins, E.A., Taylor, P.D. and Cadie, A.C., 253
Pestalozzi, Johann, 27, 101
Peters, Richard, 13, 27
Petrie, Ian, 264
Piaget, Jean, 97, 263, 278
Piaget, Jean and Inhelder, B., 66
Pidgeon, Gordon, 264-5
Popham, W.J., 257
Povey, 273
Presland, John, 256
Presland, John and Roberts, G., 256, 272
Pring, R., 272, 299

Raths, J.D., 287
Raybould, T. and Solity, J., 256, 257
Read, H., 263-4
Reid, W.A., 189
Richards, R., Collis, M. and Kincaid, D., 98, 109
Richards, R. and Kincaid, D., 112
Robson, C., 256
Rogers, C.R., 308
Rosen, C. and Rosen, H., 268
Rosen, H., 124, 291
Rousseau, Jean-Jacques, 10, 11, 27, 312
Rowe, M., 188

Rowntree, Derek, 266
Ruddock, J., 285
Russell, Bertrand, 44, 55, 313
Ryle, A., 188

Scheffler, I., 288
Serpell-Morris, G., 272-3
Shearer, M.S. and Shearer, D., 251
Sinha, C., 248, 278
Skilbeck, Malcolm, 250, 262
Smith, Frank, 75
Southgate, V., Arnold, H. and Johnson, S., 59, 77-8
Spencer, Margaret, 35
Stabler, T., 265
Stenhouse, Lawrence, 10-11, 13, 14, 183, 189, 203, 250, 257, 261-2, 287, 292
Stevens, Mildred, 258-9, 273
Swann, Will, 272, 274
Swann, Will and Briggs, D., 277

Taylor, P.H., 186, 252, 253
Tizard, B., Mortimore, J. and Burchell, B., 59, 76
Trudgill, P., 79
Tucker, N., 66
Tyler, Ralph, 14

Vygotsky, L.S., 58

Wastnedge, E.R., 96-7
Weir, R., 58, 64
Wells, Gordon, 59, 62, 76, 269, 270, 278
Wheeler, D.K., 253
Whitehead, Alfred North, 13
Wilkinson, A., Barnsley, G., Hanna, P. and Swan, M., 76
Willes, M., 37
Williams, R., 14

Young, M.F.D., 12

SUBJECT INDEX

accountability, 15, 28, 207, 250
  and record-keeping, 162
active nature of learning, 36-8, 60, 106, 120-8, 259, 281, 288-9, 314
  see also developmental basis of education
Aims in Primary Education Project (Schools Council), 20
  across the curriculum, 115-30, 299-300
art, 98, 119-20, 134, 145, 149, 246, 267, 299-300
Aspects of Secondary Education in England (HMI), 292
assessment of pupils, 48-50, 87-9, 109-10, 266-7, 302 see also examinations; record keeping
  forms of, 88
  in special education, 266-7
  reasons for, 181
  teachers' ability to undertake, 223

basic skills, 12, 16, 18-20, 29-56, 116-17
  basics view of language work, 78-9
  in Special Education, 275-7
  inhibiting aspects of, 19
  place in overall education, 29-30, 38
  planning to teach, 38-50
  problems of teaching, 32-8
  separate approach to, 30-1
behaviour modification, 246, 249, 264, 272
behavioural psychology, 14, 19, 21, 246, 249, 252-7
  influence on skills teaching, 30
Belfield Reading Project, 77
book marking, 39-41, 53-54, 68-70, 228-230,

Bristol study, 59, 76
British Institute of Mental Handicap, 252-3
Bullock Report, A Language for Life, 1975, 60, 74, 264, 293
Bullock Revisited (HMI), 68

Centre for Advanced Research in Education (CARE), 281
checklists, 62, 79, 163, 302
child-centred education, 10, 163, 183, 259
child development, 61, 97, 220, 246
child population, increase in, 236, 237
child-produced books, 39-41, 53-4, 68-9, 70-1
children with special needs, 115, 230, 248-78
children's interests, as resource, 39-41, 69, 89-94, 97-8, 117, 314-15
classroom control, 37
classroom language, 61-3
classroom observation procedures, 186-7
classroom organization, 86, 92-4, 109
Cockroft Report, Mathematics Counts, 1982, 32
cognitive development, see intellectual development
communication, 22, 71, 78, 79, 105-6, 116, 189, 180, 191-2, 194-5, 209, 267, 300-302
Communication Skills in Early Childhood Project (Schools Council), 22
concept development, 87, 107, 110, 210, 285, 299, 303
confidentiality, 207
consultants, see curriculum support schemes
content, 1, 16, 109

content model of curriculum planning, 13-14
Craft, Design and Technology Project (Schools Council), 20
creative arts, 3, 71, 74, 115-56
  and learning generally, 115-30, 299-300
creative nature of learning, 60, 115
Crediton Project, 76
Crowther Report, *15-18*, 1959, 312
curriculum development
  defining the task, 189-91
  funding, 193, 198
  implementation of, 190-5
  inhibitions, 16-22, 159
  planning, 13-14, 22, 184-90, 202
  principles of, 11-13
  recognising the need, 184-9
  responsibility for, 192
  support structures, 159, 195-9
  time for, 192-5
  traditions, 10
curriculum dissemination models, 189, 212, 214
curriculum guidelines, mathematics, 84-5, 171, 175
curriculum support schemes, 200-17
  contract, 213-15
  follow-through activities, 214
  philosophy, 203-8
  role, 203
  strategies, 208-13
  task models, 209-13
curriculum support teams, 160
  headteachers and, 204-6
  process consultancy, 208
  task consultancy, 208-9
  teachers and, 204, 210-13

dance, 116, 128, 267
decision-making, 116, 205-6
degree courses, syllabuses for intending teachers, 225
developmental basis of education, 12, 14, 18, 221, 274, 278, 288-9, 299-300, 310-15
  see also active nature of learning; intellectual development
discipline, *see* classroom control
drama, 128-30, 259, 260, 264, 265, 267, 276-7, 300
  in special education, 264
  educated man, 13

Education: A Framework for Expansion (DES), 239-40
Education 5 to 9 (HMI), 315
enactive mode of representation, 281
environment, and language development, 58-9
equipment for skills teaching, 41-3
evaluation, 14, 19, 28, 37-8, 67, 75-8, 109-10, 181, 184, 186-8, 271
  of curriculum development, 190, 195, 201, 207
  of record systems, 171-81
  teachers' ability to undertake, 223
examination, 9, 246-7, 280-81, 302
  at 11+, 9, 10, 159
  CSE, Mode 3, 301-5
experience, 12, 30, 67, 71, 89-94, 109, 118, 124-27, 156, 163, 210, 226, 228, 246, 262, 287, 299, 314
Extending Beginning Reading Project (Schools Council), 77-8
extending strategies, 51-2

feelings, 115, 116, 119, 120, 150, 156, 285, 298
flow diagrams, 90-1, 163-74, 191, 195-7
Ford Teaching Project, 186-8

group discussions, guidance of, 293-4

HM Inspectorate, 185
  see also publications by title
Hadow Report, *Primary Eduction*, 1931, 9-10, 12, 261, 308, 312
Hester Adrian Research Centre, 252, 255-6
Higher Education, 2, 236, 237
History 13-16 Project (Schools Council), 294
home and school, 76-77, 270
Humanities Curriculum Project (HCP), 10, 186, 188
Humanities, 280-307
Huddersfield Polytechnic, 255

iconic mode of representation, 66, 281-2,
ILEA
  curriculum support scheme, 200-17
  Notebook, 165, 172-3
Illings test of Psycholinguistic Abilities (ITPA), 255, 277
imagination, 66, 116, 129, 139, 142, 144-45, 146, 300

impersonal learning, 35-6
incompetence, fear of, 32
individual learning, 33-5
individuality of the pupil, 220-1
induction training, (teachers), 222, 240
infant schools, 9, 69, 101, 110, 163
innovation, reactions to, 184-9
in-service education, 87, 113-14, 160, 185, 191, 192-4, 218, 236-7, 238-42
    effects of economic recession, 240
    school-based, 193, 215-16, 241-2
    school-focused, 215-16
integrated curriculum see unified curriculum
Integrated Studies Project (Schools Council), 184
intellectual development, 35-6, 59, 65-6, 106-7, 108, 115, 187-8, 262, 275-6, 281-2, 289, 298-9, 310
    language and, 291-2
interactive nature of learning, 57, 58-61, 80, 110, 186, 278
interests, 39, 50, 69, 93, 97, 106, 114, 163, 165, 265, 308, 314
Interdisciplinary Enquiry (IDE), 10
intervention, 62, 205-6, 293
intrinsic motivation, 283-4
intrinsic values of education, 11, 21

James Report, *Teacher Education and Training*, 1972, 239-40
judgement, teachers' 219-20
junior schools, 9, 71

knowledge, 106, 221, 224-25, 232-33, 246-47, 314-15
    'form' of, 18, 288
    undifferentiated, 12, 17
    see also unified curriculum

LEA advisory service, 17, 19, 20, 185, 198
LEA inspectorate, 185, 200-1, 203, 206-8
language across the curriculum, 60-1
    see also Bullock Report
language development, 57-80
    back to basics, 78-9
    importance of talk, 64-5
    in realistic situations, 62-3, 72-3
    Secondary, 291-4
    Special Education, 254-5, 269-70
Learning through Science Project (Schools Council), 18, 22, 98, 108-14
learning *through* subjects, 224, 299

Linguistics and English Teaching Project (Schools Council). 184
literacy, 29, 30, 32, 34, 35, 38, 61, 64, 65-9, 74, 78, 80

Man: A Course of Study (MACOS), 11, 281-6
    benefits for teacher development, 285-6
    development beyond, 286-9
    emphasis, 285, 298
    goals, 286-7
    themes, 284
materials
    ability to create, 223
    development from, 44-5
    for language work, 63-4, 67-71, 74
    for MACOS, 284-5
    for science teaching, 111-13
    for skills teaching, 43-6
mathematics, 3, 18, 19, 30, 32, 36, 39, 43, 54, 81-95, 98, 117, 118, 120, 128, 131, 135-6, 138, 145, 146, 191, 201, 209, 211, 227-28, 230, 267
    fear of, 81
    insight, 85
    record-keeping, 171, 175
    special education, 268-9
    strands, 85-6
mixed-ability grouping, 11, 280-1
modes of language, 60
modes of representation, 66, 281-2, 284, 302
monitoring of 'standards', 15
motivation, 283-4
morals, 115, 230
music, 128, 130, 134, 138, 260, 276

Nuffield Junior Science Project, 96-7, 111
numeracy, 29, 30, 34, 38
Nursery schools, 21, 76, 110

ORACLE study, 34, 315
objectives in curriculum planning, 11, 13, 14, 16, 20-2, 79, 94, 97, 159, 163, 183, 233-4, 246, 287, 289, 303, 313
    in special education, 249-50, 252-7, 272-73
Open University
    Curriculum in Action course, 186
    Reading Development course, 188
    Special Needs in Education course, 274
oracy, 60

organization of schools, 205-6, 208-9
  organizational health, 190
  see also classroom organization

parental involvement, 46, 76-7, 271
  special education, 270-1
passive learning, 36-8
personal autonomy, 296, 304
personal nature of learning, 35-6
  private journals, 73
play, importance of in Special Education, 259, 263-5, 267
Plowden Report, *Children and their Primary Schools*, 1967, 10, 59, 183, 261, 312
policies, school, 60-61, 108-10, 114
Portage Guide to Early Education, 251
precision teaching, 256-7
Primary Education in England and Wales (HMI), 10, 17, 19, 22, 108, 315
probationary year, *see* induction training
problem solving, 284, 288, 295-6
procedural principles, 13, 94, 246, 273, 287-89
processes in curriculum planning, 1, 3, 11, 13, 15, 21-22, 30, 55, 57, 61, 97, 114, 203, 206, 219-21, 233, 246, 247, 248-78, 279-308, 315
  language development as paradigm, 57
  processes of science, 98-101, 106, 107
professional types, teachers, 184-9
Progress in Learning Science Project (Schools Council), 98
public control of curriculum, 15-16
punctuation, 79
puppets, 40, 116, 118
pupil as researcher, 302-3
pupil expectations, 36-7, 307

qualified teacher status, 238
questions, 103-4
  open-ended, 294

reading, 19, 30, 31, 34, 35, 36, 43, 49-50, 50-51, 60, 65, 66, 74-75, 77, 78, 134, 171, 175, 180
  learning of, 67-74
  teaching of, 35, 49-50, 77
record-keeping, 3, 48, 162-82
  and planning, 162, 163-15, 172, 181
  as scientific activity, 105
  coverage, 163-71
  evaluation, 171-81

for future planning, 94
  for mathematics, 171, 175
  for reading, 171, 175, 180
  individual child, 48-50
  in Special Education, 266-67
  of achievement, 87, 88, 170-5
  of activity, 87, 90-1, 164-5, 167-8
Record-Keeping in the Primary Schools Project (Schools Council), 21
relationships, 64, 65, 70, 88, 205, 262
religion, 115, 280
research
  by pupil, 286, 302-3, 306
  by teachers, 61, 75-78, 250
  in education, 7-8, 15-22, 27, 57, 77, 185, 186
  influence on practice, 57-60
resources, 97, 98, 214, 227, 230
  for science teaching, 110-11
  for skills teaching, 39-41, 52
  in language work, 64-5, 74
  resource centres, 110-11, 208
routine tasks, 37, 46
rules, discussion of, 74
  for basic skills, 46-8, 50-1

school and college closures, 235-6
school-centred innovation, 3, 160, 183-199, 200-217, 241-2
school practice, 163-4
Schools Council,
  Curriculum Bulletin 8, 254
  funds, 16
  structure, 17
  Working Paper 63, 253
  see also projects by title
science, 3, 18, 27, 39, 63, 73, 96-114, 115, 128, 129, 138, 209, 211, 230, 308
  art work and, 126-7
  benefits of, 106-7
  defined, 98-100
  historical perspective, 96-8
  policy (school), 98, 108-9
  slow learners, 113
  themes, 109
science across the curriculum, 98, 107
Science 5-13 Project (Schools Council), 97-8, 111
Secondary education, 10-11, 246, 279-308
  application of process model, 280-307
senses, use of, 101-3

sequential learning schemes, *see* structured learning programmes
social nature of learning, 33-5, 57-8, 105-6, 115, 120, 260, 291
Special Education, 4, 245, 246, 248-78
  application of process model, 258-72
  package approach, 251
  recent developments, 272-7
special educational needs, *see* children with special needs
  see also Warnock Report
spelling, 72, 78
spiral curriculum, 282
spoken language, 58-60
spontaneous application of skills, 54-5
'standards', 310
  monitoring of, 15
story-telling, 44, 64, 65, 67-9, 71, 73, 124-6, 226, 270
  in special education, 270
structured learning programmes, 30, 34, 43, 83-4, 307
  extension of, 71
  in special education, 251, 253, 273-5
subject-based approach to education, 10-13, 15-18, 60, 128, 221, 246, 315, *see also* content model of curriculum planning
learning *through* subjects, 224, 299
  see also teacher education, knowledge acquisition
supporting structures (curriculum development), 159, 195-9
symbolic modes of representation, 282

talk, 64-5, 74, 270, 292-4
  teacher-to.teacher discussions, 87, 171-5
task development, 190
teacher education, 16-17, 160-1, 218-42, 315-16
  concurrent courses, 225-8
  for Special Education, 256

inadequacies, 231-5
integration within, 222-3
knowledge acquisition, 224-5, 231-3
non-degree courses, 236
one-year courses, 221, 231, 232, 234-5, 237-8
process approach, 219-31
professional skills, 223
recent trends and developments, 235-8
retraining, 237
theoretical understanding, 223-4, 232
  see also in-service training; induction training
Teachers' centres, 198-9
technology, 115, 247, 311
theory and practice of education, 1, 185-87, 223-24, 226, 232, 250, 316
Teaching Primary Science Project, 111
ticksheets *see* checklists
Thomas Coram Research Unit, 252

unified curriculum, 3, 38, 48, 50-55, 98, 108, 109, 127, 299

values, 115
  implicit in teaching materials, 43-4
  intrinsic, of education, 11, 21
  teachers', 191
vocational (utilitarian) education, 310-13

Warnock Report, *Special Educational Needs*, 1978, 113, 254, 258, 263, 273
writing, 34, 42-3; 58-9, 60-61, 65, 66, 69-75, 105, 116, 129, 130, 134, 136, 139-40, 145, 146, 229-30
  art work and, 120-8
  purposes of, 72-3
  Secondary schools, 292
  teacher reactions to, 71-2
  'voice', 72-3